BY BREAD ALONE
The Story of A-4685

by

Mel Mermelstein
Author and Lecturer

Dedication

I wish to dedicate this book to the youth of America, Europe, Asia, Africa and, in particular, to the youth living in Russia, China, Argentina and the Middle East because, while these young people may be aware of the "Nazi Holocaust" and its consequences, they are no doubt unaware that Hitler's rallying point for his vile hatred of mankind began with the persecution of the Jews.

M.M.

NOTE: Czechoslovakian Fifth Grade graduation photo taken in May 1938. *Author Encircled.*

MAP OF EUROPE 1939

About the Characters in this Book

Though the characters in this story are real, I felt their names had to be changed to protect their privacy. I have not consulted with any of the survivors mentioned here, because I know how some might feel if the story of their part in the Holocaust were brought to them once again to be dealt with.

TABLE OF CONTENTS

Gen. Patton, Gen. Bradley & Gen. Eisenhower inspecting the liberated Nazi concentration camps in Germany toward the closing days of World War II.

COMITÉ INTERNATIONAL DE LA CROIX-ROUGE

SERVICE INTERNATIONAL DE RECHERCHES
3548 Arolsen · République fédérale d'Allemagne

INTERNATIONAL TRACING SERVICE   INTERNATIONALER SUCHDIENST
3548 Arolsen · Federal Republic of Germany   3548 Arolsen · Bundesrepublik Deutschland

E/Fi/Go/ej   Téléphone: Arolsen (05691) 637 · Télégrammes: ITS Arolsen

Arolsen, 3rd September 1971

Mr. Melvin Mermelstein
Ideal Pallet System, Inc.
1660 East Firestone Boulevard

LOS ANGELES, California 90001
U.S.A.

Our Ref. : T/D - 359 391
Your Ref.: MM:jms

Dear Mr. Mermelstein,

May we refer to your letter dated 3rd August 1971, concerning
yourself as well as your father Mr. Bernard MERMELSTEIN, born on
11th January 1899, and your brother, Mr. Lajos MERMELSTEIN, born on
12th February 1925.

Please be advised that only the following particulars are contained in our records concerning you:

1) MERMELSTEIN Moric, born on 25th September 1926 in Muńkacs,
Kom. Bereg, Hungary; Nationality: Czechoslovak; Religion:
Jewish; Parents' names: Hermann and Fany née KLEIN;
Occupation: automobile mechanician, engine-fitter; last
permanent residence: Oroszveg 272, Kom. Bereg, or Mugaczewo,
Czechoslovakia; entered Concentration Camp Buchenwald,
Prisoner's No. 130508, on 10th February 1945, coming from
Concentration Camp Gross-Rosen; former Prisoner's No. A-4685.

Category or reason given for incarceration: "Polit." (= Poli-
tisch i.e. political); "Jude" (Jew).

On 5th March 1945 he was still incarcerated in Concentration
Camp Buchenwald.

Records consulted: "Häftlingspersonalkarte, Schreibstuben-
karte, Häftlingspersonalbogen, Revierkarte, Arbeitskarte, Nummernkarte, Blockbuch, Zugangsliste" and "Veränderungsmeldungen"
of Concentration Camp Buchenwald.

2) MERMELSTEIN Mor or Moric, born on 25th September 1926 in
Mugaczewe, Czechoslovakia; Nationality: Czechoslovak;
Religion: non Orthodox, Parents' names: MERMELSTEIN Hermann
and Fanny, née KLEIN; Occupation: automechanician, locksmith;
last permanent residence: Mugaczewe, Czechoslovakia; Marital
Status: single; was in DP-Camp Eschwege on 30th March 1946,
4th June 1946 and on 20th July 1946. He emigrated from Bremen
to the USA aboard the SS "Marine Perch" on 22nd August 1946.

Records consulted: Two DP-2 Cards, dated 30th March 1946;
list "U.S. War Shipping Administration, U.S. Lines, General
Agents".

vii

Furthermore the following information is available in our records:

The name MERMELSTEIN Moric, born on 25th September 1926 in Mukacevo; Nationality: Czechoslovak; last permanent residence: Mukacevo; Occupation: locksmith; appears in a list "Gerettete Personen im Lager Buchenwald".

As to your request concerning photostatic copies of our records, kindly note that, in accordance with our regulations, we do not submit copies of our records to private persons, but merely to the competent authorities.

We are very sorry to have to advise you that no particulars whatever are available in our records pertaining to your father, Mr. Bernard Mermelstein, and your brother, Mr. Lajos Mermelstein.

Trusting nevertheless to have been of some assistance to you with the information we could give, we remain,

Yours sincerely,

A. de Cocatrix
Director of the ITS

AUSCHWITZ-BIRKENAU

Author's Parents

2 Sisters and Brother

"I SPEAK OF JEWS
WHO DIED AT AUSCHWITZ
OF HUMANITY THAT DIED AT AUSCHWITZ
FOR WHEN HUMANITY KILLS JEWS
IT KILLS ITSELF."

Professor Elie Wiesel
Boston University

ACKNOWLEDGEMENTS

I wish to express my gratitude to the many students, teachers, professors, and administrators at numerous high schools, colleges and universities who urged me to publish my personal story of the Holocaust. I wish to thank them, as well, for the many times I have been invited to speak and share with them my personal experiences during the Holocaust.

I also wish to thank the many newspaper reporters and radio and television announcers who have interviewed me, and especially Ray Briem of KABC Los Angeles for inviting me twice to appear on his talk show.

My thanks to those who read my manuscript and gave me their opinions and assessments of my work.

FOREWORD

Atrocities had been committed long before the creation of Nazi death camps. But never before in man's recorded history had men gone about with such vigor and determination to design, build, and operate death factories specifically to exterminate the Jews. I do not mean to minimize the horror of war and senseless destruction of the innocent bystanders of war. But, the Nazi Holocaust, the systematic destruction of European Jewry, had no connection with acts of war. These men, women and children were lured and driven into gas chambers disguised as shower rooms because they were Jews.

How was it possible for a Holocaust to take place in such a highly advanced society? How and what happened during this awesome period? Can it ever happen again? If so, where and under what circumstances?

This book may not have all the answers, but a reader of my first-hand experience will be enlightened and perhaps a little better informed about this awesome era known as the Holocaust.

I've been asked by various individuals of different backgrounds, "Why study the Holocaust? Why not forget such horrors?" My answer, as a survivor of the Holocaust, is, "Because never before in recorded history has man revealed himself more than during this period. The mask of mankind had dropped and we must therefore take the opportunity to learn what it is in man that makes it possible for such a Holocaust to occur. What can we do to avoid future Holocausts? What role are our political, social, economic and religious institutions to play before, during and after a Holocaust? Who is to blame for it and whom shall we hold accountable?" All these questions and more we must ask if we are to prevent the destruction of civilization. "THE STUDY OF THE HOLOCAUST IS THE STUDY OF MANKIND."

Mel Mermelstein

PREFACE

The picture of my life is sundered; it is broken in two. First, there is the familiar man, friendly, outgoing, smiling, successful, often relaxed. The other is but a number, a figure. I didn't invent that number, nor is it a literary gimmick; it is very real and will always be a part of me. If I let my mind wander for a moment, the number appears, and the images it casts are frightening and disturbing. The scenes are repeated endlessly, the settings always the same: Birkenau, Auschwitz, Gleiwitz, Blechammer, Gross-Rosen, Buchenwald. Those places are strange to many of you, but not to me, nor to my number. The images come from far away, and the places are far apart, but they melt together in my mind. They are all concentration camps, death camps. In those camps I became A-4685. I, and my number survived, while six million did not.

With my number I was a prisoner among prisoners, walking on raw, bare feet, standing in the rain, huddled against the cold, fear permanently knotted in the deep pit of my empty gut. Even then my mind wandered, it always asked the same question. Should I fight and die? Try to escape and die? Or should I endure beyond endurance and live? My number now leads me round and round, over and over, in that place with so many punishing questions. It leads me round not only in memory, seeing those same images repeated but also in real life. It takes me by the hand and makes me go: in recent years it has led me back eight times to where it all began, to Auschwitz, to Gleiwitz, to Buchenwald, to the shrines in Israel, to Auschwitz again, to the mass graves at Babi Yar—where I was inflamed with anger as I beheld the monument raised to the Soviet heroes, but not to the Jews! Were the thousands who filled the graves at Babi Yar Jews or not? And again it leads me to Auschwitz-Birkenau, back to see, to wonder and to reaffirm my liberation at Buchenwald.

It never leaves me. It never recedes into the past. It never fades away, but only urges me on. It spends my money and it collects books on the Holocaust, which line my shelves at home. It collects hundreds of photos of the past, and snaps new ones of the places that still dot the old battlefields, the ghettos and the death camps. It drives me to write scores of letters, pushes me into lecture halls, it guides my pen, it remains the master, and I have no choice but to do its bidding.

This is my story, and now I am asking that you share all of my tragic experiences. I'm not requesting that you absorb it deeply into your subconscious mind. I don't expect all of you to jump up, scream, beat your head against the wall, or dwell on how it was possible that some men could so coldly and routinely inflict such mad and cruel tortures on others created in the same image.

I'm not asking you to feel the heel of a boot kicking against your skull, or the pang of helplessness in watching little children being driven naked to flaming pits. I'm not asking you to stand in horror and watch men, women, and children marched or driven into a chamber to be gassed. I am not asking you to look beyond, at the frozen, suppressed horror of those who were forced to move the corpses, "their mouths wide open, leaning one upon the other, especially close to one another near the door, where in their deadly fright they had crowded to force it...their twisted limbs grown stiff with the gas" (memoirs of Perry Board, SS Auschwitz). I'm not asking you to feel the numbness of the sondercommando, the Jewish crematorium squad, that had to shove the bodies into the ovens, watch them come out as black smoke, and later when the furnace was cooled, dump the ashes into a peaceful pond that swallowed the debris which was once human flesh with a terrible belch and resume its natural tranquillity.

How can I expect you to feel all of this, or even a portion of it? Why should you? Surely we all hope that it is a nightmare that will never be repeated. No, I cannot ask you to do all this; I can only ask that you read, with or without a full and comprehending mind. Perhaps you would like to hide some of your awareness away as you read, to let your mind wander. That's natural, just as you would turn your face aside if you were to come upon the mangled body of a head-on auto crash. Look out of the corner of the eye, or just see it all as a bad dream. Again, all I'm asking is that you read my story. That will mean a great deal to me.

For you see, even as you follow my advice—rushing through, possibly turning aside occasionally, thinking of pleasant music as you read—still a fleeting memory is bound to remain, and you will inevitably understand a bit of what it meant to be out in that rain, the door bolted against you, the warmth of the fireplace out of reach, with no raincoat, the wind chilling you through. And there you stand, five minutes, an hour, five hours, even a whole day....

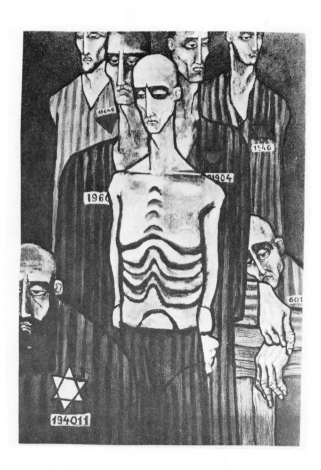

"First the Nazis went after the Jews, but I was not a Jew, so I did not object. Then they went after the Catholics, but I was not a Catholic, so I did not object. Then they went after the Trade-Unionists, but I was not a Trade-Unionist, so I did not object. Then they came after me, and there was no one left to object."

Pastor Martin Niemoller
A German Theologian

CHAPTER ONE
"Exile"

The first German tank I ever saw looked as if it had gone through a war. Of course it had—a war that had been raging continuously for six years, in my country and in a large part of the world, with no apparent end in sight. It was already 1944 and it looked like the end would never come.

To my seventeen-year-old vision the tank was puzzling and odd; it seemed as though the crew simply didn't bother to maintain it. However, sitting in the shade the tank provided, the crew didn't look much better than the over-used vehicle. There the Nazis sat, eating their rations and brewing coffee in a helmet. The streaks of dirt on their uniforms resembled the oil smears on the sides of their tank; their unshaven faces seemed to match the huge clumps of dirt that had accumulated on the axles, around which the treads revolved. If the Germans were depending upon these tanks and soldiers to win the war, then it was no wonder they were losing it.

Although the war had to this point lasted about six years, seeing that metal monster in our small town came as a surprise. It appeared on a fresh spring morning in March, when everything seemed quite normal, much the same as any other day. Peasant women, many of them barefoot, in their embroidered blouses and coarse skirts were on their way to the city to sell or barter their produce. We walked to work as usual; my father to his wine shop; my brother Lajos, aged nineteen, to the watch repairman's stand where he was apprenticed; my sister Magda, fifteen, to the corsetiere where she was learning to make hats; I, to the machine

1

shop where I was an apprentice. My oldest sister Etu, 20, remained at home, helping my mother. Being youngsters, we had no idea of the gigantic events beyond our ken which had brought the Germans to us that spring.

We lived in a mountain region which had a special character all its own. Located in the Carpathian Mountains, a chain linking former Czechoslovakia with Poland, it formed a natural geographic and cultural entity. It was filled with streams, sparkling lakes, rushing rivers, dense forests, and bounded by lofty mountains, which hovered over us to create a heavenly scene. In one minute the sun would be shining brightly and in the next, thunder and lightning would break loose. Heavy rains would fill the rivers, flooding cities, towns and villages; the people would run for cover—the Czecks, the Slovaks, the Moravians, Germans, Bohemians, Gypsies, Ruthenians, Magyars and Jews. Each was independent of the other, each conscious of the other's life. Far from being autonomous, our region was constantly subjected to political and military struggles, conflicts that made us part of the Austro-Hungarian Empire, then part of Czechoslovakia, then briefly independent as Ruthenia, and finally Hungarian again.

There we lived in the remote mountain region of Eastern Czechoslovakia best known as the Carpatho-Ukraine. To the east, west, north or south of us a range of mountains reached into the sky. In the winter and spring its alpine and snow-covered slopes, barren crags and heavily forested valleys would give us the feeling of being protected, secure in our isolation.

All this was an illusion. As far back as 1928, the region had been reduced to the status of a province, and called sub-Carpathian Russia. Politically, it was of little importance until the years 1938-39 when Nazi Germany began mixing politics with nationalism in Eastern Europe. With the rapid shifting of boundaries, this little outpost on the tail end of Czechoslovakia suddenly acquired prominence. After the "Munich Agreement" it was granted autonomy within a disintegrated Czechoslovak state, and on October 26, 1938, a Ukrainian Nationalist Cabinet took office, headed by Monsignor Augustin Voloshyn, who advocated independence for Ukrainia.

In November 1938, because of a decision made by the German Nazis and Italian fascist representatives, the "Horthy Magyars," the Hungarian fascists had been granted a considerable part of the region, including its capital, Uzhorod. However, the Carpatho-Ukraine continued its existence in a federative relationship with the remainder of Czechoslovakia, shifting its capital to Hust. The official language of this small, chopped up region became Ukrainian, with Hungarian and Yiddish as minority languages. Determined to remain independent, this tiny governing body created an army, a small one, called the *Zaporozhian Sitch Sharpshooters,* the ZSS.

On January 6, 1939, at dawn, the sharpshooters clashed with the superior and well-organized Hungarian army. January 6th fell on Friday that year, the eve of the Sabbath, a holy day for the Jews.

Determined to have their Sabbath as usual, Jews from all over town flocked to the city under the roar of cannon fire and the screaming of rifle bullets. No Jew would dare to ignore the observance of the Sabbath, even if it meant getting shot and killed!

While not ultra-religious, we followed the crowd. My father went to buy fish and fresh *halla,* the traditional Jewish Sabbath bread, from the bakery for the holiday. Briefly, there was joy and peace again. The Hungarian and Ukrainian guns quit momentarily, the dead were gathered and buried, and silence once again reigned at the border.

At the age of twelve I was curious as to what this battle was all about, so my friend Tibi and I decided to go to the front. It was only walking distance from our home. Barbed wire had been strung all around. Soon, we could see the soldiers crouching, trying to find places to hide, their rifles slung on their shoulders and their hats pulled over their ears, swinging their arms in motion to keep warm. We didn't stay long. A light snow began to fall and Tibi, nearly fifteen, wisely decided that we should return home.

While we were heading back we ran into young recruits, soldiers who were guarding the entrances and exits. They were Hungarian and seeing us, appeared bewildered.

"Where in the hell are you coming from?" one of them asked.

Tibi and I became numb with fright. Getting no reply, another soldier joined in the interrogation. This one swore he'd lock us up if we didn't tell him where we came from and what we were up to.

"You know we shoot spies!" another shouted. There was silence and then Tibi whispered, "We were just curious."

"Curious?" interrupted the youthful guard. "I'll teach you a lesson, you little sons a bitches!" He removed his rifle from his sling arm position, reached to the bolt and pulled it to the rear, placing a bullet in the chamber. "Now are you going to tell us what information you took to the enemy? Who sent you here? How much were you promised for giving information to the enemy?"

From all sides Tibi and I were bombarded with interrogations until we both broke down and cried. The tears in our eyes didn't seem to help and our pleas of innocence seemed to fall on deaf ears. We were dragged into the guard house and ordered to sit on the bare floor. The doors were slammed shut. We broke into a sweat. We shivered. Our fright numbed us and we shivered some more. Soon the wooden plank doors screeched open and a tall, well-groomed officer walked in, his brass shiny and ornamental, pure white gloves in his right hand, and a pistol inside a holster attached to his broad belt.

"Good morning," he greeted us in a friendly manner. Still frightened, neither Tibi nor I could respond. "I am the Sergeant of the Guard," he said. "Are both of you members of the youth brigade, the Hungarian Levente?" he asked.

"No, sir," I replied, "I'm too young."

Tibi noticed my fright and explained that he was older than I and that he was a Levente, but that I was not.

"Good," replied the guard master. "What is your nationality?"

"We're Jews," responded Tibi. "But we're not spies, we haven't done anything wrong. We wanted to see the front and all the fighting. We walked along the river where the barbed wire was strung."

"We didn't go any farther and talked to no one," I said.

"I believe you," he said. "I'm going to let you go, but you

must remember to be good Levente. We're at war and we'll need you to defend the motherland. We don't want the Bolsheviks to set foot here—do you?''

"No, sir!" we shouted.

He moved closer to us, stroking our hair and putting us at ease. "Now go home, and remember that you're Magyars." We went home.

Soon after, the battle resumed and continued until a cease-fire was arranged. The Magyar and Ukrainian guns were finally quieted and a border peace was established.

In March of 1939, while Hitler was sending his elite troops across the remainder of Czechoslovakia, Carpatho-Ukrainia was proclaiming its independence with Voloshyn as president. But the Magyars, with the consent of Hitler and Mussolini, surged through the Carpathian Mountains with lightning speed, overcoming the gallant resistance by the *Sitch Sharpshooters* and annexing the entire region to Hungary. Thus, the Jews in the Carpathian Mountains became Hungarian again, but now under the hostile and despotic regime of the Regent, Horthy Miklos.

As in many parts of Eastern Europe, the Jewish population in Carpatho-Ukrainia was considerable. In some regions the Jews were more numerous than all other religions and creeds combined. Those Jews who acquired any type of wealth were the first targets of discrimination. In the city of Munkacs there were about thirty-six thousand people, of which sixteen thousand were Jews. The majority of the Jewish inhabitants were of the strict Orthodox religious sect, and their livelihood, or more precisely, their means of subsistence, depended largely on charity.

As the Horthy regime extended its reign over the territory, anti-Semitism raged. It was felt day by day. No Jew was spared; your friend of yesterday turned against you. My thirteen-year-old friend Joncsi was no different. Because of all the anti-Semitism, I wondered if he would turn enemy because I was Jewish and he was Gentile. I soon found out. School had opened again. As usual, kids met to play, but this time it was different—the faces were no longer happy. They expressed a mood of fear and hesitation. My friend was no exception.

5

By Bread Alone

Los Angeles Times

POLES HUG HUNGARIANS AT NEW BORDER

Polish border guards embraced Hungarian soldiers, left, when 20-year dream of common frontier came true through Hungarian occupation of Ruthenia. This picture was sent by telephoto from Warsaw to London and radioed to New York yesterday.
(AP) Wirephoto

Hungarian Soldiers Welcomed by Poles

WARSAW, March 16. (Thursday) (AP)—Hungarian troops today established a common frontier with Poland, marching across the Carpatho-Ukraine and reaching the Polish border at Lavoczne and at Sinaki at 1 a.m.

The small detachments of Hungarians, who had fought their way across the eastern tip of demolished Czechoslovakia through a raging blizzard, were received into the Polish guard stations and given a warm welcome by Polish troops.

They received food and hot drinks immediately.

The Hungarians had advanced across approximately 60 miles of mountainous terrain by way of the Ung River valley to Sinaki and by way of the Latoriza River valley, farther east, to Lavoczne.

Polish military sources said they were "happy that the 20-year dream of a common frontier with Hungary has now been realized."

With supporting forces expected to follow the Hungarian advance guard, the eastern tip of Carpatho-Ukraine and its capital of Chust was cut off from Slovakia and the Czech capital at Prague.

MARCH 16, 1939.

Ukraine Battles Hungary Army

Invaders Shelled on March Northward Toward Polish Border

BUDAPEST, March 15. (AP)—Hungarian troops marching northward to occupy Carpatho-Ukraine of the fallen Czechoslovak republic were being resisted tonight by artillery and machinegun fire, a Foreign Office spokesman announced.

The spokesman admitted that there had been Hungarian casualties, but said the number of dead is not known.

Trains and trucks were rushing more Hungarian troops into the region and tens of thousands of soldiers were on the move.

A general of the Hungarian staff said resistance was so vigorous northeast of Munkacs on the Hungarian-Carpatho-Ukraine frontier that "a field campaign may be necessary."

The fighting was going on despite the fact that some Hungarian troops had already reached the Polish border. Officials of the former Federal Czech regime had accepted a Hungarian ultimatum order withdrawal of all Czech troops, it was said here, but in the meantime Premier Augustin Volosin, of the Province of Car-

patho-Ukraine, reportedly declared the state independent and defied the ultimatum.

IRREGULARS IN FIELD

It was presumed the resistance was coming from Ukrainian irregulars, possibly reinforced by a few detachments of regular Czech troops who refused to withdraw.

The Hungarian soldiers under fire were considered more than halfway across Carpatho-Ukraine to the Polish border.

They were advancing through snow which in some places in the mountains is six feet deep.

Hidden machine gunners harassed them by sporadic fire.

The Hungarian military command reported Czech military authorities in the region had asked for a five-day period to evacuate all Carpatho-Ukraine.

ORDERED TO DISARM

The Hungarian answer was that even more time for evacuation would be allowed, but Czech troops must give up their arms at once.

Safe conduct was promised all Czech soldiers wishing to return to Moravia, Slovakia or Bohemia.

The Foreign Office stated the purpose of the military operation is to create a Hungarian corridor, in the region of Munkacs, to Poland.

With such an operation completed the tip of old Czechoslovakia would be cut off with all Czech troops and Ukrainian irregulars bottled up.

HUNGARIAN INVADERS BATTLE CARPATHO-UKRAINE TROOPS

Carpathian Area Seized by Hungarians

WITH THE HUNGARIAN ARMY IN CHUST (Carpatho-Ukraine) March 16. (AP)—Hungarian troops stormed this little Carpatho-Ukraine capital late today and after an hour and a half of energetic mopping up smashed all Czech and Ukrainian resistance.

Tonight Chust was a quiet, bullet-marked city completely under Hungarian control.

In Budapest the entire province was declared formally annexed to Hungary.

TROOPERS DRIVEN OUT

Ukrainian storm troopers whose dream it had been to establish an independent Ukraine state, and a few Czech soldiers who had decided to fight rather than flee to safety to Rumania, were driven out into the snow-covered mountains which circle the city.

They will be hard to dislodge from their mountain hideouts, but the tired Hungarian soldiers were preparing to pursue tomorrow.

The bitterest fighting occurred in a system of shallow, barbed-wire protected trenches seven miles east of Chust.

HAND-TO-HAND FIGHT

After a brief artillery bombardment of the defense works, the Hungarians made a bayonet charge and for half an hour there was bitter hand-to-hand conflict.

In one trench the bodies of 37 defenders were counted.

Most of them wore the uniforms of the Czech army.

But there were a few in the blue uniform of "Stitch," irregular Ukrainian guards.

Once past the trenches the Hungarians made rapid progress toward the city. There was a pause at the outskirts while the commanders debated whether to bombard the town.

LITTLE RESISTANCE

It was decided artillery would inflict unnecessary hardships on civilians.

So the infantry advanced and met comparatively little resistance.

6

Los Angeles Times MARCH 16. 1939.

10,000 Facing Nazi Questions

Many Arrested in Bohemia and Moravia Areas

PRAGUE. March 18. (AP)—At least 10.000 residents of Bohemia and Moravia were known to-night to have been ordered to report for questioning by the new German masters of broken Czechoslovakia.

The orders did not mean. how-ever. that they would all be de-tained. but numerous arrests are known to have been made.

The partitioned republic was kept in ignorance of the fact that the United States. Britain and France had denounced Ger-many's absorption of Czecho-slovakia.

NEWSPAPERS CENSORED

Newspapers of the Bohemia-Moravia protectorate. brought under Nazi control. made no mention of Friday's statement by Acting Secretary of State Sumner Welles or of the French and British notes calling Hitler's action illegal.

Only those few Czechs who heard foreign news broadcasts had any inkling the outside world was showing any interest in their fate.

Newspapers were filled instead with announcement of the ap-pointment of Baron Konstantin von Neurath as Reichs-protector over Bohemia and Moravia and that Karl Hermann Frank. as-sistant leader of the Sudeten struggle last year. would become his secretary of state.

SILENT PROTESTS

All day Prague residents con-tinued their silent demonstra-tions before the Rathaus war memorial honoring patriots who were killed in 1620. when Czechs once before lost their independ-ence.

Men. women and children—few without tears—stood with bared heads before the memorial flanked by two eternal flames. Inside the Rathaus (city hall.) citizens complied with a military order requiring them to surren-der all armaments. Revolvers. old muskets and antique wea-pons of all sorts were carted into the building and turned over to authorities who gave receipts in return.

MANY HIDE IN WOODS

Reports from Prague suburbs said at least 200 women and chil-dren had spent last night hiding in the woods.

Foreigners today were forbid-den to enter the Y.M.C.A. which had been headquarters for relief

NAZI SALUTE GIVEN BY BOHEMIAN WOMEN

In the midst of boos and hisses, Hitler's invading troops were welcomed by these Bo-hemian women as they marched through the Province on the way to Prague. — Wirephoto

work among political refugees before the German conquest.

The Nazi campaign against Jews continued. A Jewish syn-agogue in Bruenn was destroyed today by fire of unknown origin.

"No Jews wanted" signs ap-peared in coffee houses of Maeh-rischostrau (Moravia-Ostrava.) Other signs appeared in stores designating the owners as Ger-man. Czech or Jewish.

JEWS ARRESTED

Nazi leaders indicated that one of Hitler's first acts would be to introduce the Numberg racial laws. which were applied to Austria immediately after its annexation a year ago yesterday and to Czechoslovakia's Sude-tenland after its surrender to the Reich early last November under the "peace of Munich."

It was understood that numer-ous Jews already had been ar-rested in Prague—some of them on charges of Communistic ac-tivities—by the 800 members of the secret police sent there by Heinrich Himmler. chief of the Gestapo.

TRAPPED BY TROOPS

Several thousand Jews had fled into Prague from the province of Slovakia. which on Tuesday pro-claimed its independence and became a Nazi vassal state.

The Jews of Bohemia and Mo-ravia. and those remaining in Slovakia. found themselves trapped by the German troops. There was virtually no escape. Airplanes were grounded. Rail communication to Poland was cut and they could not reach Ru-mania because it was impossible to cross Slovakia.

SUBVERSIVE LEAFLETS

The Voelkischer Beobachter published photographs purport-ing to show Germans killed by Czech Jews in recent days.

A minor sensation was caused by the appearance of subversive leaflets attacking Hitler's anti-Semitic drive and asserting that "the November pogroms and anti-Semitic policy ruined not only the Jews in Germany but de-prived Germany of her friends abroad."

LIKELY MEASURES

Among the measures which Hitler probably will proclaim are:

1.—Incorporation of Bohemia and Moravia into the financial and customs system of the Reich.

2.—Incorporation of the Czechs in Field Marshal Hermann Wil-helm Goering's four-year plan of economic self-sufficiency.

3.—Germany will reap a rich prize by taking over all the gold reserves of Prague's national banks. The Czechoslovak na-tional bank has $83,000,000 in gold, excluding about $11,000,000 of gold held in special funds against gold liabilities.

4.—The Czech army. number-ing 180,000 well-trained and ex-cellently equipped troops and 1,300,000 reserves before the "peace of Munich" will be dis-banded and Germany will as-sume the defense of Bohemia and Moravia.

"Joncsi, Joncsi!" I yelled. "Let's go..." I kicked the ball to his corner but Joncsi would not play.

"I don't want to play with you—you Jew..." I looked at him, puzzled, and he turned and began to run away, in the opposite direction. The atmosphere was full of poison and hate.

Government restrictions became gradually more severe. Business permits for Jews were cancelled and their stores closed. Jewish children were limited to primary grades. "Incidents" were manufactured, and innocent Jews were constantly arrested. An anti-Jewish propaganda campaign was in full swing, and anti-Semitism was taking a carefully directed course throughout the entire region. In the midst of all these difficulties, the Jews still hoped that some day this imposed hatred would subside and that common humanity, truth, and the Christian principles their neighbors proclaimed would prevail. But political realities had already decreed otherwise.

As regent and head of state, Admiral Horthy, a nationalist with extreme rightist leanings, led Hungary into World War II as an ally of Nazi Germany, on June 22, 1941. The Magyars were moving men and equipment through the mountains across the forests into Russia. "On to Moscow!" was their slogan. "Rejoice at last!" they proclaimed. "We shall defeat the enemy— Bolshevism and International Jewry."

The radios were broadcasting the swift success achieved by the Nazis every day. The Magyars were proud to boast of their Nazi comrades. Simultaneous attacks with the Nazis were launched by the Magyar armies from the Carpathian Mountains near where we lived. Jews were conscripted in special battalions; for forced labor no longer were they trusted with rifle in hand.

My father, too, was drafted. He came home on June the 25th only to pack and to inform us of his fate. "Goodbye, goodbye," he cried.

"But you must take your warm clothes along," insisted mother. "It gets cold in those mountains. What about food?"

"No," said father, "I have but twelve hours before I am to report. There are no trains headed in that direction and I'll have to walk over mountains. Let me go now. I'll write." He moved

8

Conscripted Carpathian Youth into Para-Military Training and Forced Labor.
Note: Non-Jews with military caps & uniforms while Jewish youth are in civilian clothes.

HORTHY　　The Hitlerizing of Hungary　　HITLER

By Bread Alone

Czech Jews Face New Drive

Hitler Raids on 300,000 in Country Expected in Berlin

BERLIN, March 15. (U.P)—Chancellor Adolf Hitler's Nazi party organ, the Voelkischer Beobachter, said tonight that a campaign probably would be undertaken immediately against, the 300,000 to 400,000 Jews in the Czech provinces of Bohemia and Moravia.

As Propaganda Minister Paul Joseph Goebbels ordered Germans to hoist swastikas and celebrate the Nazi "liberation" of the 7,000,000 Czechs, the Nazi press broke into an inspired chorus against Czechoslovakia's Jews.

Jews in Prague and other cities occupied by the German army were accused of waging "pogroms against the Germans" and it was predicted that "speedy justice" would be meted out to them.

dictator of Soviet Russia

FREE SPEECH FOR NAZIS URGED

Civil Liberties Union Maps Main Fight

BALTIMORE, March 19. (AP)—Arthur Garfield Hays, national director of the American Civil Liberties Union, today labeled "defense of the right of free speech for the Nazis" the principal problem facing advocates of civil liberties in the United States.

"The only way to combat these people is to grant them constitutional rights; let them speak and then ignore them," he said. "The more persons who come to speak about Nazi principles in German-American accents, the better. There isn't any crackpot movement that could not attract 2,000,000 members in this country in a few years."

He asserted, "if in fear of dictatorships we deny the right of free speech, even to the Fascists . . . if we are stupid enough to believe their false ballyhoo . . . then their ideas will triumph and democracy will be destroyed."

Adolf Hitler, on whose next political move the peace of Europe rested last night.

Los Angeles Times

FRIDAY MORNING.

MARCH 17, 1939.

Ruthenia Taken by Hungarians

Capital Occupied After Brief Battle; Many Bodies Found

Even Hungary, which profited from the break-up of Czechoslovakia through the annexation of Carpatho-Ukraine—proclaimed to a cheering Parliament by Premier Count Paul Teleky today—shared the anxieties of other southeastern states.

Worried Balkan chancelleries which watched Bohemia and Moravia pass into the German Reich and then Slovakia join them as a Nazi protectorate were wondering where the Nazi "drang nach osten"—"drive to the east" —would make itself felt next.

DIRECT PRESSURE

Hungary was uneasy because the collapse of Czechoslovakia greatly increased Germany's direct pressure upon her. No buffer remains between her and the expanding Reich.

Pressing her conquest of Carpatho-Ukraine's 4206 square miles and 550,000 inhabitants, Hungary, through her general staff, announced occupation of Chust, the Carpatho-Ukraine capital.

Other Hungarian detachments already had reached the Polish border, to establish a common frontier with Poland.

Admiral Nicholas Horthy, Regent of Hungary, issued an order thanking the soldiers for their excellent accomplishments in penetrating the Carpathian Mountains under arduous conditions.

PLEA FOR CLOTHING

Lady Horthy appealed through the radio to all Hungarians to supply warm clothing to the Hungarian soldiers.

The Premier told Parliament that "Carpatho-Ukraine becomes a part of the kingdom of Hungary," that it was "set up as an autonomous region" and would "enjoy sweeping rights of self-government."

The immediate Hungarian reaction to Germany's advance was to do nothing to offend the Reich. In the same speech in which Teleky announced Carpatho-Ukraine's annexation he proposed immediate adoption of the long-pending Jewish control law.

Parliament ended a debate which had been raging six weeks and passed the law within an hour.

CURBS JEWS

It bars Jews from many occupations and limits Jewish participation in professions and business to about 6 per cent of the total persons in those callings.

Balkan states are worried by the fact that Germany has gone beyond the racial principle hitherto followed in her expansion and that non-German peoples now are being absorbed.

Hitler Painted as Power Mad

Thomas Mann Says Nazis Seek to Be Rulers of World

CHICAGO, March 15. (Exclusive)—"Roosevelt now plays Benes' role in Hitler's personal fight. The aims of National Socialism are unlimited and embrace even the Americas. England errs in supposing that, by giving Hitler a free hand in the east, Western Europe can avoid war."

Thomas Mann, German author and 1929 Nobel prize winner in literature, said this here today.

Speaking smoothly and rapidly in German, of which many of his countrymen regard him as foremost living master, he declared that Germany is unprepared for war and was unprepared last September.

SITUATION TRAGIC

Though his assertions came without hesitation, they had the sound of matured conclusions.

"The present situation in the East," he affirmed, "is tragic, but not unexpected. We know that England wishes to give Hitler the freedom of the East, hoping in that way Nazi aggression may be deflected from the West."

Rumania Will Ban Refugees

Cabinet Decides to Halt Influx From Carpatho-Ukraine

BUCHAREST, March 16. (AP)— Private sources today said the Rumanian Cabinet has refused the request of the Carpatho-Ukraine Premier, Augustin Volosin, to annex the former Czechoslovak territory as a protectorate.

Premier Volosin, who fled to Rumania, sent a telegram to Bucharest asking annexation immediately after reaching the frontier at Siget.

Apparently he had not heard of the formal proclamation of annexation by Hungary at Budapest earlier in the day.

TO HALT INFLUX

The Cabinet also decided to halt immediately the influx of refugees from Carpatho-Ukraine, particularly Jews.

The only exceptions will be well-known political refugees and others already in Rumania will be expelled.

Among the refugees reaching Bucharest tonight was the famous Czech shoe manufacturer of Zlin, Jan Bata, sometimes known as the "Czech Ford."

He arrived from Zlin, now a part of the German protectorate of Moravia, in his private airplane.

GOING TO ENGLAND

He refused to make a statement, but it was reliably learned his intentions are to settle in England where he also has large business interests.

Thousands of other refugees are joining the trek through Carpatho-Ukraine's snowy mountain roads toward the Rumanian frontier.

Three Czech infantry battalions crossed the border at Siget and surrendered their arms. Three units of armored cars and two artillery regiments followed them.

By Bread Alone

Los Angeles Times

FRIDAY MORNING,

MARCH 17, 1939.

Rioting Flares Among Poles

Celebration Turns Into Demonstration Against Germans

WARSAW, March 16. (*P*)—A celebration marking the establishment of a common Hungarian-Polish frontier t h r o u g h Hungary's annexation of Carpatho-Ukraine developed tonight into anti-German and anti-Jewish demonstrations.

The boisterous scenes here in which a crowd estimated at 1000 shouted "down with Germany" and "down with Jews" was in contrast to those at the Polish-Carpatho-Ukrainian f r o n t i e r where the Hungarians were greeted by kisses from Polish soldiers and civilians.

The crowd here tried to march on the German Embassy, but was thrown back by a strong force of special police around the building.

SHOPS ATTACKED

The demonstrators then turned their fury on Jewish shops in the vicinity. Several windows were smashed before police finally restored order.

The demonstrations were the first anti-German disorders in Poland since students paraded and shouted Feb. 28 in protest at treatment of Poles in Danzig. Those disorders lasted over a period of four days, while the Italian Foreign Minister, Count Galeazzo Ciano, was paying a visit to Warsaw.

Tonight civilian refugees arriving at the border town of Awoczne from snowbound Carpatho-Ukraine told of hardships encountered in fleeing their homes.

LOSE THEIR WAY

The refugees said many of their companies lost their way in raging blizzards and it was feared they had frozen to death.

They said they left their homes in such a hurry they were unable to bring any belongings.

Many Czech soldiers were reported to have been wounded in encounters with the Hungarian army of occupation.

Hungarian troops arrived at the border and found a number of Polish soldiers and civilians at the frontier.

Their colonel advanced immediately to the Polish colonel in charge and kissed and embraced him to symbolize comradeship in arms of Hungarians and Poles.

In Warsaw, officials reserved comment on the situation in Central Europe.

SAD AND DEJECTED

The plain Polish folk, however, were sad and dejected expressing deep sympathy for the Slovaks, who today came under German protection.

Wieczor Warszawski, Polish nationalist newspaper, tonight called German occupation of Bohemia-Moravia and Slovakia Reichsfuehrer Hitler's "first important mistake."

This step in expanding Germany's empire, the newspaper said, followed "the bad tradition of the Hapsburgs."

It attributed Nazi successes to Europe's fear of becoming involved in another war but declared such alarm did not exist in Poland.

Italy Expects Early Departure of Jews

ROME, March 15. (*P*)—A government communique said today that all of the 7000 foreign Jews in Italy, excepting those given special authority to remain, are expected to "leave the kingdom within a short time."

The communique said the government would recognize "extraordinary" cases due to "illness or special family situations."

An estimated 2000 "foreign" Jews—a term applied to all those who entered Italy after Jan. 1, 1919—left the country Sunday before the expiration of the midnight, March 12, deadline set for their departure. Many made their way across the Alps on foot into France. The French government said that those whose papers were not in order would be returned to Italy eventually.

𝕷𝖔𝖘 𝕬𝖓𝖌𝖊𝖑𝖊𝖘 𝕿𝖎𝖒𝖊𝖘

SATURDAY MORNING.

MARCH 18, 1939.

Czech Prison Camp Set Up

Concentration Plans Rushed as Suicides Keep Hearses Busy

PRAGUE, March 17. (U.P)—Nazi rulers of Czechia (Bohemia and Moravia) and Slovakia tonight are understood to have set up a concentration camp on Czech soil to hold an estimated 12,000 persons arrested as "enemies" of Fuehrer Adolf Hitler's protectorate.

The Nazis, flooding the subdued but still hostile city with "S.S." storm troopers and police, speeded up their repressive campaign and reports of suicides among Jews, Czech army officers and businessmen increased by the hour.

There were riots at the frontier, where refugees found escape cut off by German authorities. The fright of the people led to many reports—one that as many as 250 Czech officers had committed suicide after being stripped of their rank by the Germans.

HEARSES BUSY

In one house alone four Jews killed themselves by leaping from windows.

Three hearses were kept busy carrying away the bodies of Prague's suicides as fear and despondency tightened their grip upon the city that until two days ago was the capital of a sovereign nation.

New graves appeared in the Jewish cemetery.

. The arrests and terror reached from Bohemia and Moravia eastward into Slovakia, over which Hitler proclaimed a protectorate Thursday before departing from hostile Prague for Bruenn, thence to Vienna where tonight he rested from his tour of the Reich's newly won lands along the Danube.

SUICIDE WAVE SPREADS

The wave of suicides spread to Bratislava, chief city of Slovakia across the Danube from Vienna.

In Prague and Bratislava Nazi patrols searched homes under orders to seize all arms, ammunition, explosives and radio sets.

In Bratislava Hlinka guards and German vigilantes confis-cated money and jewels, it was reported.

"This money is being taken into custody to prevent it from being smuggled abroad," they told protesting Jews.

Communists, radical Marxists and anti-German Jews were arrested along with Jews in Bratislava.

Thousands of the 120,000 Jews of Bohemia, Moravia and Slovakia were hiding with friends, or fleeing to the countryside. Many were arrested when they reached the border and were unable to produce blue cards, stamped by the German high command, permitting them to cross.

Everywhere in the streets were Hitler's police.

The Czech concentration camp was reported to have been established at Milovice, 18 miles from Prague, because of the difficulty of transporting the anti-Nazi prisoners across the border to German soil.

LEADERS ARRESTED

The gestapo, or German secret police, seized a number of Prague residents who tried to leave the country. Three hundred Jews who sought to escape to Poland by way of Maehrisch-Ostrau in the north were halted.

Among the 12,000 persons estimated to be under arrest at nightfall were many prominent figures. They included Ferdinand Peroutka, political writer, and the editor of the newspaper A-Zet, who was understood to have been seized on the grounds that he published an unflattering picture of Hitler.

It was understood that Emil Hacha, last President of independent Czechoslovakia who "trustingly" surrendered to Hitler, would organize a new state party under Nazi control and that a one-party system would be established as in Germany. Parliament would consist only of the Chamber of Deputies, which would meet only perfunctorily to approve Hacha's actions which in turn would be entirely dictated by the "Reich's protector."

toward Lajos and put his arms around him. "You're now the head of the family and you'll have to work at the brewery in my place," he said.

"But I'm only fifteen years old, father. Will they let me work in your place?"

"I've prearranged everything," father answered, "all you have to do is report to work at six."

"Yes," nodded Lajos. Then father walked toward mother, gave her a warm hug and a kiss and by then Etu, Magda and I were in tears. As was the custom of our home, we escorted him across the bridge into the city. There we met scores of Jews with rucksacks and yellow armbands on their left arms. Father, too, slowly pulled out his creased and soiled armband and put it on. It was getting late in the evening and all around the big guns could be heard. This was all-out war with Russia. Trucks and ambulances loaded with casualties roared by. I could hear the cries and moans of young soldiers. "Help, help, help me. Mother, mother, my dear mother, please help!" There was havoc all over, I could not stand it. We bid a final farewell to father and went home.

Days went by and we had no news of him or his whereabouts. We worried until a post card arrived two months later. "I'm well," is all the post card said. We gathered around the kitchen table and analyzed the card thoroughly. Etu finally reached a conclusion. The post card came from Russia. Father was in the Ukraine, behind the advancing Hungarian army.

"But there's a war raging there!" exclaimed Lajos.

"They're making them dig trenches," replied Etu.

"I wish they would stop fighting, so father could come home," said little Magda. She was hardly thirteen. I noticed the pathetic look on her face as she got up and went to join her friend.

Weeks went by and we had little news from the front. We heard rumors of atrocities. The Nazis were killing civilians at random. Men, women, and children from all over flocked in for safety. They came to Munkacs, our town, a distance well-removed from the battlefields. They became refugees overnight, and had to be sheltered, fed, and hidden from the *Arrowcross bandits,* who were comparable to the Nazi fascists.

Los Angeles Times MARCH 18, 1939.

TRIUMPHAL ENTRY INTO CARPATHO-UKRAINE HAILED

Townspeople on either side of the highway gave the Nazi salute yesterday as a detachment of Hungarian troops, riding in a small truck, passed through a decorated arch in their entry into Taseo, Carpatho-Ukraine. Hungarians took possession of the province's capital, Chust. This photograph was sent by radio from London to New York.

Wirephoto

15

By Bread Alone

Los Angeles Times

MARCH 19, 1939.

CARPATHO-UKRAINE'S CAPITAL FLIES CZARIST RUSSIA FLAG

UNGVAR (Hungary) March 20. (*P*)—The flag of Czarist Russia was hoisted today over this capital of Carpatho-Ukraine, annexed by Hungary and granted political autonomy a f t e r the breakup of Czechoslovakia.

Groups of White Russian officers, wearing Czarist uniforms, gathered before the posters on which the Hungarian government announced autonomy.

The posters were printed both in Russian and Hungarian languages.

OFFICIAL COMMENT

"Sub-Carpathian Russia (Carpatho-Ukraine) can be expected actively to fight Bolshevism," said one Hungarian official.

"They hope they may have a chance to help free their oppressed brothers in Ukraine proper."

Hungary has adhered to the anti-Comintern pact with Germany, Italy and Japan and it was explained that the autonomous government here would of course take an active part.

CZECH ACCUSATION

The G e r m a n Consulate at Chust, former capital of Carpatho-Ukraine, has been accused by Czech leaders of working to further Adolf Hitler's plan to u s e Carpatho-Ukraine as a springboard to seize the Ukrainian territory of Poland, Rumania and Soviet Russia.

The German Consulate, with 30 officials, will continue operating, it was announced, but may be moved here from Chust.

REPORTS ON VLADIMIR

Grand Duke Vladimir, 21-year-old pretender to the throne of the Russias, was reported last December to have a place in Hitler's plans for the Soviet Ukraine.

These reports said a r d e n t White Russians planned to gain Hitler's support for an upsetting of Communist rule in the Soviet Ukraine.

The Grand Duke visited Berlin Dec. 19 but said he did not see Hitler.

Jews Fleeing Central Europe

Exodus Starts From Carpatho-Ukraine Seized by Hungary

B E R E G S Z A S Z (Carpatho-Ukraine) March 18. (*P*)—Sandwiched between advancing columns of soldiers, hundreds of Jews were moving southward on highways and trains today hoping desperately to get out of Central Europe.

RESTRICTIVE LAWS

Most of them seemed to be comparatively unconcerned by the military phases of the Hungarian annexation of this former Czechoslovak district. But they knew that Hungary has j u s t a d o p t e d legislation restricting Jewish participation in business and the professions.

Their greatest concern and the question m o s t frequently asked is "When is Hitler coming?"

NEAREST APPROACH

The nearest that Germans approached, however, was to the village of Nagyszalancz in Slovakia on the Carpatho-Ukraine border.

There, at one point, German and Hungarian soldiers w e r e quartered on opposite sides of the road. There was nothing to indicate that the Germans contemplated moving farther east but their presence appeared to be to assure that the Hungarians would not move west into Slovakia.

OUSTED PREMIER
Augustin Volosin, who fled to Rumania as Hungarians seized Carpatho-Ukraine.

The Nazis heard that the Jews were fleeing, and demanded that they be handed over to their special SS commandos. There was some haggling over their demands, but the Nazis won all the arguments. Roundups became a common practice for the Nazis. It was not unusual to see them hauling people off the streets twenty-four hours a day. The Jews from Poland and Ukrainia were a frightened and pitiful bunch. They had reason to be, of course, for they stood no chance if captured by the vicious Nazis. It was apparent that every man, woman and child caught, would be crammed into boxcars and shipped off to the battlefields. There they would be handed over to the SS special commandos, the *Einsatzgruppen*, Hitler's hand-picked killing squads.

There were others, too; Jews born and raised in Munkacs were rounded up and carted off to the slaughter. No one was exempt from the powerful clutch of Hungarian fascism. We were frightened, but we gathered with our neighbors to protect ourselves from the Arrowcross bandits. It was winter; the cold brisk air chilled our bones. We dared not to go out until the roundup ended.

During the middle of the night in January 1942, a knock on our door brought shivers to all of us. I approached the door quietly and peeped through the keyhole. I couldn't tell who it was. I didn't answer, but waited and listened. Soon, there was another knock accompanied by a gentle sound. "It's me...Apu!"

"Everyone come here!" I yelled from the top of my lungs. "It's father, come quickly!" I shouted over and over. I opened the door and there he was, pale, frightened, but also relieved at seeing all at home and alive. Still bracing himself at the door he began to tell us why he had to make this unauthorized journey home from the front. We knew, too, that if he were discovered at home he could be shot. "But, it was a chance I had to take," he said. "My life had no meaning when I saw the long string of boxcars rolling by and in it I spotted what I thought was Lajos. And then I visualized Etu and all crammed into those boxcars. I wanted to save you or at least go with you, so I followed the tracks."

"I couldn't understand where they were headed. My inquiries went unanswered. But I knew that they were Jews in the boxcars,

17

By Bread Alone

Einstein Sees Threat of Early Barbarism

NEW YORK, March 21. (P)—Albert Einstein said tonight the "war" against Jews in Central Europe threatened a "reversion to the barbarism of ages long past."

In a radio speech in behalf of the United Jewish Appeal for Refugees and Overseas Needs the scientist asserted the aim of the anti-Jewish movement "is to exterminate not only ourselves, but to destroy together with us that spirit expressed in the Bible and Christianity which made possible the rise of civilization in Central and Northern Europe."

Final Jewish Plan Offered

London Conference Expected to Fail as Rejection Forecast

LONDON, March 15. (P)—Great Britain tonight submitted to Jews and Arabs her final plan for the future of Palestine.

It was made clear that the plan, which is understood to recommend creation of an independent Arab-dominated state, will not be modified except in minor details.

It is believed the Jews, who would have a minority status in the proposed state, will reject the plan, and thus terminate the Holy Land peace conference which has been going on here for five weeks.

ORIGINAL PLAN

Details of the proposals were not made public, but a British spokesman said they follow closely the original suggestions presented by the British government Feb. 27.

After a five-year immigration period the question of further immigration would be considered by the British, the Arabs and the Jews.

German-Jewish Rally Gets Roosevelt Greeting

AUBURN (N.Y.) March 21. (P) President Roosevelt congratulated Auburn's Germans and Jews tonight for following biblical precepts by uniting in a dinner at a German church.

"This coming together of Jews and Christians in common worship of the ever-living and true God exemplifies in a striking way the highest teachings of the Old and New Testaments," the President wrote Rev. Ralph A. Philbrook.

Reading of the letter and singing songs banned by Nazi Germany featured the gathering of the only German church and Jewish synagogue here.

A dispute has arisen between the Jews and the British over Britain's right to change the basis of Jewish immigration without consent of the League of Nations' Council.

The Jews contend the British must get the League to consent in order to limit immigration to 75,000 for the next five years, as they propose. The British insist they do not need such consent.

POSITIVE POLICY

Although it is believed the Arabs, as well as the Jews, might reject the plan, a British spokesman said:

"What has been needed in Palestine is a positive policy, and we shall not be stopped in enforcing this one."

Colonial Secretary Malcolm MacDonald is expected to announce the plan to the House of Commons next Wednesday or Thursday.

After a two-hour conference with MacDonald and Viscount Halifax, the Foreign Secretary, the Arabs asked to be given until Friday to answer. The Jews, who received the plan in a half-hour meeting tonight, said they will inform the government of their decision tomorrow.

THREE DIVISIONS

The proposals were understood to be grouped under three main divisions:

1.—Future development of a constitution for Palestine, the question to be worked out when the Arab and Jewish populations are working amicably together.

Rabbi Calls on President

Wise Voices Jews' Gratitude for Aiding in Refugee Work

WASHINGTON, March 21. (P) Rabbi Stephen S. Wise of New York told President Roosevelt today that Jews the world over appreciate his "fine understanding and concern and deep sympathy" in connection with efforts to aid Jewish refugees.

BACK FROM LONDON

The Jewish leader had just returned from London, where he attended the conference on Palestine for the Zionist Organization of America. He said he gave the President his personal impressions of the conference and discussed the refugee problem particularly with reference to children.

Rabbi Wise was accompanied to the White House by his successor as head of the Zionist organization, Dr. Solomon Goldman.

ZIONIST'S PREDICTION

"There is already in Palestine, with a Jewish population of nearly half a million, a de facto Jewish homeland," said Dr. Goldman. "The ultimate decision as to the future of the Jewish homeland in Palestine will be made, not by the British government, but by the Jewish people in Palestine and their Jewish supporters and Christian friends throughout the world."

2.—Jewish immigration. It is reported the plan calls for entry of only 15,000 Jews a year into the Holy Land for the next five years, after which time the question would be reconsidered.

3.—Land sales to Jews. Informed sources said the plan provides for division of Palestine into three tracts, with land sales permitted in one, restricted in another, and forbidden in a third.

September 1, 1939, Hitler sends his shock troops across and into Poland. In a matter of weeks he stands outside Warsaw the capital of Poland and says, "We are putting an end to the eternal movement of Germanic people to southern and western Europe and turning our eyes towards the east." Adolph Hitler, Mein Kampf.

By Bread Alone

Los Angeles Times ** SUNDAY, APRIL 25, 1943

B'nai B'rith Calls Meeting for Discussion of Unity Plan

To consider problems and plan action needed to meet "the most serious situation faced by Jewry in the 100-year history of the B'nai B'rith," all members of all Los Angeles area B'nai B'rith lodges and auxiliaries will meet in emergency session Thursday at 8 p.m. at Sinai Temple.

The call was issued by Robert Bogen, president of the Southern California B'nai B'rith Council, and Mrs. Eleanor Weissberg, president of the Southern California Conference of B'nai B'rith Auxiliaries. In a joint statement they said:

"This is the most critical hour ever confronted by the Jewish people. The enormity of the crisis demands immediate co-operation of every man and woman regardless of other plans and commitments."

Speakers will be Rabbi Max Nussbaum of Temple Israel; David Blumberg, vice-president of the Supreme Lodge, and Mrs. Rebecca Rosenthal, first vice-president of the Women's Grand Lodge, District 4.

MONDAY, APRIL 26, 1943 ** Los Angeles Times

Day of Compassion Scheduled for Jewish Victims of Nazis

NEW YORK, April 25. (AP)—The Federal Council of the Churches of Christ in America said in a research bulletin issued today that "the suffering of the Jewish people in Europe is beyond anything the civilized imagination can picture."

The bulletin, titled "The Mass Murder of Jews in Europe," was prepared by the council's department of research and education to guide Christian churches in the observance of a day of compassion for the Jews on May 2, the council said.

Material presented in the publication, the council stated, shows that the Nazis have pursued a policy not merely of discrimination against the Jews but of deliberate extermination.

Of the approximately 600,000 Jews who were in Germany in 1939, according to the council, it is estimated that not more than 40,000 remained at the end of 1942.

20

Jews from Poland and Russia. Jews from the Carpathians too. I swear I saw Lajos in one of the boxcars. I yelled to him but he wouldn't answer. I hitched onto the back of the car, riding through the night. Then the trains came to a halt and I was driven off by a railway inspector. I decided not to go back to my unit until I knew. So I came home. But now that I see that everything at home is fine I must leave. I must not be discovered missing from my unit."

And then father was gone again.

The heavy snows melted and the warm spring days were approaching. The war raged as before, but no one seemed to care anymore. Perhaps we developed an immunity to it. There was a serenity throughout our region. People walked around unnoticed, uninterrupted, disregarding the war and the persecution; they were only concerned with the present. As time passed the Jews were beginning to come home from labor battalions and the few Jewish soldiers still under arms were discharged from the military. Father, too, came home and went back to his winemaking.

As the years and the war dragged on and Russian strength grew, Marshal Zhukov sent forces into the Carpathians. Horthy cynically turned coat and shifted his allegiance to the Soviets. Horthy sent an armistice commission to Moscow and announced the surrender of Hungary. But he was too late, as German troops had already occupied Hungary. They forced Horthy to rescind his order and resign. And we were in the middle of all this the morning the Nazi tank arrived, scruffy, worn, and, as it turned out, a herald of our destruction. The tank was not alone. With it, blueing the air with exhaust fumes, choking our narrow cobblestone streets and destroying the quiet of the morning, came armored cars and trucks, loaded with German SS soldiers, who quickly dismounted and set up camp in every open space. The vehicles looked much like the first tank in their state of dilapidation. The Germans, weary, short-tempered, and fed up, made no effort to impress the natives with a display of military spit and polish. Of course, we didn't go out of our way to impress them either.

I arrived, as always, in the morning for work at the machine shop. Just behind me came Hans, the other apprentice. He had seen his German soldiers up close, that same morning.

I greeted Hans and Snukly cheerfully. Snukly was the elder apprentice, and as usual nodded his recognition. But not Hans, the "Schwab" as we nicknamed him.

"What makes you so happy?" demanded Hans. "Those aren't Palestinians who have come to save you. Those are the Fuhrer's soldiers. They'll finish you off."

"Did you see them?" I asked. "Go look at your master race. They're kaput."

"Oh yeah?" exclaimed Hans. "They're still powerful enough to wipe out all of you Jews." Hans became furious.

Snukly stepped between us to stop what was to be an inevitable fight. During the morning Hans grew more and more restless. Looking through the open doors of the shop, we saw no indication of the presence of the Germans, no Nazi flags flew over the town, no shots were heard, no orders barked. In fact, until lunch time there was no indication within the walls of the shop that anything at all unusual had taken place.

As I began eating my lunch, a vehicle pulled into the yard. Out of the German army scout car, came two German officers. They were SS. They raised their hands in a lazy Nazi salute, but their "Heil Hitler" was snappy and commanded attention. Hans made the approach and greeted them in a similar fashion. I could see the pride and joy in Hans as he raised his hand in a similar Nazi salute. He achieved the ultimate, his ancestors had arrived; he was finally a true and pure German.

They needed repairs for the car. Hans, anxious and extremely excited, began talking to them in Schwabic, a German dialect that sounded like Yiddish to me. Before the Nazi invasion, the Schwabians, a German people living outside Germany, were regarded as second-class citizens. Actually they were bigots and ranked highest in their hatred of Jews. Many of their young people joined the German SS as early as 1938, leaving their homes and their parents for the fanatical Nazi cause. Hans was not ready for the SS yet, not until he finished his apprenticeship. Now, with two Nazi officers present, he was in his glory.

The mechanical trouble was only minor. Hans couldn't fix the modified jeep alone, and reluctantly he had to turn to me for assistance. Together we examined the engine, worked on the carburator, jiggled a few things, changed the oil, adjusted the starter, gave the car a reflective kick on the rear and the job was done. The Nazis missed the symbolism of my gesture. They paid Snukly the mechanics' fee, thanked us, and drove off very satisfied with a job well done.

With no further interruption from the occupying forces, the day continued like all others, most of it spent trying to repair a diesel engine which was expiring of old age. Hans and I kept apart, but before the afternoon was over we were talking to one another once again.

"After all," I reasoned, "if you're going to defend supermen, they ought to at least look the part." Our unexpected visitors hadn't looked the part, and Hans' boasts about German superiority were less spirited than usual.

But there were others among the visitors who came silently and unnoticed—a special commando of SS and Gestapo—who were far deadlier for the Jews than the mechanized units.

I arrived back home that evening to find that my calm mood was not matched by anyone else at home. The kitchen, where we ate our meals and where, on chilly nights, we gathered for warmth, seemed unnaturally quiet as I opened the door to the house and strode in. The hush was like that at the bedside of a dying man.

My mother sat by the stove, slightly concealed by the huge soup kettle, her hands tightly clasped. "Moishi, Moishi, my child," she said in a quiet voice. "Pour yourself a bowl of soup. The rest of us have already eaten...you too must eat a warm meal." She was concerned, and she cared more for her children than for herself. It was more evident now than ever before. I felt the anxiety in her more than ever.

My father stood near the window, staring at the dark sky. I knew the mood; it meant he was angry, really furiously angry. His habit was to get more quiet and withdrawn as his anger grew. Now he was completely silent.

Magda sat in her favorite chair, a book in front of her. But, she wasn't reading.

Etu sat next to the sewing machine, her fingers flat on the table. Her face, usually bright and gay, was filled with sadness.

Only Lajos moved at all. He sat by the kitchen table, assembling a dismantled wrist watch. I sat next to him sipping my bowl of soup. "You should've seen Hans today," I said. "Two Germans came in with a heap. It was worn and busted. We fixed it for them. Hans was really mad. They looked so scruffy. Don't they wash in the German Army? Don't they care for their equipment?"

My voice broke the silence. My father turned towards the room, speaking perhaps to me, maybe to everyone, possibly to himself. I never heard him talk with such bitterness. "So, they've found us," he shouted. "No one thought they would. God, what can the end be? What will it mean?"

"The meaning is, father," said Lajos firmly, "that we never know the meaning of war until it's too late. And too late it is. The Nazis wouldn't allow the Jews to be liberated. Nor would the Red Army rush across the mountains to save us."

The inner meaning of all this was too much for me. I had never seen my mother sit like that, quiet, tense, looking as though she were about to explode, tight as a cord about to snap under strain. It frightened me more than I would have admitted to anyone. I remembered an appointment to meet my friend Tibi, and explained to my family, "We're going to visit a traveling carnival, Tibi and I."

I put the soup dish aside and slipped out the door. Ordinarily my departure would be the signal for considerable commotion; questions about my destination, warnings to be home on time, a check by my mother on my appearance, and perhaps a few cents in my pocket from my father. Tonight there was not a sound. All of them were frozen in their positions like a tableau. It was the most frightening moment of all and I fled.

Tibi was not at the carousel where we had planned to meet, but the Nazi soldiers were there, and in great numbers. They seemed attracted by the lights and music and mostly by the girls of the town. I watched with a certain fascination as they walked around the attractions. Their marksmanship at the shooting gallery was impressive. They laughed, shouted and slapped each other on the back, and that surprised me. They were having so much fun, and didn't seem too different from the Hungarian and Czechoslovakian soldiers with whom I was more familiar. Suddenly I found nothing to fear in them. In fact, I began to mingle with them as they stood around wondering what to do. Since I knew little German with Yiddish inflections, I decided to greet them openly, and in a friendly manner.

"You'll like the carousel and the roller coaster too," I said. "It's thrilling."

One of them burst out laughing, "We're not looking for more thrills. We get enough of those on the battlefield."

His companion, an SS trooper, listened as I spoke a mutilated German. He once again looked at me strangely, then with a sudden outburst snapped at me, "*Jude*, scram!"

I was startled. Without thinking I immediately froze with fear.

"Scram," he said again, "before I kill you, you Jew!" The temporary illusion of Nazi humanity was gone. For me, the evening was over and I turned pale with terror and raced back to the safety of my home and family. When I got there, my mother had gone to bed and my father and Lajos were talking quietly. The lights were low, the conversation seemed not intended for my ears.

I climbed into bed and pulled the cover over my head. It was an old trick I employed to go to sleep when I was anxious or frightened. It had worked for me since I could remember, but that night it failed. Determined that whatever disasters threatened, they could wait until morning, I finally fell asleep. It was a hard, undisturbed sleep.

The next morning not much was to happen. Each of us went to our respective jobs. The tank, however, remained parked near our house. The Germans washed, ate, slept, walked around and made no attempt to clean up their foul-looking vehicles.

The calm did nothing to ease fears among our elders, although for me it was a period of relaxation. The atmosphere at home remained tense. Friends came by and stayed for hours; people sought out familiar faces, voices and reactions for assurance. It was a time to feel the closeness, the reinforcement of an old friend.

But at the shop things became suddenly more interesting. I was getting an opportunity to learn about the construction of German army vehicles; the Volkswagen of the first day was succeeded by many others in the following days. There was little friction in the shop, as we were all too busy to argue. Furthermore, the Germans paid on time and tipped us well, not always with money, but delightful luxuries such as chocolate, an occasional cigarette and even for Snukly, a small bottle of wine. I found these Germans at the shop friendly, never too busy to give me a pat on the head and a word of encouragement. If it had not been for the situation at home and the brief encounter at the carnival, I would never have thought twice about the change in our town. I was quite unprepared when suddenly my world exploded around me.

On the fifth day after the Nazis arrived, a Gestapo ordinance was posted all over town ordering all Jews to wear yellow armbands on their left arms. Women and children were not excluded. The penalty was severe, so all Jews wore the armbands the following day. Then, to confuse and terrorize us even more, the Gestapo ordered the yellow armband to be replaced by the yellow Star of David.

On the eighth day Jewish shops were marked with yellow paint and all non-Jews were forbidden to trade there.

Two days later the Jews were ordered to be off the streets by six in the evening. The curfew was in effect for all regardless of profession or protocol. In two short weeks the process of identification and confinement was well under way. The Nazi tactics worked well elsewhere in our region too, and finally, all Jews were placed under house arrest.

My career as an apprentice was over.

My life as a Nazi prisoner had begun.

CHAPTER TWO
"The Brickyard"

Before the house arrest, the men had been gathering hurriedly in groups, in homes, in the synagogue. From conversation, I grew aware that the Nazi terror had spread all over town. Jewish shops had been smashed and looted. Each new day confusion turned into fear, and fear into mourning. This was indeed a dark hour for all the Jews in Munkacs.

In the evening of April 10th, father came in, an anxious look on his deeply lined face and said, "They're gathering in the synagogues, in temples to chant the Psalms by candlelight. They carried sacks from the mill, ripped them open and wore them and poured ashes upon their heads. Let's join them," he urged.

Lajos and I looked amazed, puzzled. "Have they gone mad? It's not prayer we need." I responded with anger. "We need our Allies to come to our rescue. Why isn't the Red Army here to prevent our persecution? We need God, too, but where is He when we need Him most?" I demanded.

"Bite your tongue," said father. Then he quoted from the book of Esther, Chapter Four. "In every province reached by the royal command and decree, there was a great mourning amongst the Jews, with fasting and weeping and sackcloth and ashes."

But there was no Mordechai, and no Esther came and no "permission granted to the Jews in every city to unite and defend themselves." Would there ever again "For the Jews be light and joy and gladness and honor," as we had read yearly in the Megillah at Purim time, celebrating the defeat of Haman?

27

In all the confusion and fright we forgot that it was Mother's birthday. She had turned forty-four.

Then, in the midst of desperation, a ray of hope appeared. The Nazi-appointed leadership in Munkacs, a sizable city by European standards, was notified by the Gestapo that they would issue a proclamation of safety for all Jews, provided we raised a certain sum of money. This was one of the many nefarious schemes to spring from the mind of the despicable Adolf Eichmann. It was indeed a large amount but not unrealizable, and in every Jewish community of the four corners of Munkacs, ours included, a campaign was begun to raise funds. Whatever we could spare was sacrificed. All contributed to try to save their own lives and the lives of all Hungarian Jewry.

For days we waited for the proclamation. Hour after hour our tensions increased, our fears deepened. Would there be a sufficient amount of money raised? No one could tell us. Rumor after rumor was spread until finally the proclamation, in large Gothic German letters, was posted. All Jews living in towns and villages were to be ready for immediate shipment to camps; all Jews living in cities would be relocated to ghettos. There was no explanation of what happened to our money or the promise of safety. My heart sank when I read it.

For the first time I began to feel panic. Until now I had looked on events with some detachment, as if I were a bystander. Perhaps the appearance of the first Nazi tank, dirty and uncared for, so little in keeping with the image of the Master Race and its tradition of military preparedness, had lulled me into a false sense of security. The anti-Jewish decrees had not affected me very much either. I had no store to be robbed, and the yellow star did not bother me. I suppose it was my youth. This old and weighty old Jewish burden somehow wasn't intended for me.

But now I was threatened with a physical change. The idea of moving to a ghetto or camp and the immensity of this danger began to make itself obvious even to me. My parents joined in the town's sudden curiosity. Which classification would we be placed under? Our picturesque and meager town of Oroszveg was always considered part of the ancient city of Munkacs. Separated by the

Latorca River, the small suburb was but a bridge from Munkacs, the only adjacent city for about 25 miles. If we were classified as a suburb, then we would go to a ghetto. If we were a town or village, then the camps would be our destination. Of the two, there was no question about which was preferable. We had hoped that we would be regarded as part of the larger city, even though Oroszveg did have some local officials. But knowing that we would be moved from our home in either case, we began packing what we needed.

We had barely begun sorting our clothing when there was a knock at the door. A surge of fear hit us. My father, acting bravely, walked to the front door and opened it slowly. There stood Tibi, who slipped quietly into the house and closed the door quickly.

"Moishi, Lajos!" he exclaimed. "We're going into the woods. You have to come with us."

"Us?" we asked.

"Samson, Moses. We're getting everyone, even the girls. Etu and little Magda, you must come too. We're going to fight!" he said with great intensity.

"With what?" we asked.

"I have a pistol and some ammunition. We have food and there are partisans in the woods. We'll find them and join up. If the Nazis want to kill us, let them pay for it," he replied.

I was stunned. The idea of fighting back had not occurred to me at this crucial point in time. But before I could even think, my father stepped before me. Putting a hand on Tibi's shoulder he said, "Tibi, don't do this."

"Why not?" Tibi was confused and embarrassed. He respected my father, but he had expected his support.

"It's too late, for one thing," my father answered. "You have to have time to organize, otherwise you're just going to the slaughter. And you cannot do anything without Christians to help you; there are only a few of you."

"But there are partisans out there," he insisted.

"And what's happening to them?" my father demanded.

"Their efforts are futile! They are too few. Do you think the Hungarian fascists will hide Jews? The Magyar Arrowcross bandits will hunt you down. The Ukrainian peasants will give you away to the Nazis."

"Mr. Bernard, everything you say is true. But isn't it better to die fighting than to wait for them to kill us?" he countered.

"Tibi, my dear Tibi," father pathetically replied, tears rolling down his flushed cheeks. "I beg you—don't do this thing. It's not meant for a Jew."

I felt the burning of his tears as I watched his face, understanding something of the centuries of the martyrdom Jews suffered, often chose, I had been taught, rather than give up their faith and their existence as Jews. What I saw in my father's eyes was not cowardice; nor was it fear. Instead it was a hopelessness in the odds of this world, curiously mixed with a faith and hope in the odds of the next.

Lajos proposed another argument. "Listen, Tibi. We know the Nazis can't last much longer. Look at them in the village. The Allied armies are finishing them off. The damned Nazis are stronger than we are here, but they're being whipped every day on the battlefields."

Etu joined him. "Let's stay together. The Germans are almost done for, and we'll be freed by the Russians."

There was a hint of pleading in Etu's voice. No longer was she the militant she had grown up to be with Tibi in the Betar Zionist Youth, a militant group of youngsters who dreamed of settling in Israel one day. Surely he could see that she could never go with him against her father's wishes; and yet, if he walked out that door without her, she would be betraying him.

But Tibi clenched his fists. It was no longer Tibi of the gentle face and laughing eyes. His face was set hard in the struggle with himself as he quietly turned to the door and went out.

The next day the drums were beating aloud. The young and old alike ran to hear the ancient drummer, as our radios were long confiscated and this was the only direct way to get the latest news. What news could the drummer give the Jews in these trying days?

We pushed and shoved to hear this old and gray newscaster, but all he did was keep hitting the parchment, turning out an ancient drum beat for all to gather, to come to bear witness of the latest proclamation. For a quarter of an hour he just kept banging away. Then he stopped.

"Silence!" he proclaimed. "Hear ye! Hear ye! Orders from Gestapo headquarters: All Jews without exception, living in the vicinity of Oroszveg will be ready for shipment to internment camps by six a.m. tomorrow morning. Those not ready will be shot. End of news report, April 18, 1944."

April 19, 1944 dawned with a spring chill and dampness to suit our mood. Passover, the festival of freedom, had ended just four days before, and we were about to enact our own Exodus; but someone had gotten the signals mixed, as all the plagues were falling on the Children of Israel and not on their oppressors. We sat on packed bundles, our spirits had left with Tibi as he walked out our door for the last time. None of us would admit it, but we wondered if we had made a mistake in not joining him for a final run for freedom.

We had slept little, on chairs and stripped beds, Lajos and I on the floor, side by side with our heads resting on our bundles, our bodies warmed by each other. My father slept not at all, sitting by the window, taking a drink of water from the pitcher, pacing a while until my mother stopped him so that the others might sleep. The moon was smothered in scurrying clouds, and I watched it hide and reappear countless times as I lay on the floor. Both of us (the moon and I), I imagined, trying to sleep and both of us being interrupted; the moon by the lowering dark clouds, I by fears as unformed as the clouds, equally dark and gloomy.

With the coming of light we ate our last meal in our old home, a cheerless repast, bread and butter and cold tea. We scarcely poured the tea, stirring it, trying to gain the last trace of flavor from the tired leaves, when there was a knock at the door. My father moved to open it; we sat knotted in fear.

Instead of a Nazi SS or a Hungarian militiaman there stood Ana, our friend and neighbor, about 44, slender, meticulously

31

dressed as usual, but highly agitated. Her friends had persuaded her to join the pro-Nazi Arrowcross party, never dreaming, she now protested, that they would go to such extremes.

"What will they do to you?" she kept repeating. "Where could they take you? After all, the war's nearly over. The Red Army is just around the corner, over those mountains," she pointed to the east. "It's only a matter of days or weeks before they'll be here to rescue all." Her arms laden with packages, she pushed her way indoors and placed them on the table.

"Here's a carton of cigarettes, some fresh bread, tea. Here, take them, you'll need them..." Her words, which started in a rush, faltered and she broke into sobs. Ana, a devout Catholic, believed in prayers and thus recited, "Jesu, that you should let such things happen. Jesu, where are you?" Her voice rose sharply and then stopped. Only her walking broke the silence.

My mother went to comfort her. "You'll pray for our safety and perhaps the Lord will hear you."

But Anushka was beyond such hope. "Jesu, where are you? Jesu, where are you?" she kept repeating over and over. Finally, ignoring my mother and all else, she rose, stumbled towards the door, and never even bid us goodbye as she left, still sobbing, into the street.

My mother placed the cigarettes and food inside our bundles and we continued to sit again in silence. Ana's brief visit forced me, for the first time, to the realization that I was actually going to leave my home, my birthplace, my friends, my work, my school, the world in which I had spent all of my seventeen years. My moments of reflection did not last long.

"It's time that we left," my father said, and he picked up a suitcase and some bundles. Not questioning, the rest of us did the same, and without a look backwards, we stepped out onto the street, leaving behind the home which we had cherished, and built with love, care and hard work. I glanced at the *mazzuzah* on the doorpost. Had father forgotten to take it off? Did he think we'd be back some day, or that another Jewish family would ever live in this house?

Outside we stood near the wooden fence by our house and watched the slow procession of our neighbors as they moved down the street, escorted by two Hungarian policemen with rifles slung on their shoulders, bayonets fixed and gleaming in the sun. They moved in the direction of the town square, toward the school yard.

Our friends, Tibi's mother and father, his sister and my schoolmate, Karen, her lovely golden hair flowing down to her waist, were all there. The youngest sister Angel, Magda's playmate, whose lovely complexion now seemed drawn and wan, walked slowly past our home. I tried to step toward them to say a few words of farewell but was intercepted by the guards.

"You'll soon be together," said one of them, a large, kindly man, whose pleasant manner and reassurance did something to relieve my anxiety. I recognized him. His son played football on a team that competed with mine. Even as he ordered me back, Tibi's family trudged by, waving slowly as they neared the house. They moved like drayhorses, nodding their heads with the strain of each step, burdened with their suitcases and bundles.

So far no one had come to fetch us to tell us to join the procession. We stood quietly in our yard watching more and more of our friends and neighbors walk by. Finally, we saw several local officials and two Hungarian policemen head down the road toward our house. They entered through the gate and greeted us courteously. They knew my father well, as they were old friends who had gone to school with him and were members of the same clubs. They frequently played cards together; in a town as small as ours, people could not help but know and respect one another. One of them took my father by the hand. His voice echoed the deep concern he must have felt.

"Bernard, you must be calm. All shall be well with you and your family. This action is taken for your safety. The Germans are sending you to a labor camp where you'll work together safely until the end of the war. Then you'll come back. Believe me," he emphasized. "You'll come back! There are worse things that could happen to you..."

"Yes, yes," father nodded. Whether or not he believed what he heard, I did not know. To me it seemed possible, especially since we had not seen a German soldier all morning. If they were still in town, they were certainly keeping out of the way.

"Now," continued my father's friend, "deposit with us your cash, jewelry—whatever is of value. We'll care for it until you return."

Father reached into his pocket and pulled out whatever money was in his pocket. He handed it over to his friend and motioned for us to do the same. My mother, silently, removed her wedding ring, my sisters their earrings; but I contributed nothing, having never owned anything of value.

I looked around to see what Lajos was handing over to the official. He was nowhere to be seen.

Surprised, I asked, "Where is Lajos?"

"He will be back in a few minutes," said my father.

"I hope so," said one of the policemen. "The penalty for hiding is death, and he would be foolish to try to escape. He can't get very far, and when they find him..." He didn't finish his sentence. It wasn't necessary that he did.

Lifting our belongings, we moved slowly out of the yard to join the continuing stream of Jews heading toward the center of town. The door to our house was locked and the key tagged as the embarrassed officials bid goodbye to us, wishing us a pleasant journey.

Loaded with baggage, I struggled along, trying to keep it on my shoulders, and not allow it to fall in the street. By this time the street had become a crowded thoroughfare, with men, women and children all heading in the same direction. Accompanied by the Hungarian militia, we soon arrived at our destination, the school yard. We sat there on our belongings for hours, as the yard and the school filled up. It took most of the day before the entire Jewish population of Oroszveg was collected. The yard, which had seemed so gigantic to me as a youngster, could hardly hold the mass of humanity pressed within it.

Over us hung the dust and the haze, obscuring the sunlight of midday. There was an awesome silence as well. Children huddled by their parents in fear or for reassurance; people spoke quietly to one another, seemed more considerate, shared what they had to eat and worked out a kind of system for sharing the limited toilet facilities, each making sure that it was his or her turn before using them. Several of the older children took on the responsibility of seeing that the younger ones had places to sleep amidst all of the people and luggage. Older people were given places in the shade. It was as though a strange civility had suddenly been developed to ease the strain of our tragic day, replacing all rudeness and harshness.

We endured our stay in the school yard with great patience, but while we were waiting, we could see groups of SS mechanized forces passing, many just circling around the school yard on their motorcycles. We had no way of knowing that this was a special detachment trained to insure our orderly relocation, a part of Hitler's "final solution" to the "Jewish problem." They did not speak to us nor did they order us around. They were there to assure strict enforcement of the master plan and to put down any resistance, quickly, ruthlessly, either quietly or publicly, depending on whether open terror or silent elimination would go further in bringing about total submission.

At about four in the afternoon, just as the light and warmth of the sun began to dissipate, with the school yard filled to its capacity, the gates opened one more time. Through them trundled several horsedrawn hay carts, the kind which every peasant in the province owned, the mainstay of transportation in the rural section of the Carpathian Mountains. We were told to load our luggage aboard the carts. The older people and smaller children were then placed atop the luggage, and the carts started out, the rest of us, under the watchful eyes of the special detachment of SS, trudging behind.

The procession moved through a silent town. As we moved across the ancient castle-like bridge which spanned the river, I could hear the sounds of the waves crashing against the foundation stones. I looked deep into the river Latorca, leaning over the rail, thinking: Would I ever see you again? Would I ever again

35

be able to swim and play here, as I had summer after summer? Would I ever be able to follow the Bulgarian vegetable growers to the river, where they rinsed the mud off their bundles of carrots? Would I ever be able to dive again for loose carrots, and make feasts of them with my friend Tibi or my playmates Karen and Angel?

But for the Jews, there was no one in sight. The non-Jews remained hidden behind their shades and doors, occasionally peeking out, but never venturing to bid us farewell or give a comforting word.

Whole families marked with the Jewish Star of David are forced into Ghettos as a prelude to deportation and "resettlement."

"Jews: Driven from their homes."

Deportation of Jews begins in Nazi occupied Hungary, 1944.

Ukrainian SS collaborator guarding the rounded up Jews.

Why me? Oh, God!

By Bread Alone

A Jewish father and daughter frightened and lost are awaiting "resettlement."

Jewish children in the Ghettos often lost their parents and were left out in the cold to starve and die.

"JEWS: SURROUNDED BY BARBWIRE FENCES."

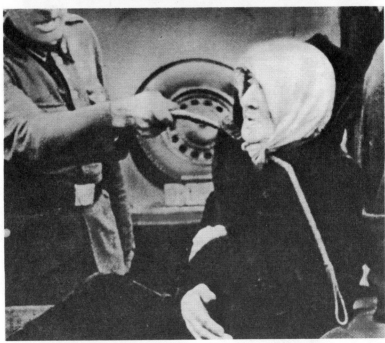

A Jewish woman brutalized and beaten by a Nazi guard.

Deprived and persecuted Jewish children begging for a crust of bread inside the Ghetto.

The pattern of identification of Jewish shops and the persecution of the
Jews of Poland are copied from that of Nazi Germany.

45

In the Ghettos

Jewish "Civil Police" in Action

The Warsaw Ghetto consisted of half a million Jews from all over Poland and other parts of Europe. It was guarded by three different police. The German, Polish Blue and approximately 2,000 Jewish police. The German and Polish police carried firearms but not all of the Jewish police did. They carried clubs and many of them used them in an awesome brutal way against their co-religionist. Their brutal behavior will never be understood by those who were not directly involved in the tragedy of the "Holocaust". It is a study by itself and someday we hope to understand what made them so brutal toward their own fellow man.

Jewish police force inside the Warsaw ghetto.

46

After a short debate the Nazi leadership under the direction of Himmler decided that Auschwitz-Birkenau in a remote part of Poland is to be the site for a mass killing operation complete with gas chambers and crematoriums.

Heydrich

Adolf Eichmann

Rudolph Hoess

Kramer

Heydrich, head of the security police was in full accord with his boss Himmler and so was Adolf Eichmann, Chief of Gestapo dealing with Jewish matters. Thus, Rudolph Hoess was chosen the first commandant of Auschwitz. Later Kramer took over from Hoess the command but in 1944 during the Hungarian mass exterminations Hoess was once again called upon to assume the awesome responsibility of mass exterminating the Hungarian Jewish transports.

One of the SS Azerbaijan platoons

Oskar Dirlewanger, the SS penal regiment's commander.

Oskar Dirlewanger was born in Wurzburg in Southern Germany in 1895. He was a doctor of political science until Frankfurt University deprived him of the title in 1935 when he was convicted and imprisoned for molesting a minor. The General SS gave him a dishonourable discharge. However, he had a mysterious and close connection with Gottlob Berger who had risen from the shadowy and murky underworld of the Black Order and gained quick promotion in the SS.

Russian SS Assault Brigade RONA led by Brigadier Mieceslav Kaminski.

Hitler: 'Wipe them out'

Some of Kaminski's RONA soldiers

Russian SS Brigadeführer Mzzieslaw Kaminski

Ukrainian mercenaries of the German army

Es gibt keinen
jüdischen Wohnbezirk
- in Warschau mehr !

The Warsaw battle is raging for weeks on
ends as the SS General Jurgen Stroop de-
clares that the Warsaw Ghetto is no more.
Jewish resistance is crushed, the Jewish
fighters executed and the women and children are on their way to Auschwitz-Birkenau
and Treblinka for "resettlement". May 1943.

JEWS: ROUNDED UP

Like at "Babi Yar" here too the Nazis used the same tactics of mass killing in remote parts of town near a ravine. Note the number of Ukrainian collaborators serving as mass executioners as well as guards.

They could not believe that they would be hanged.

or shot.

Zionist: **Mendel Fisher Is Here to Rally S. F's Jews**

"Land for victory!"

That is the slogan of Zionists throughout the world, who have united in an effort to settle homeless Jews on farms in Palestine, to raise food for themselves and contribute to the Allied war effort.

In San Francisco this week is Mendel N. Fisher, national executive director of the Jewish National Fund of America, the land purchasing agency of the world Zionist organiaztion.

On a Nation-wide tour with "Land for Victory" as his slogan, Fisher will stay in this city until Thursday, and will speak in the various synagogues during the Yom Kippur ceremonies tomorrow and Wednesday.

His organiaztion, Fisher said, sent $500,000 to Palestine during the month of September, and averages about $2,000,000 annually. "The Jewish National Fund, established 40 years ago, has acquired 134,500 acres in Palestine and settled 285,000 refugees there since the advent of Hitlerism."

"There are 8,000,000 homeless Jews in Europe now. After the war we hope to settle 3,000,000 of these in Palestine. This project, which we expect will take 10 years to complete, will be the greatest colonization project in history."

Fisher said that the whole Jewish population of Palestine was deeply concerned with helping the Allies win the war. "Eight thousand Palestinian Jews are already in the British army. A Jewish army

MENDEL N. FISHER
"Land for victory"

is now being organized—called the Maccabeans, resolved to fight just as the Maccabees did 2000 years ago.

"The Jews are lovers of peace, but every Jew would give everything to see the Allies victorious. There is no hope for mankind—Christian or Jewish—should Hitler win—as he will not."

Jewish Ghetto fighters before their execution.

What could this little boy have done to warrant SS troopers ordering him "hands up."

They will not surrender their honor.

By Bread Alone

"Mordchai Anielewicz and his colleagues in the Jewish fighting forces."

Chil
Grynszpan

Jakub
Praszkier

Michal
Rozenfeld

Lejb
Rotblatt

Michal
Klepfisz

Edward
Fondaminski

Mordchai Anielewicz, born in Poland 1919. In November, 1942 he organized the Jewish Fighting group known as the Z.O.B. He initiated the uprising of the Warsaw Ghetto and led his group until May 8, 1943 when he was hopelessly surrounded by the ruthless SS Nazi commandos, he took his life instead of yielding to the Nazis.

Iccak (Antek)
Cukierman

Niuta (Wanda)
Tajtelbaum

Abram
Sznajdmil

W.
Krawczynski

Tosia
Altman

Luba
Fondaminska

Zofia
Zatorskn

Samuel
Zimmerman

Eszel
Bielski

Mira
Fuchrer

B.
Chaimowicz

Dr. Adolf Berman
"Borowski"

Hilel
Cajtlin

Icchak
Kacenelson

Dr. Emanuel
Ringelblum

Rywa
Wojskowska

Los Angeles Times

EQUAL RIGHTS

LIBERTY UNDER THE LAW   TRUE INDUSTRIAL FREEDOM

WEDNESDAY MORNING, MARCH 22, 1944

Poles Report Mass Murder

LONDON, March 21. (*Æ*)—The Polish Ministry of Information said today that more than 500,-000 persons, mostly Jews, had been put to death at a concentration camp at Osweicim, southwest of Krakow.

In a lengthy report on Nazi atrocities the ministry declared three crematoriums had b e e n erected inside the camp to dispose of 10,000 bodies a day. Gas chambers were said to have been attached to the crematoriums.

The report asserted that men, women and children arrive by truckloads and are removed to the gas chambers where 10 to 15 minutes are required for execution, but since the supply of poison gas is limited some persons are not dead when they are thrown into the crematorium.

Los Angeles Times WEDNESDAY MORNING, MARCH 22, 1944

F.D.R. URGES JEWISH HAVEN

Shelter Jews

WASHINGTON, March 24. (*P*) President Roosevelt, saying hundreds of thousands of Jews face death as a result of Hitler's grasp of the Balkans, called on the peoples of those countries and the Germans themselves today to hide intended victims from the Nazi executioners.

The Chief Executive also asked in a statement that "the free peoples of Europe and Asia, temporarily open their frontiers to all victims of oppression."

Refuge Promised Jews

"We shall find havens of refuge for them and we shall find the means for their maintenance and support until the tyrant is driven from their homelands and they may return," he said.

Mr. Roosevelt read the statement to his press conference. He said the American Interdepartmental Committee on Refugees has had considerable success in actually getting people out of Nazi-dominated areas.

Foreign Policy Stated

He indicated that he considered the first paragraph of his statement to be a summary of American foreign policy, commenting after he read it that it should answer people who have been going around asking bellhops whether this country has a foreign policy. The paragraph reads:

"The United Nations are fighting to make a world in which tyranny and aggression cannot exist; a world based upon freedom, equality and justice; a world in which all persons regardless of race, color or creed may live in peace, honor and dignity."

Keep War Guilt Record

Mr. Roosevelt's appeal to the Germans and the Balkan peoples, asked that they record the evidence against Nazis guilty of savagery and promised that those having a part in such acts —leaders, subordinates and functionaries—will all be punished.

"All who knowingly take part in the deportation of Jews to their death in Poland or Norwegians and French to their death in Germany are equally guilty with the executioner," he said. "All who share the guilt shall share the punishment.

Appeal to Germans

"Hitler is committing these crimes against humanity in the name of the German people. I ask every German and every man everywhere under Nazi domination to show the world by his action that in his heart he does not share these insane criminal desires.

"Let him hide these pursued victims, help them to get over their borders, and do what he can to save them from the Nazi hangman. I ask him also to keep watch and to record the evidence that will one day be used to convict the guilty."

Many Reach America

Prompted by the President's appeal for free countries of Europe and Asia to open their borders to refugees, a reporter asked if the United States planned to do the same. Mr. Roosevelt said we are already taking care of all we can get out. There are a good many now in North Africa, he added, but not enough to come to this country.

In another foreign policy development Mr. Roosevelt issued a statement reaffirming America's pledge to drive the Japanese from the Philippines and grant freedom to the island people. The occasion was the 10th anniversary of the Philippine Independence Act.

62

Los Angeles Times TUESDAY, APRIL 25, 1944

Story of Death in Poland Relayed by Underground

WASHINGTON, April 24. (AP) From the Polish underground has come a document purporting to show how the Nazi extermination policy has reduced Poland's prewar Jewish population from 3,500,000 to 50,000.

Contents of the report were made public John W. Pehle, executive director of the War Refugee Board.

Ghetto Liquidation

The underground report said: "Last month (October) we estimated that there were only 250,000 to 300,000 Jews left in Poland. It is our opinion that in a few weeks there will only remain about 50,000 . . .

"On Aug. 17 there began the liquidation of the only large ghetto in the east of Poland, in Bialystok, where there were approximately 40,000 Jews. During the first three days of this action seven transports of victims were taken to the death camp at Treblinka. In addition a passenger train, filled with children, left Bialystok. There were two Jewish nurses in each car.

"It is the general conviction that, before going to their deaths, these children were to furnish their blood for wounded German soldiers.

Germans Set It Afire

"On the fourth day of the action the fight began. Bloody combats took place in a number of streets. Just as in Warsaw, the Germans entered the ghetto in armored trucks and equipped with field artillery. They brought along about 1000 gendarmes and S.S. men and a number of Ukrainian detachments.

"The Jews retaliated mostly with grenades and incendiary bombs; they also had a few machine guns. Several hundred Germans and Ukrainians fell or were wounded.

"In order to crush the uprising the Germans did what they had done in Warsaw—they set the ghetto afire."

While the Germans still were trying to put down the Bialystok uprising, the report continued, "the final lipuidation of the ghetto of Tarnow took place" in early September.

Dig Own Graves

"All the children were concentrated in one building," the story said. "They were told that they were to be taken away to a nursery. The building was then hermetically sealed and blasted into the air.,,

Two months later, "on Wednesday, Nov. 3, at 6 a.m., all the men in Trawniki (concentration camp) were called out for the alleged purpose of digging air-shelter trenches. After two hours they were encircled with machine guns and all of them, without exception, were shot down. In the meantime 50 trucks drove into camp. All the remaining women and children were loaded on them and taken to an extermination point where they were forced to strip off their clothing and were then machine gunned in the same fashion as the men. After this massacre 3000 Italian Jews were brought to this camp and the same fate awaits them."

63

By Bread Alone

Los Angeles Times TUESDAY, APRIL 25, 1944

NAZIS IMPRISON 240,000 JEWS IN TOWN OF 17,000

STOCKHOLM, March 19. (*P*)— The small Czechoslovakian town of Marie Theresienstadt, with a prewar population of 17,000, now accommodates 240,000 Jews from all corners of Europe, imprisoned there by the Nazis under the doctrine of Aryan superiority.

Some details of this huge concentration camp, between Prague and Dresden, reached neutral Sweden by accident.

When the Nazis deported 500 to 600 Danish citizens of Jewish origin to Marie Theresienstadt, they made the error of sending away several of pure Aryan stock. After four months of unspeakable experiences, the mistake was "corrected" and they were returned to Denmark.

Danish patriots have since reported their experiences through the underground news network.

Jews from Holland, Norway, Belgium, France, Greece, Italy, Rumania, Serbia, Croatia, Hungary and Poland comprise the population of Marie Theresienstadt.

There are no Russian Jews; reports say the Germans always shoot them.

Los Angeles Times, 1944

Danish Minister Pleads for Postwar Tolerance

The United Nations will win the war but one cannot be certain of who will win the peace, Henrik de Kauffmann, Danish Minister to the United States and spokesman for all free Danes outside of Nazi-occupied Denmark, last night told an audience of 400 Jewish welfare leaders.,

He spoke at the annual dinner of the Federation of Jewish Welfare Organizations at Wilshire Blvd. Temple House, 636 S. Hobart Blvd.

"The day will come," de Kauffmann warned, "when the people will have to make the choice of another war, far worse than this once, or a world with much greater tolerance and decency existing among different national groups than we have today. There is no third choice.

Loyalty to Humanity

"We must develop and believe in not only loyalty to our own country but also in loyalty to humanity. The standards of decency we apply to relations between individuals must be applied between nations."

The Danish Minister told of 80 per cent of Danish Jews being evacuated from Denmark by the "underground" and was paid tribute for the Danes' pledge to recompense Sweden with funds liberated after the war for the care of refugees from Denmark.

New Trustees

Rabbi Edgar F. Magnin presided.

Jean Hersholt of the films, president of the National American-Denmark organization, introduced de Kauffmann.

David Tannenbaum, retiring president of the federation, and Dr. Maurice J. Karpf, executive director, also spoke.

Fourteen new members were elected to the board of trustees of the federation, which is composed of 16 social welfare agencies affiliated with the Community Chest and the War Chest. The new members: Ben Solnit, Col. Samuel Briskin, Mrs. E. Basthein, Jack Y. Berman, P. Karl, Joseph P. Loeb, Rabbi Magnin, Mrs. L. S. Nordlinger, Isaac Pacht, Mrs. I. Pelton, Ludwig Schiff, David Tannenbaum, George Thompson and Henry Weinberger.

Rabbi Max Nussbaum delivered the invocation.

65

By Bread Alone

AT JEWISH WELFARE DINNER—Left to right, Rabbi Edgar F. Magnin, Henrik de Kauffmann, Danish Minister to the United States; David Tannenbaum, Jean Hersholt.
Times photo

CHAPTER THREE
"The Demon"

The carts struggled uphill, and it was not long before I realized that our destination was to be the brickyard on the far side of the neighboring city, Munkacs. It made sense. That was the only site in the area that could hold the several thousand of us, and there was no indication that we were being taken for a long march.

Soon, we arrived at the brickyard, only to discover that we were not alone. For the past several days the SS and their Hungarian henchmen had been rounding up Jews in the other towns and villages, driving them to the Kalus brickyard. How little we knew! How much we had been deceived! For many days, during which time the vigorous fund-raising campaign had been in full swing, men and women and children from nearby villages were already being incarcerated! It was ironic that none of the so-called leaders of our communities were aware of it. Then a thought dawned on me. What if they did have full knowledge, but saw that either way we would be rounded up? Was there anything, short of the ultimate sacrifice, that we could have done?

By now, most of us were resigned to a ghetto form of existence, as long as they left us alone. In the past month we had been stripped, haunted and brutalized, our homes and livelihood taken from us, we were no longer human, rational or civilized.

I looked through the fence and saw men, women and children roaming about aimlessly. The men who had been there for some days had already built a wooden fence around the yard. There was a gate and a guardhouse, and several dozen newly recruited militia were posted at various locations around the yard.

The gate was closed and we sat for awhile, weary and drained, waiting for someone to tell us what to do.

The pause ended with the appearance of a tall, skinny-looking SS trooper, who strode out of the guard house. Around his arm was the SS brassard, in his hand a long whip.

He abruptly ordered us to rise. "I am your Commandant," he declared. "You obey my orders, and you are to move in orderly fashion into the camp." He waved his whip in the direction of the brickyard, and went on with a stern warning. "You are restricted to this camp and anyone attempting to escape will be shot without warning."

Hastily he pushed open the gates. We lifted our bundles and began to move into the brickyard. He stood behind us sadistically swinging his whip as we pushed our way through the gate. Once inside each family looked for a place to set itself down. There were no quarters, only huge brick ovens which were already occupied by earlier arrivals. So were the several rotting huts and a barn located within the camp area.

Together with another family, we found an unoccupied space behind the barn. We set down our luggage, spread coats and blankets on the ground, collected a bit of straw from the barn, and lay down for the night. At dawn we woke up shivering from the cold and fear. We were soon ordered to build our shelter, and so we began to obtain the needed material. There were lots of bricks around but no mortar to hold them together. There was disarray and more confusion as the day progressed, and finally by night we still found ourselves under the skies without a roof over our heads.

I was just about asleep when I felt a gentle tap on my shoulder. It was little Angel who had settled for the night with Karen alongside the wall near me. She was frightened, I could tell.

"Are you asleep?" she whispered.

"Just about," I whispered back. I knew she wanted to talk because it was always her way to deal with a problem.

"Let's talk," she said. "I can't sleep..." And so we talked through the night. "We should have listened to Tibi and Samson and Lajos, too, and gone to the woods to fight," she said, "rather than to die in this rat hole." "No," I responded, "it's not that simple...we have no weapons to fight with, and no contact with the partisans in the mountains. We'd be gunned down by the fascists," I said convincingly. "They fill the mountains and the forests. They'd just kill us before we ever had a chance to fight." Angel listened wide-eyed. Although I couldn't see her, I knew I had convinced her that it was best for us to stay here, and that the Allies would soon rescue us. I began to believe it, too, and my hopes along with Angel's were much brighter. On and on we talked, and only then did we realize how happy we had been. I kissed her and she responded warmly. As I kissed her again I felt the tears on her cheeks. Gently, I wiped them away and comforted her as best I could. I told her once again that I was sure that we would soon be liberated. The Red Army was a short distance away and their guns could be heard in the background. I sat beside her until she finally fell asleep in my arms.

Daybreak came. Men, women and children dragged themselves from under the cover, lost and frightened. Those of us who woke first moved slowly, so as not to disturb the others, but soon all the newcomers awoke fitfully. The "old-timers" who had been there two or three days were able to sleep longer.

We had brought food with us, and there was water from pumps and wells in the yard. Latrines had been hastily improvised by the first arrivals; though they were much too modest, they were at least adequate, so that sanitation was not the problem it might have been.

Far more serious was the lack of shelter, but in this we were coached by Bram, a young man whose camp experience dated back to 1940 and 1941, when he was a recruit in the Hungarian army. He was a born organizer and his energy was infectious.

Bram collected six families around him and proposed a simple plan.

"There may not be much else that we need for our comfort, but it's obvious that a brickyard has bricks."

He organized us into a human chain. Every single person in the six families moved bricks all day, built four walls, padded a floor with clumps of grass, made a roof of rotting lumber, and by nightfall thirty people had a home they had built themselves. But there was little energy left for pride in the achievement; we were weary from carrying the bricks and apprehensive about the future.

By nightfall the six families had become one. But Bram's usefulness did not end at homebuilding.

Later in the evening, as we were resting, Bram called a meeting of all the men and older boys among the families. He included people from other groups also. We were not unique. All around us families had banded together in what might be called tiny villages, or tribes. Several of these "villages" were represented at the meeting. Bram, whose background included a term at forced labor as well as a year as a Hungarian soldier, explained what was on his mind.

"Unless the Russians speed up their campaign and rescue us, we are doomed," he began realistically. "Our task is to see that we live long enough to enable them to save us."

He paused while his message sank in. Then he continued.

"Only if we organize can we expect to survive. Now we've built homes for ourselves, and that's a start. But it's only a start. Tomorrow we have to build a home for all those who have none. We have to set up a medical dispensary. We need a storehouse. We need a great many things. Thank God we have bricks. Now if you are ready to work..."

No one contradicted him. Finally someone asked the question that had been on everyone's mind.

"How do you know how long we'll be here? They may move us out tonight, tomorrow, even next week."

"It doesn't matter. For as long as we're here, we'll work to keep alive. How long do you think some of our people will live if they are forced to sleep out in the rain?" Then he dropped a bombshell. "How many here will volunteer to serve as watchmen?"

We were all stunned. At first I thought he meant for us to join the Hungarian police. Then I realized he was talking of forming our own guards. It made a lot of sense to me, but it didn't go over so well with the others. But Bram persisted.

"Look. We have to worry about the safety of our families. I'm talking about guards who'll help us get through this, who'll see that order's kept, that one person doesn't abuse the next. We'll try to protect the old and the children. Not only that, but we'll resist orders, slow down their projects, even foil the Nazi plans wherever we can. But we also have to avoid any disturbance which'll bring the Magyar guards down on our heads."

Bram argued with us for another half hour, but before we went to sleep, the ablebodied, myself included, were newly enrolled Jewish guardsmen.

For the next few days, we had two strokes of luck. One, the rain, never very far away in our mountain spring, held off. Also, both the Hungarian militia and the Nazi SS personnel were kept busy elsewhere, perhaps with the newcomers who were added to the camp roll daily. It seemed as though every Jewish village for a hundred miles around was being emptied into the brickyard.

During those days the camp began to take shape. With bare hands we helped each other build shelters. A rude mess hall was set up, where we distributed the food and supplies we received from the ghetto in the city, some donated by friends and some a contribution from the Jewish community there. We also built a dispensary of sorts, where the ill were brought to be kept in a warmer place with some semblance of professional care. Some among us had been trained in nursing, but there were no medicines and no doctors. Our doctors had run for safety, some out of the country and others to Budapest, where Eichmann promised a haven for those who could pay the ransom he demanded.

Word of our plight was passed to the surrounding region, and some of our non-Jewish friends began to help in our fight for survival.

Parcels of food and medicines were received each day and distributed to the fortunate recipients; however, combing through the various bundles I found none for us. Bitterness began to grow in me. I asked myself, "Have they forgotten about us so soon? Where are the good neighbors and our Gentile friends?" I wondered.

Then one morning I bumped into a huge bundle wrapped in corrugated paper and tied with heavy rope. It looked strange; it was the biggest package in the bunch. But it can't be ours, I thought. Why would anyone send us that? "No, no," I kept repeating. I hardly glanced at it, first shoving it aside, then kicking it, wishing it were ours. I walked away, dejected, beaten, sad. Then Tibi ran after me, excited. He grabbed me by the hand and yanked me back to the parcels.

"Hey, can't you see? This hunk of baggage is yours. Read it." Tibi was beside himself.

The package was addressed to me, from my boss at the machine shop.

"Come," said Tibi, "let's take it to the hut and see what Master Wilmos sent you." Tibi and I grabbed the bundle, lifting it slightly off the ground, and together we lugged it back to our quarters, where we dropped it inside on the ground.

I wanted father to open it.

"You open it," hinted father, "it's for you. Yes. Yes. It's addressed to you," he kept repeating.

All of his life my father taught us to help others in need. To be charitable. I remember him saying over and over, "It's better to give than to receive." Now I began to understand what he meant by it. I reached for the sharpest knife in our hut, quickly cut the ropes and gently unravelled the package.

Huge chunks of lard, sausage and soup bones first appeared. Digging deeper inside, I found beans and barley; in several bags, mushrooms, and most precious of all, bread. Freshly baked rye, with seeds sprinkled on top. We made a feast of it as we all joined in the traditional blessing of the bread.

Buried within one of the bags I discovered a note. It was written in Hungarian and directed to me:

"Escape to the mountains. Go to the vineyard in the hills. The gates to the cellars are open. We shall care for you in hiding." The note was signed "Master Wilmos."

I didn't know what to make of it. I looked around to see if there was any reaction as I was reading the note. Everyone looked puzzled. Not father. I looked into his eyes and began to understand. He and my boss, "the Master" as we used to call him in the machine shop, were good pals. They met frequently in the gambling parlors and in their union hall for a game of cards and a friendly discussion. My escape had been prearranged.

It was a good offer, and generous, too. My heart leaped at the idea, but then, strangely, I found that the chance to escape the camp did not appeal to me. Hiding day and night in a cellar in the mountains was not freedom. Nor was I tempted because of any immediate threat to my life. I somehow felt safe and even secure in this compound in the brickyard. The few days without appearance of the SS commandant, and with no overt threat on his part, had diminished my sense of danger.

All, including Magda and Etu, agreed that I should leave the brickyard.

"They'll never know you left, in all of the confusion," said Etu. "Getting out will be easy and it's a short walk to the mountains."

"Go," said Magda. "We'll cover for you."

My mother and father were united in their desire that I take the offer. However they left the final decision to me. From then on I had to make such choices over and over. Hide? Resist? Fight? Try to run away, or stick it out and ... what?

How I wished Lajos was here to give me advice. In the end I chose to stay with my family, Karen, Angel and Tibi, too. I couldn't bring myself to leave them. I remained, and all else followed from that.

Within the next few days our good fortune changed. The rains began to fall, and those who had been ill became worse; even the healthy began to suffer from the chill and the dampness. The first deaths among us took place, most of them old people, who succumbed to the weather, to depression, or because of their inability to adjust to the new conditions. A few were babies, children born in the camp, who might have lived under better circumstances, but who had no chance in the brickyard.

As the mud and water began to rise, some of the huts collapsed or were swept off their rude foundations. There was little we could do for those who were thus suddenly thrust out into the rain. Influenza was widespread, and the sounds of dripping water and people coughing were heard constantly throughout the camp.

Then, just as things seemed to be as bad as they could get, they suddenly became much worse.

One morning, during our second week in the brickyard, we were driven out into the rain and ordered to stand at attention. Even the sick were ordered out, and Magyar guards went from hut to hut to see that all were present and accounted for. We were new at this, and the order seemed frightening. Even the sick in the rain? But there had been no mistake, and those who couldn't walk were carried, propped up by others. It looked like an assembly of the damned.

In front of us stood the SS commandant, whip clenched tightly in hand. The rain dripped off the visor of his army cap. His boots were muddy, his uniform wet, but you could see that he was enjoying himself.

What could he see as he viewed us? A weary group of harried, wet, sick human beings, standing before him, trying to preserve some element of pride, of their humanity, of their confidence in themselves and their hope for their future.

If he saw any of this he said nothing, except to command the Hungarian militia to have us move a huge pile of bricks from one side of the camp to the other.

It took us hours of slow shuffling to accomplish this, each carrying what he or she could, even the sick and the aged doing what they were able to do.

When this assignment was finished, we waited for further orders. They were simple. He emerged once again from his guardhouse and gave another order: move the pile back to where it had been.

"The Demon," someone whispered. That whisper was to be his name among us from then on.

Shifting, compulsive, always on the move, blaming, shouting, striking out everywhere, sifting out every weakness, pouncing on the slightest infringement, the Demon was a marvel of nervous sadism. Quite mad. But there was no defying him. The whip was in his hand, the pistol in his holster and guns in the hands of the Magyar police. We were helpless. Those who fainted or collapsed, as many began doing, were left to lie in the rain, or crawl furtively for shelter as best they could. Those caught were dragged back to the center of the camp and left lying there.

By late afternoon the pile had been moved twice, and was now where it had been in the morning. We were dismissed and allowed to return to our sodden places of rest.

The brickyard became a mass of exhausted, hopeless, sick people for whom, in the past few days, life itself had lost meaning. Yet we must have been clinging to some hope. For the second time the Passover story forced itself into my befogged brain as I thought of the Children of Israel, slaving in the Egyptian brickyards under the whip of the taskmaster. But in the end help came to them.

Early the next morning, the call came again to assemble in the center of the brickyard. I expected that we would have to undergo the same routine, and this time, I was sure, some of us would not survive. My parents, dazed and exhausted, were near collapse. They had spent much of the previous day lying in the mud. Another such experience would kill them. Anguish befell me, and yet I had no idea how to help them. Nor did Etu or Magda, both of whom had fallen asleep the night before only after hours of hysterical sobbing. I watched them this morning, their eyes glazed with weariness and fear, stumbling out of the hut, walking the short distance to the assembly.

To my great relief, they were all sent back except the able-bodied, including me. A suspicion gripped us that something rotten was in store. We stood rigid at attention, wondering all the while what the Demon was up to now. We worried and waited.

Tibi standing beside me said, "Let's kill the bastard before he kills us."

"They have guns, " Bram replied, "and lots of them."

"They can shoot us and then our women and children," I remarked.

The Demon strode before us, his whip under his arm, and finally spoke.

"You are the chosen few. I picked you for a special task. As of now, you are the official members of the Camp Police. The following are the six basic orders you will obey.

"One, you'll wear a yellow armband."

"Two, you will always obey the Hungarian militia."

"Three, when confronted by an SS man, you'll freeze to attention and salute by removing your cap."

"Four, you'll be held responsible for escapes or rioting within the camp."

"Five, you will be in charge of work details and will see that my instructions are carried out to the letter."

"Six, you will carry a stick at all times, and will use it vigorously, or we will use our weapons instead."

"YOU WILL BE SHOT IF YOU DISOBEY MY ORDERS!"

There again: Hebrew foreman over the Hebrew slaves.

Clubs and armbands were issued, and each was given a post to control. Unlike our self-created guard unit, the inauguration of this one was not to be accomplished without ceremony.

Later in the day an urgent call for the entire police to assemble was heard.

"On the double," the Demon yelled. "Let's go, on the double ... line up in front of the guard station."

We ran to the guardhouse, where we were received by yet another SS man. He looked dapper, white gloves in hand, neatly dressed. He was a high-ranking Gestapo officer from Budapest, and the Demon was to put on a show on his behalf.

As we stood at attention he screamed, "You dirty swine, if you don't assemble quicker I'll make you crawl on your hands and knees. Dismissed," he shouted even louder, "but when you hear my whistle I want you to assemble with greater speed—understand?"

"Yeah—Yeah," we shouted back.

We rushed to our posts, and after a few seconds the whistle sounded again. Over and over we ran the same course until our breath gave out.

"It seems that you're not pleased with your new responsibilities as police," the Demon said. "Once again, return to your posts and come running as you never did before."

This game was repeated over and over until his egomania was satisfied. For hours we stood at attention and then the Demon drove us to perform calisthenics at his command. Not until we were completely exhausted did the Demon order a halt to the torture; it was late in the afternoon, after hours of pointless effort, that the Demon finally let us return to our posts.

But our day was not yet over. After sundown the Demon's whistle sounded once again as we were called to assemble. This time he redoubled his efforts, ordering us outside the gate into a swamp, where we stood in muddy water half covering our bodies. Finally, when he was satisfied, he ordered us to return to the camp and to our posts. We first rushed to our huts to strip ourselves of the muddy clothing. I had barely managed to take off my pants when the call to assemble was heard again. Half naked we rushed back to the assembly point, only to discover that the Demon had finally given up. He dismissed us for the night.

The brickyard was not an isolated area. Hundreds of people passed it every day on their way to work or to the marketplace.

There were many Ruthenian peasants who had their homes in the vicinity.

One day a peasant, dressed in Ruthenian garb of crude linen, stopped to gaze at the newly created camp. He must not have known what was inside. His horse-drawn cart, loaded with a few sacks of potatoes, drew close to the fence. A mob soon gathered. They were his fellow villagers, from nearby.

"Please, comrade, please bring us food. Please do not forsake us. Give us potatoes and bread. We need flour, beans, eggs and milk for our babies. Please, please," they begged.

The peasant was beside himself. He couldn't understand why we were here in the brickyard. I heard him promise to return with more produce. He tossed over a few bags of potatoes and a bag of flour, all he had in his wooden cart.

The guards spotted the peasant, as well as the crowd inside, and fired a volley of rifle fire in the vicinity. The horse became frightened and the peasant drove off, but not until he steered close to the main gate, stood up, his whip high in the air shouting and cursing. "You Nazi pigs! God will smite you for your evil deeds. He'll swallow you up for your criminal acts. Death to the Magyar Arrowcross bandits." He drove off at full speed, avoiding a chase and reprisal.

Similar incidents took place daily, especially on weekends when people crowded outside the gates, looking for friends and shouting messages to those inside.

Then one Sunday morning the Demon decided to pick six of us from the camp police to assist him in a raid to drive off the spectators by the gates. He took us into the gatehouse for a briefing. It was a short one. "You'll follow me when I give the order."

When the crowd had formed, we assembled quickly in front of the gate. With clubs in our hands we were led past the gate by the Demon, his whip in one hand and pistol in the other. At his command, we sallied forth against the mob, shouting an order to disperse and to leave the area. In this wild and maddening pursuit, I caught a glimpse of Aunt Sari, my mother's younger sister, who like others had come to seek out family and relatives. I rushed toward her and began chasing her away from the crowd toward the far reaches of the field to safety.

"Run, run!" I shouted repeatedly. "Don't get caught. You must go back."

Looking behind she quickly recognized me and plopped to the ground. I noticed she had a small food parcel under her arm which she wanted me to take for our family, but for fear of the Demon I couldn't take it. Getting caught with it as I returned might have been the end of me. I ran back to the gate where several peasants had been rounded up for punishment, to be meted out by the Demon. Most of those caught, I noticed, were elderly women who couldn't run away. He whipped them and ordered them to cross the fields for added punishment.

Some of the women pleaded with the Demon to be released because they were not Jews, but it did not help. Only their heavy clothing saved them from serious hurt.

Suddenly he shoved an elderly woman to my side where I was standing a distance from the group. The Demon moved closer and handed me the whip shouting and ordering me to give her twenty-five lashes. As I looked at this stooped and wrinkled elderly woman, trembling with palsy, I simply couldn't bring myself to hit her. I stood helpless wondering what to do. "What are you waiting for?" the Demon shouted. He yanked the whip out of my hand, slashing me across my face and neck, shouting and raging, "You Jewish swine. I'll put a bullet through your head if you don't carry out my orders!" He pointed his pistol to my head. I fought to keep my self-control. The gun itself didn't frighten me. Still I remembered, and at this moment I thought I could get the gun away from him and kill him. But what would happen to my family if I failed, or if I succeeded?

The Demon began to fidget, but the gun was still pointed at my head. He was just crazy enough to shoot me. I tried to visualize myself whipping the woman. Another self stepped out of me whom I had invested with anger and who raised the whip to strike the innocent old lady. But I couldn't even complete the image.

"That's someone else," my mind kept repeating, "someone else. Not me, not me."

Now the poor woman who had been awaiting a blow recognized my plight. "It's all right, my son." She nodded her head and her lips and eyes said, "Go ahead, I understand."

That decided me. I swung the whip easily and merely dusted her ruffled skirts pushing her away shouting at her never to come back again. I looked cautiously to see if I had satisfied the tyrant's wrath, but he had already turned away to torment someone else.

The beatings ended, but the attempts of our friends to communicate with us continued. The packages of food they had been bringing served us well, but our situation became much worse as time went on.

The Demon then organized his "policemen" into special work details, placing me in charge of the group assigned to book burning. I wondered why he had chosen me for this job: then I noticed him carefully choosing among the pious and most religious for the task of tossing the books and Holy Scriptures into the ovens.

He had us all gather around him and gave us a little speech.

"This will be your job until all the Jewish books and articles are burned to ashes. If I catch anyone loafing or sabotaging the work, I'll shoot you one by one."

Most of us took him at his word, and so the brick ovens were fired up. From every community in the area books were taken from Jewish homes and from synagogues and thrown into the barn. Torahs, prayerbooks, pamphlets, newspapers, in Hebrew, Hungarian, Yiddish, it made no difference—everything on paper, valuable or valueless, was brought in carts and dumped, waiting for the flames.

As I watched I felt I was a part of a great sin. I winced as the Hebrew books began to burn. I tried to slow the holocaust but it was no use. The Demon was always there checking to see that all that was brought in was quickly tossed in the ovens. The flames consumed our holy books, the hand-written scrolls of the first books of the Bible.

I was pain stricken each time I saw those flames. After all, how could I be a part of it, when I had been taught as a boy of three to respect the book. Each time I concluded a prayer I was taught to close the book gently and kiss it. I was to recite a prayer of forgiveness when I ripped a page in the holy book, and now I was part of the holocaust.

I was angry and felt an enormous guilt. The guilt was not to leave me for a long time. I ran to meet our Rabbi, to tell him I was not to blame.

"What am I to do?" I pleaded.

The Rabbi placed his hands upon my head and began to say a prayer. I did not hear him. I felt only guilt for the scrolls I helped to burn and for the woman I almost whipped.

"This is the Lord's will. Go in peace; God will forgive you," the Rabbi kept repeating.

It was already dawn and my time to sleep had long passed. I could not sleep; all I could do was think.

"Why do I feel so guilty?" I wondered. "Why not he, the Demon?" Did I, in my young mind, begin to perceive the truth? I felt guilty, because *he* didn't. There was heavy, painful guilt hovering in the air, and it had to find a resting place. Guilt is a phenomenon that must find a body. But why me, I kept repeating to myself. Why me, of all the people in the world? I didn't quite understand all of that yet, but it was settling in upon me.

The vision of those flames on the books was full of foreboding. I heard about ovens and fires, and pushed such thoughts away from the level of consciousness. Yet, if they could burn the printed words of books ...?

Then there was the fervor with which the Nazis went about the burning, as though they had a fear of the printed word. They practiced no discrimination. Copies of pro-German newspapers somehow were picked up along with everything else. As long as the print had been in a Jewish surrounding it was to be destroyed.

I now realized that we would not be returning to our homes, at least not until the war was over, and certainly not to the homes we had left. Until now, most of us treasured in the back of our minds the hope that this was a temporary situation, and that somehow, from somewhere, an order would come sending us back to our homes. After all, we were still so close. We were still in our home town.

Along with all of this, the rain continued incessantly. The mud in which we lived permeated our clothes, our blankets, our few belongings, our bodies and our hair. It seemed to cling to everything we had and everything we were. There was no way of draining the water from the bottom of the huts. Those who were fortunate had natural drainage caused by a ground slope, but more often, more water poured in from a higher elevation, and in many huts there soon developed small channels on the floor, along which the water would run in ceaseless rivulets.

The roofs, too, leaked, as did the walls, and the constant dripping of the water added to the discomfort we all felt. You couldn't sleep without shielding your face from drops of water, without waking a dozen times in the night from the trickle of cold water moving through clothes and coverings and reaching the skin. The effect on people's nerves coupled with the uncertainty, fear, and illness that surrounded us all, the unending coughs and hacking, the moans of those in pain, and the cries of children and infants made the night an unforgotten horror.

One morning I watched as the Demon and a fully armed goon squad stood outside a hut, protected in their slickers from the pouring rain. He ordered all the occupants outside. A family of eight or nine came out into the rain. They stood dripping in front of him, the mother holding an infant child, an ancient crone of a grandmother barely able to stand, the rest doing what they could to help the less fortunate.

"Your hut is not waterproof, is it?" he asked in a solicitous tone.

"No, sir," replied the father of the infant.

"Then," he sneered, "why don't you lazy Jews put bricks on the floor?"

"There aren't enough bricks to go around," replied the helpless father.

He turned to his Nazi underlings, "Comrades, you hear? The poor Jews are wet and uncomfortable in their huts. Then why don't we get them all out?" He laughed harshly at his jest, and his men joined in. There was doom in the jest. He drove them out of their huts to stand in the rain. "Come," he turned to his cohorts, "get them all out quickly."

They went from hut to hut, ordering the occupants out to stand in the rain. He strode among the huts, peering inside to see if they were empty. As he entered a hut, a young woman, crying hysterically, pleaded with him to permit her mother to remain inside under cover. Her mother was critically ill with the flu and was unable to stand, let alone walk. But he was adamant.

"So? She'll die anyway," the Demon barked. "This is as good a time as any. Bring her out, you bitch."

The girl rose from her mother's side, pulled herself together and approached him. I was aware of her lovely face, brightened by flushed cheeks and her feminine body. The effect on the SS men must have been total, though I could but dimly grasp the scene being played. The girl's choice had been cruelly thrust upon her— to spit in the face of this dumpy, petty despot, or to try to win his favor.

"Have pity. My mother is ill. Very ill. She'll die out there in the rain ...," she pleaded.

For a moment he hesitated, his eyes bulging out of his leering face. He glanced at his men and saw his own lasciviousness reflected in them. He turned viciously and slapped his whip across her face. As she staggered, I tensed and automatically moved toward the Demon, but the girl fell against me, grasping and dragging me to the ground with her.

"No," she whispered, "he'll kill you ... and us too."

The Demon apparently thought she had knocked me down in her fall. We lay there in each other's arms for a moment.

"Now, get her out," he screamed. His voice was snarling and angry.

I gathered the mother in my arms, carrying her outside in the rain. I propped her against the side of the hut, but she slid down into the mud, her head flopping to one side. The girl, herself covered with mud, knelt beside her, holding her mother's head out of the mud and protecting her from the rain. Blood from the slash in her cheek mingled with the rain on her face and dripped into the mud below. We stood in the rain until it stopped. As the sun came out the order was lifted, and we were permitted to return inside.

The next morning orders came that all men and boys were to shave their heads, beards and sidelocks. It was our Rabbi who registered a plea with the Commandant that the Orthodox be excepted. It was a rare moment as I watched our Rabbi, honored and respected in the community. He was the only Rabbi we had known. His father, his grandfather, and his great-grandfather had served us in our town. We watched as, quietly and with dignity, he approached the Commandant to make his simple request for exemption from cutting for the pious Jews. He began explaining what a serious infringement of the religious discipline it would be.

"Who do you think you are?" the Demon let loose at the Rabbi. "An order is an order, and that doesn't exclude you from it." He delivered a slap, and then another, that sent the Rabbi reeling to the mud. He picked up a two-by-four lying on the ground and swung it, barely missing the Rabbi's head. The Rabbi gently lifted himself off the ground, wiping the mud mixed with blood off his face. He stood erect, unmoved and without pain. No one dared to interfere. The Demon, surprised at the Rabbi's courage, made a brisk about-face and returned to the guardhouse.

If the Rabbi's faith subdued a question, it rose quickly enough to my mind: Where was the God he was to serve?

And the barbarisms went on and on, limited only by the Demon's imagination.

And then one day it ended. It was on May the 19th, a beautiful, sunny day. We were told that the entire camp would be shipped to Germany in two transports. Those wishing to leave first must be ready and packed. A great hurrying and bustle arose everywhere. Many rushed to prepare themselves, fixing and mending their scruffy duffle bags, stuffing their mildewed clothing into sacks or whatever they could find to serve as a valise.

There were no limits to what we could take along. Some took even their pots and pans, since we were told it was a work camp we were being shipped to. There was excitement mixed with anguish and relief.

I became a busy young man, since I knew how to fix suitcases with locks on them. I did not charge for the work, but I always managed to be rewarded for my efforts. A lady, whose elegant suitcases I fixed, rewarded me with twenty cigarettes. I fabricated a small key to fit the lock to her suitcase where she stored the beautiful gowns and dresses that she had succeeded in safeguarding throughout the miserable days at the brickyard. I wondered how she did it and was envious of her beautiful wardrobe.

I headed back to our hut to help with our packing, but everyone seemed to be already in motion, except father who was listless and bewildered. I handed him the few cigarettes I'd earned. He gently placed them in his vest pocket, gesturing with his head and quietly murmuring and reciting words from the Scriptures. All I could hear were the words, "God help us," followed by what sounded like "Where are you, Lord?" I walked away and began to gasp for air. I took a deep breath to calm my anger and frustration.

We had been totally cut off from all the news sources of information. We didn't know what was happening around us or in the next village or town. We did know that German armies were retreating throughout Eastern Europe and that in the West the second front was imminent. What we did not know, as yet, was the extent of the German extermination program for the Jews. Hans, at the machine shop, used to taunt me with "You'll get yours, you Jew bastard. The Nazis will finish you off once they get you to Germany. They'll gas you, that's what they'll do." It was natural for me to slough off the impact of his words. What sane human could ever accept such remarks as real, I thought.

A game of duplicity and blackmail for human lives had been in process. We heard rumors of a deal ... Jews for trucks. The Jews of Hungary became pawns in a secret deal. It remains unbelievable, still unknown, to this day.

The collection of money in our town was not just a small-time official's idea. It was an attempt to meet a payoff arranged by Eichmann and his gang. They agreed to allow some Jews to escape from the fate of Auschwitz for money. Pay or die was the deal.

Weeks of waiting in the brickyard turned out to be part of a larger pattern in which hundreds of thousands of us were held in brickyards, in city ghettos, in transit, in camps all over Hungary, waiting for the consummation or the failure of the "Big Deal." If the money was to be paid some might be saved. At least that was the agreement. And money was not the only acceptable ransom. Jewish children without their mothers were to be exchanged for military hardware and supplies. A high-pitched fund-raising campaign went into full swing. Jewelry was demanded and received from those who had no currency. There were arguments among the self-styled Jewish leaders over the cash and the gold. The ghettoized and doomed Jews raised the money, while our brethren in the four corners of the free world were silent, could not hear of it, or would not believe us. Five million, five hundred thousand of their immediate brothers, sisters, mothers and fathers, aunts and uncles, grandparents, cousins and friends had been systematically exterminated. Urgent messages were sent stating: "We're lured and driven into gas chambers disguised as shower rooms. Help us!" they cried. Churchill was advised, Roosevelt was given first-hand information, and Stalin could smell the stench of burning flesh. Aerial photos were sent to Eisenhower, Patton, Montgomery, and Zhukov. The five chimneys at Auschwitz-Birkenau stood tall. All twenty-four death camps were spotted and marked. The nine hundred slave labor camps had been identified.

Deception played a big role. We were the last to realize fully what was happening. Post cards stamped "Aussee" were received by many. "All is well, arrived safely," they read. My uncle, Moshe-Aaron was relieved when he received a post card from us. It was from Auschwitz-Birkenau dated May 21, 1944: "Just

Los Angeles Times TUESDAY, APRIL 25, 1944

Poland Bridges of Nazis Blasted by Underground

New York Times

LONDON, April 26.—The Polish underground army, in the most daring and effective blows it has yet struck, has blown up railway bridges on two lines leading to Lwow, key to German defenses in Southern Poland.

These strokes, carried out on orders sent into Poland over secret routes by the Polish government in London, have seriously hurt the Germans' capacity either to resist further pressure from the Russian armies or to counterattack effectively. At the same time they are welcomed here as further evidence that Polish guerrillas are willing to co-operate with the Red army even at terrible risk to themselves.

One bridge destroyed was near Prezmysl on the double-tracked main line running from Berlin to Lwow via Breslau and Krakow. Over this line alone 92 or more German supply trains pass each 24 hours. The other bridge was near Sanok on a parallel line south running between Krakow and Lwow. That line is the only connection between Lwow and the Carpathians.

Copyright, 1944, New York Times

IRONIC: They bombed and blasted bridges but, were unable to destroy the railway lines leading to Auschwitz-Brikenau.

By Bread Alone

Los Angeles Times, April 27, 1944

Mr. Roosevelt's Call for Protection of the Oppressed

The President's statement in which he called on the people of Axis-occupied countries to do their best to shield persecuted minorities of whatever race or religion is a shrewd move which may do a good deal of good. It is about the only practical step that can be taken at this time or which can be taken until the Nazis and the Japs are finally driven back into their respective homelands.

As the President says, the refugees who may have found shelter in Hungary, Rumania and Bulgaria are exposed to new peril through the Nazi occupation of these countries. A few may be able to escape to neutral countries and the President assures the neutrals that they will be aided in carrying the burden if they give them temporary asylum.

Reiteration of the intention of the United Nations to punish the oppressors and persecutors also is useful as a warning to the people under the occupation not to join in any persecution; and the request to them to take note of outrages and those responsible for them may provide some useful witnesses when the war is over.

Coupling the Japs with the Nazis and mentioning their barbarities as well shows that none of the savages will be neglected when the day of reckoning comes.

Baruch Gives $1,100,000 to Aid Physical Medicine

NEW YORK, April 26. (AP)— Bernard M. Baruch today gave $1,100,000 to extend the oldest branch of the healing arts, physical medicine, which started among cavemen with the "laying on of hands."

Simultaneously the Baruch Committee on Physical Medicine, headed by Dr. Ray Lyman Wilbur of Stanford University, recommended a nation-wide, scientific boost of this art, particularly for returning soldiers.

IRONIC: Bernard Baruch, an American of Jewish ancestry should be donating $1,100,000 to aid physical medicine at a time when the dollar could have helped save Jewish victims from the gas chambers.

88

Hungarian Jewish Forced Labor Youth 1944.

arrived in Poland at a labor camp in Aussee. Hope to see you soon, too. Signed Etu and All.''

With Hungary occupied, the Nazis had a whole population of Jews to gamble with.

Their threat to exterminate us was recognized by many who knew what was going on in Poland and in the Ukraine. Some of our own self-styled leaders knew that Auschwitz had proved itself capable of disposing of ten thousand people a day. They knew that Auschwitz-Birkenau—located close to the Slovakian border in a corner of Poland, with rail lines, radiating in all directions—had proved itself capable of disposing of ten thousand people a day.

In Budapest, three Jewish committees were set up to cope with the plight of the Jews. The first was the Jewish Council, which was ineffective. They attempted to placate the Nazis through cooperation and submission.

The second was the Palestine Committee, which was pressuring the Jewish Agency in Palestine to get an increased allotment of certificates from the British, so that a select few could migrate to Palestine. They succeeded in getting nearly two thousand Jews to Palestine, and many more to Ecuador and the Dominican Republic.

The third, the so-called Jewish Rescue Committee, was headed by Dr. Rudolph Kastner. He made a direct approach to the office of Adolf Eichmann. Through Eichmann's top SS officers, Wisliceny and Clages, Kastner was to raise 6.5 million pengo, about 1.6 million dollars, to get six hundred Jews released for Palestine. As the money began pouring in, the Nazis agreed to raise the number to be freed to sixteen hundred—sixteen hundred when there were eighteen thousand doomed Jews in Munkacs alone! There were three-quarters of a million condemned in all of Hungary, yet Kastner, Joel Brand and his rescue expert, in committee, managed to select only sixteen hundred. This hand-picked few left for Switzerland in specially arranged transports.

In New York, Boston, Los Angeles, San Francisco, a few Jews met to discuss the plight of their brethren. The New York and Los

Angeles newspapers reported on the meetings. The banquets were filled with the illustrious guests, such as Rabbi Edgar F. Magnin, and Rabbi Tannenbaum. Jean Hersholt met with Danish ministers to call for post-war tolerance, while Rabbi Mandel Fisher was to rally the Jews in San Francisco.

The Civil Liberties Union got into the act to demand freedom of speech for the Nazis. It was April, 1944 when another Rabbi said that all was well, and that the prospects for the rescue of the European Jews looked much brighter.

Meantime in Budapest another new development was in the offing. Eichmann, acting on Hitler's orders, was to make direct contact with the Allies. No longer were they interested in negotiating with the Jews. After all, it was the American trucks and material that they were after. The Jews in Europe had been plucked clean of their money, gold and other possessions. He was to tell Kastner that this was the route Hitler wanted to go.

On May 8, 1944 the offer was submitted by a self-styled Zionist leader, Joel Brand, to the Jewish Community in Turkey. According to William O'Dwyer, Director of the U.S. War Refugee Board, Eichmann, through his Jewish emissaries, demanded two hundred tons of coffee, two hundred tons of tea, two thousand cases of soap and ten thousand trucks. In return, Eichmann promised to shut the gas valves at Auschwitz-Birkenau, to stop the transports from leaving Hungary. "And you better get with it," he said, "if you don't want 'all the Hungarian Jews fried.'"

Brand, accompanied by a double agent, a Jew named Bandi Gross, was the wheeler-dealer in this episode. Both were captured by the British and removed to a Cairo jail.

It made no difference to us, since the ransom would have to come from the Allies—from the Americans, specifically. They were silent and unresponsive—not a word, not a gesture, while we were slushing around in the mud, in a brickyard, tortured by a Demon.

Thousands of Jews were rounded up daily and sent off in freight cars to the death factory of Auschwitz-Birkenau. But from

Joel Brand

Rezsö Kastner

SS Dieter von Wisliceny

the brickyard it seemed as though a transfer to Germany meant that the Nazis were moving us away from the advancing Russians. There would be no purpose in doing that if they did not want to preserve us.

At noon, boxcars especially ordered for us were spotted on the railway tracks adjoining the brickyard. The car doors were opened widely, while the small windows were wired with barbed wire so none could escape. Magyar armed guards quickly surrounded the group.

We were told that the entire population of the brickyard would soon be leaving in two shipments, one on the nineteenth and the other on the twentieth. Many rushed to be on the first transport, but my family and I decided to wait it out until the second shipment. The brickyard might not be a place we would recall with joy, but it was close to home. Germany, whatever fate awaited us there, was a strange and fearsome part of the world.

The first group moved off to the nearby tracks, where the long line of freight cars had been strung out to take the first transport. They crowded on, one by one, with the old and the sick heading the columns, followed by the women and children. The doors were rolled shut and sealed. As soon as the train began its slow journey away from the yard, the rest of us, unnerved, were filled with tears. We stood in front of our huts, speculating on what was to become of us, and one could sense the rising feeling of panic.

Some felt that the move to Germany would be to our advantage, because those camps must be older than the ones put up in Eastern Europe and therefore better built for protection against the weather. Besides, the Germans, however cruel they might be, were noted for their order and efficiency.

There were others who were angered at not going first, because arriving there first would have given them the better accommodations. They feared they might end up without a roof over their heads.

It seemed to my young and imaginative mind that the later we arrived in Germany, the better chance we had that our liberators would already be there, and that we would be riding to our freedom, rather than to servitude.

Some rumors spread that our baggage would be taken from us when we arrived. We packed only the things we could not attach to our bodies. We put on as many pairs of pants as possible, and other garments, one over the other. We were uncomfortable, but the feeling that we were out-maneuvering the Nazis seemed worth the discomfort. The following day we dragged our bundles to the railroad tracks and waited until the second train appeared on the siding, slowly huffing and puffing its way in, and then gradually coming to a halt with a squeak of badly oiled brakes. Specially designed planks were moved toward the boxcars. They served as a platform, a kind of loading dock, as columns of men, women and children lined the way, preparing to mount. They shoved and pushed to get on, and everyone was anxious to find a suitable spot. Children were crying for their mothers, "Mommy, mommy, don't leave me." The tender voices were heard over and over, "Water, Mommy—I'm thirsty." They pleaded for hours but to no avail. The heavy doors were shut tight and latched from the outside. The voices were getting lower and lower until they finally gave out.

The darkness that accompanied the closing of the doors came as a shock, and what arose among us was a collective sign, and a whimpering sound. It was as if the mass within the boxcar had given up hope, as if the sliding door that sealed us in had also sealed our lives forever.

Now, we were no longer considered Hungarian Jews but prisoners of the Nazis, condemned. Whatever strength we had taken from our friends, and from our sense of belonging to a particular place, was now denied us. We knew now that there would be no more parcels from the outside, no more shouted words of encouragement across the fence, no more friends to hold our keys and watch our homes until we returned. I felt for the first time that there would be no return.

There was a lot of chugging, starting and stopping of the train, and jarring as the cars clanked together and pulled apart. Through the small barbed wire window I could see that the train was not moving fast. It had hardly been underway a half hour, and had covered a distance no more than a mile, when it stopped at another brickyard. The Ostreicher brickyard had also been converted into a transit camp for Jews, but for Jews from the city ghettos, in preparation for the final journey.

Shortly after the train stopped I peeked out of the window and was startled to see a familiar face, Hana, the youngest sister of my mother. I screamed her name. Startled, she looked up, recognized me, and began running away from the train. I could no longer see her after a second or so. I stood there, wondering if I had done the right thing. Suddenly she reappeared in my field of vision. With her, also running, were Lajos and an old, stooped man whom I did not, at first, recognize.

My flush of joy was replaced by fright at seeing my brother. What was Lajos doing here? Why wasn't he in the woods among the partisans? I had assumed he was with the Resistance, and in my fancy I had imagined him spreading death among the Nazis— rescuing his people, his family, carrying us off to safety. It was a fantasy that had sustained me through many miserable nights in the mud and dripping rain.

My disappointment was great. I hardly noticed the third person. Only after they stopped in front of the tiny barbed wire window to speak did I see that it was Grandpa. But what kind of a grandfather was this? He'd always had a full beard, now it was gone, his face hidden by a scarf. He was ashamed, I guessed, to show that his beard had been cut off. Gaunt and hungry looking, weak and stumbling, "Zeide" was led by both hands, puffing and dazed. I could not believe my eyes.

Hana pleaded with the Hungarian guard to let them closer to the boxcar so they could talk to us. At first he refused, but a few minutes later the doors were unlatched and rolled back. By this time there was a sizable crowd in front of the car, as others within saw members of their families and called them over.

95

A shouting match began; the screaming for brothers, sisters, mothers and fathers was getting louder and louder. The guards got into the shouting as well, but all they could yell was, "You'll all be together, everyone is going to the same place!" Suddenly a fight broke out in the rear of the train. Someone demanded to know where we were headed. The guards stood firm with rifles and machine guns at their sides, holding off the crowd. With a burst of machine gun fire the crowd quieted down, and those who wanted to join the train did so in a matter of seconds.

Without any hesitation Lajos climbed aboard effortlessly, but Hana and Grandfather remained on the ground. "They can't come with us," said Lajos. "Don't ask them to." It was all he managed to say before we smothered him with kisses and sobs. He was now safe in our hands.

Within a few minutes the heavy doors were once again shut firm and latched from the outside. I could see Grandfather and Hana weeping as they waved us out of sight. The train slowly began picking up speed as, at last, it headed for whatever would be its destination.

Lajos was not the only one to join our boxcar, and now it was tightly packed with more elderly and sick people, not all of whom could lie down at the same time. Some sat and others stood; as the speed of the train gradually increased, the boxcars began rocking from side to side.

Lajos and I managed to find a corner well removed from the window, and he began to tell me what he had experienced during the month we were separated. He had gone into the city to stay and help relatives with small children. The Jewish population by then had swelled greatly, due to the influx of Jews from the surrounding towns and villages. All the Jews were concentrated into what were called *Jewish Houses* — the ghetto. Jews weren't allowed to live anywhere else; six to eight persons to a single room as well as bathroom and kitchen facilities.

In these circumstances there was much that Lajos, nineteen years old and a vigorous idealist, could do to help uncles and aunts and their children and other Jewish children who needed a guiding hand to keep from getting lost and dislocated. Lajos was tall and thin, slightly stooped, with a kindly, sympathetic face, and he moved like an angel of mercy amongst the youngsters he befriended. He was brave and daring.

I well remember—it was in 1943, on Yom Kippur. Lajos and I went to see a movie, *Jud Suess*. It was being shown for the first time in Munkacs, and it was the only showing. It must have been scheduled to coincide with the holiest day in the Jewish calendar. Lajos insisted that we both go to see it. He wanted me to know the hate that was spread upon us. "If you want to survive in this ugly world, you must know what's taking place." I remember him telling me this. "But it's Yom Kippur, and we must not indulge in movie going. If father finds out we'll be punished for it," I replied. "Don't worry," he said. "He'll approve this time."

The movie pictured the Jews as exploiters, and the heroic Nazis came in and rounded them up. Toward the end of the film, a Jew is hung by his neck. This proved to be too much for Lajos. He rose from his seat in the darkened theatre and shouted, "This is what they'll do to Hitler!" A goon squad of Magyar police quickly grabbed him and silenced him on the spot. Then they took him to headquarters, where he was beaten severely before being released. He wore his wounds with pride.

Now, in the dark of the rocking train, we regretted that we had been leaderless and unorganized in our town. There had been a large group of seventeen, eighteen and nineteen year olds who could have gone underground if someone had shown us the way.

"I tried to get away," Lajos said. "I thought I would join Tibi across the river and fight with the partisans, but the plan didn't work. I wasn't the only one trying to get away. They shot Zalman the tailor, because he tried to hide. And they clubbed Ben-Zion the radio man to death because he tried to escape, and lots of others, too. There was resistance in Munkacs at the railsidings; you should have been there. A whole transport refused to embark. But soon the SS, in cahoots with the Hungarian Arrowcross bandits, came to the scene and opened fire, killing the resisters in full view of women and little children. The remainder were shoved into the boxcars. The whole episode lasted a short time. If we had had outside help, that would have been the beginning of a successful uprising."

"Did Tibi make it to the woods?" Lajos went on. "Have you heard from him?" he asked curiously.

I shook my head and mumbled sadly, "Across the way," pointing to the opposite corner in the boxcar to where Tibi sat dejected.

"I was hiding for two days," Lajos went on. "I had to come to look for food and water. I walked by the ghettos, to the Ostreicher brickyard, and saw those helpless creatures peek out the fence. They were pitiful. Then I decided to join them!"

I told him how we passed the month. The rain and the mud were a familiar story to him, but their militia were far more brutal than ours.

Lajos continued, as if wanting to tell all at one time. He was full of anxiety. "Daily, countless numbers of our people were tortured and clubbed to death. The Arrowcross bandits were vicious. They spared no one. Grandfather's beard was forcefully cut. I think that killed him. He wouldn't eat. He sat in his hut, quietly reciting prayers. He believed that God wanted this to happen. 'It is God's will,' he kept repeating. I could no longer communicate with him. I think he'll die in the brickyard." Lajos just kept on and on, until he tilted his head, slowly resting it on my shoulder. Then he fell asleep.

After hours of riding in cramped quarters it became obvious that if we were to survive the journey, some organizing would have to be done. Lajos thought of it, and Tibi had a plan, but no one would listen. His plan was to break out, to lift a few boards off the floor and sneak through. It was an attractive plan but no one would buy it.

With night came darkness, and in the darkness there was silence. A kind of peace and awesome silence, only disturbed by an occasional restless child. The first part of the night we passed the test of endurance. Later others became restless, nauseous. The vomiting was incessant. The smell was everywhere. Hysteria rose when a woman panicked. "My baby's choking...she needs air...please, please give my baby air!" She kept screaming and flailing about. Within moments a fight broke out. The woman hit her neighbor and he struck back. He hit her with a hard object; she moaned and sank to the floor in silence, clutching the baby to her breast. There was nothing we could do, since adults as well, began pushing toward the one source of fresh air...the small barbed wire window in the corner.

Lajos and I sat away from the window. We were somewhat removed from much of what happened, but could hear everything. There was a subdued peace in our corner, on our side. There were no strangers among us. Angel, Karen, Magda and Etu kept together, while our parents settled on their bundles. Our plan was to whisper to each other...to keep our courage and maintain sanity.

At the first light of dawn the train stopped. Lajos and I managed to peep through a crack to see what was going on outside. We could see a Hungarian soldier pacing the tracks. Then we noticed more arriving. Finally a squad of border patrol appeared, and some kind of quarrel broke out among them. I heard one of them telling the other, "We must not allow this transport to pass."

"Yeh," said the other. "You know where they are headed."

"Yes, I heard. How can we turn them back? We're only two soldiers and the SS are all around us."

"Well, there's nothing we can do," said one soldier to the other. "At least let's give them some air."

The doors were soon opened, just enough to allow a breath of air in. It was heavenly. A sigh of relief came to all. We were alive again. People began to speak of hope. There were some kind words exchanged in and out of the cars. The soldiers began to talk to us with sympathy. They reached inside for our pails and filled them with water.

From a distance I could see villagers, the green pastures and the flocks feeding upon them. Some ran toward the train to see and talk to us, but they were turned back. The border patrol wouldn't let them near us. They looked like the *gendarmerie*. They wore high green hats with feathers attached to the back, resembling a rooster's tail. A distance beyond I could see more soldiers armed with automatic rifles and machine guns heading in our direction. It was already daylight and I could tell they were SS. I was frightened. They were dressed in battle fatigues and were laden with ammunition.

"Are they coming to shoot us?" a woman in a boxcar asked.

"No, no," replied the Hungarian soldier. "They are your new escorts. They will take you over past Kassa through Slovakia. We'd send you home if it wasn't for them."

"Only God knows what they'll do with you," said one of the Hungarian soldiers in full view of the SS.

I could not understand his language. My mind wasn't aware of what he was talking about. I felt like asking for a clarification, but I was afraid to ask. He might tell me what I did not want to hear, what I did not want to accept. I was beside myself. How I wanted to make a run for it; but how could I? My father, mother, brother and sisters were hostages, and if I made it, how could I survive, knowing they were on their way to their deaths? It was a struggle to think. Our plight was helpless. I decided for the first time to blot it out of my mind. I'd just go along.

The heavy doors were about to be shut again. At the last moment an announcement was made by one of the Hungarian guards. "You'll be leaving Hungary in a few minutes. The Hungarian currency will be of no use to you in Germany. Hand over your money."

Two hats were passed around and they were filled with money. From every corner in the boxcar people gave. I emptied my pockets with the few coins I had. I wondered why. Maybe because they gave us water, or out of gratitude for a breath of fresh air and thanks for the feeling that normalcy still existed. Whatever the reason, we felt those two soldiers were our friends. Helpless friends, but nevertheless friends, and we filled their hats.

The guards were replaced by the dreaded SS troopers. We could see them take their positions along the long line of boxcars, two "Death's Head" SS troopers to a car, one in the front and the other in the back.

Slowly the convoy began its journey again, but this time with speed. It hardly made any stops for the next day and night. It kept on moving through cities, towns and villages. The next morning the train stopped. It looked as if we were in a holding track outside a metropolis. Tall buildings were in sight and the air was thick. I managed to get to the little barbed wired window. Another train just like ours was in sight.

I began to shout across, "Who are you...? Where are you coming from...? We are Dutch Jews...We are headed for Germany...to a labor camp..."

The SS ran over to put a stop to our communication. From across I could hear a women scream to the guard, "You killed my child . . . my baby's dead . . . you killed it, you Nazi swine . . . I'll kill you!"

He turned his head toward the noise, removed his automatic weapon and delivered a burst of fire into the boxcar. I heard another SS shout back derisively, "With what will you kill me, you bitch?"

"With my bare hands."

Another burst, but this time in the air as he moved away to the other end of the transport.

It was the third day of our journey, and few were entirely rational. I found myself hallucinating, imagining that I was elsewhere, mostly at our home in the village, but sometimes in the machine shop or in school. What would ordinarily have been dreams were coming to me while my eyes were open and I was fully conscious. The people I saw were real enough; Hans, my schoolmates and neighborhood friends, my family. I seemed to talk to them and for brief moments I relived my former life; I escaped the present horror. After a while I welcomed these interludes, not understanding the danger in them, that one might escape to a fantasy, and never return.

It finally ended with an opening of the huge sliding doors and a shouted command to come out. Stumbling into the light, filthy and benumbed, we were not yet aware that we had survived.

It was a scene full of madness. Everyone rose at once and hurriedly began gathering bundles and securing belongings. Shouts and screams for loved ones to stick together filled the air. Mothers hushed their children, frightened by a strange lot of shouting men dressed in blue and white striped uniforms. Their shouts overpowered all others.

Before we could disembark, a new command was shouted: "Leave your bundles on the train. They will follow you later." This was stranger than hell to me. How were we ever to recognize our belongings, and where would they store them? A suspicion was planted in my mind; I soon became suspicious of the whole thing. I began to sense, then recognize more clearly, the awesome danger. But what was there to do? To whom could I turn? From where could help come? There was no answer. I turned to my mother who was busying herself around our bundles. Quickly she pulled out several pillows and handed me one. "Here, my son, you will need that; and remember not to sit on the cold, bare ground." With a pillow under my arm I made my way to the door, jumped off and waited to help my mother down.

We were standing on solid ground once more. Our bodies were alive and our minds functioning. We could not know it, but what we were now to undergo was far worse than what we could have pictured in the darkness of the freight train.

Many of the victims were stifled in these boxcars by the time they arrived.

Jews were driven into boxcars like herds of cattle.

Last minute farewells before cattle cars leave for shipment "east."

"The arrival in trucks."

The Auschwitz-Birkenau main gate as it stands today and as it stood in the awesome days of Nazi Extermination. This photo was taken soon after the camp was liberated by the "Red Army" in January 1945. Note prison gear such as bowls.

The arrival in boxcars at Auschwitz-Birkenau.

By Bread Alone

The Nazi selecting officer sizing up a Jew. To left meant slave labor while those selected to the right were earmarked for the gas chambers.

Alfred Wetzler-Josko Lanik   Walter Rosenberg-Rudolf Vrba

Two brave Slovakian Jews who made a daring escape from the death camps of Auschwitz-Birkenau. It was they who took it upon themselves to inform the Slovakian Jewish Community, as well as the Hungarian Jewish Community, what fate is awaiting them at Auschwitz-Birkenau in 1944.

(However, none would listen to those two brave and courageous young fighters.)

CHAPTER FOUR
"My Father's Keeper"

"Women and children on this side, men over there," snarled the guards.

Surprisingly, there was no expression of dismay at the separation. Whatever we may have felt, no one cried out in protest or refused to obey the order. While this command was frightening, we told ourselves that this was temporary and that we would be reunited as soon as accommodations were arranged. We were too demoralized by the long journey in the sealed boxcar to do anything but obey. We were too dazed at coming out into the light of day to have the possibility register in our minds that this was a final separation. We stood apart. Lajos and I and my father stood by each other as my mother and sisters were led away with the rest of the women and children. I do not even recall a shouted goodbye, although I cannot imagine that some words were not said.

And so, quietly, feet dragging with weariness and fear, the women trudged away and my mother and my sisters disappeared from sight.

We remained standing in the fog, by the side of the railway tracks for some time. Then I noticed how well tended parts of the place were. There was some grass, and there were trees on the far side, too. I had forgotten such things existed. I was calmed. Surely everything will be all right, I thought. Surely I'll be with mother soon.

Upon arrival at Birkenau right at the unloading dock men were separated from women and children. Those men who showed signs of ill health or old age were placed with the women and children.

The inside of a wooden barrack at "Birkenau." These were bunks for the working prisoners only. The others slept on bare platforms built into racks.

SS guards with automatic pistols were standing nearby, but did not interfere. From a nearby area, several inmates suddenly emerged and walked toward us briskly. They became our escort. I could see from their faces that they were somewhat different from people we were accustomed to seeing. They were inhuman in their behavior.

By their insignia, a yellow star, I knew that they were Jews. But what kind of creatures were they? I looked around, and could see a string of barbed wire fences amidst a huge railway yard, unlike anything I had ever seen. There must have been at least a dozen rail lines connected to all parts of the world.

"What could this place be? Where in the world is this?" the cries were heard. "Birkenau, Birkenau," we were told, "Auschwitz-Birkenau" voices were proclaiming to one another. We soon discovered we were in Poland, but none of us ever heard of Birkenau or Auschwitz-Birkenau.

All of us froze into one.

Staring at each other, not speaking a word, we looked and wondered at those tall chimneys spewing a peculiar reddish flame. A smell none of us had ever experienced before hung in the air. Then, a beastly looking creature appeared.

He began to mingle with us, to look us over, then another and another arrived.

What were they looking for, I wondered. What did they want? They looked fierce, angry. Some of them carried clubs and were well dressed. Then a tall, husky, well-built creature stepped forth. "Sons of bitches, hear me out," he said angrily. "You've just arrived in a Death Camp...Birkenau...do you hear me?...A few kilometers from here is Auschwitz. Birkenau has more ovens, that's why you came here first. Look at those tall chimneys...you dumb bastards. Do you see those flames? That's what'll become of you *kurvas*—whores. Do you understand? Why did you come here? Did you have to bring your kids, brothers and sisters with you? Your aunts, your uncles, your mothers, your fathers? Have you not heard of Auschwitz in 1944, you creeps? This is the end of the road. From here you'll go to the ovens. Look," pointing again, "See the chimneys? If you're healthy and strong you might get to work in the coal mines, or in the death factories. When you're used up they'll put you in, and you'll come out like smoke—there...you rotten bastards." I looked up and could see the smoke rising in the windless air.

Filled with fear, each of us was asking the other, "What's he saying? What's he talking about? He must be delirious, crazy!"

"Yah. Yah," I said to myself. "This creature must know what he is talking about. We are the ones who are delirious and crazy for having permitted ourselves to be carted here."

Without realizing it, I began talking to myself.

"There are no family quarters here. Don't you understand? There are no families here. Can't you see? Hans told me; I didn't believe him. Now this creature is telling me that all those people—women, mothers, little brothers and sisters—walked away from us to their deaths." I still didn't believe him, nor did I understand, but I could see the chimneys, and they were smoking fiercely.

A guard moved toward us and the beastly inmates stepped aside. We stood there, still uncomprehending, but gradually the full understanding of what we had learned dawned on us.

I turned my head trying to dismiss the picture of the smoking chimneys and the fires below them, but the vision did not leave. It became worse inside me when I realized that at the very moment my mother, Etu, Magda, Angel, and my playmate Karen, might be in there, consumed by the flames. I looked up. I could barely see the sky. The picture became real. I screamed.

Lajos, standing next to me, clapped his hand over my mouth. A guard came running over. He looked. But I was still. Lajos held me, in a near faint, sagging against him. The guard turned away and I regained my strength.

My father was ashen faced, and the men around us also. Several muttered under their breaths, praying, I imagine. It was as though the chilled wind of death had descended upon us. There were none who did not go mad at the thought. A month before we

113

might have exploded, run, fought, killed and died in the process. But now we had suffered the brickyard and the sealed train; we had no strength left, no will to fight.

We were called to attention. Silence fell. It didn't occur to me that we now might also be walking toward the death houses.

We were told to line up and form a single line. There in front of us stood an SS officer. Along with him was an assistant, I thought. One of them beckoned for us to come forward, while the other just motioned with a finger: to the left, to the right. It went on and on like that. I looked to both sides. There were more selected for the right side than the left.

"What can that mean?" I asked. My father standing next to me urged me to speak up for myself. "You are eighteen and a machinist by trade. Do you hear me? You, too, Lajos, tell him you're a good hard worker. Be snappy, and stand up straight and look tall. Do you both hear me?"

Both of us clung to our father for safety. Then our time came. I went first. I snapped to attention. Then I froze for a brief moment, afraid that I might be separated from Lajos and my father. Quickly I said, "I'm eighteen and a machinist." My anxious eyes followed his finger, and I briskly ran to the left. It was but a moment before I was joined by Lajos and father, too. We were driven to a row of barracks alongside the barbed wire fences, facing a row of chimneys.

Five abreast, side by side. I looked behind and saw the eldest and the very young left behind, still standing to the right. I wondered what they'd do with them. I heard dogs barking. Each hound was led by an SS guard with leather thongs in his hands. They were headed toward a tunnel, a tunnel close to the chimneys, near where the old and the very young were standing. As I looked again I could see them no more. They disappeared in the night and the fog.

Once inside the wooden barracks we were ordered to undress.

"On the double," this strange creature in blue and white prison garb yelled. We were to keep our shoes and belt.

Suddenly an SS guard, whip in hand, rushed into the barracks, screaming, *"Rauss! Rauss! Out! Alles Rauss!"* He was flailing wildly with the vicious thongs in his hand. We shoved and pushed to escape his wrath and the bite of the whip. Outside we were met by other SS men, also with dogs. They drove us along a road close to the electrified barbed wire fence.

"Faster, faster, you filthy dogs," shouted the guards. I was joined by Lajos and Tibi. I was unable to find father among the running men. No wonder. There were hundreds of men running, all naked, pushing, shoving and scrambling.

What a mad and crazy sight we must have presented. Suddenly the road burst upon the scene—a scene right out of Dante's *Inferno*. Ahead were three huge pits dug deep into the ground. In each a fire was raging. Around the flaming pits naked men were running in an endless circle.

All around I could see SS guards and prison "Kapos" swinging their leather whips and driving the prisoners from behind into the pits. I couldn't believe my eyes. Fear mounting, we gripped one another to hang on to every moment of life.

Shouts of *"Shma Yisrael*—Hear O Israel" were heard everywhere as the pious screamed the last words a believing Jew must utter before he perishes. *"Adonai Ehod!* The Lord is One!" In the midst of all the panic and confusion I became separated from Lajos. Their fate was now my only concern. "Oh, God," I kept repeating, "they must not be in there, in that flaming Hell." I kept pushing myself away from the pit but something kept drawing me back. I was torn between two worlds, the living and the dead. I pushed my way closer to the edge of the pit. My God, I could see humans in the fire, writhing and moaning.

As I began to make my way back to the rear I was forced to the ground by the oncoming crowd. I lay there until I had regained my strength. Slowly I inched further away from the pit.

I called for Lajos and father, but received no reply. How could they hear me in all that confusion, when everyone was shouting for someone or something? I reached the outer circle of the crowd

By Bread Alone

"Auschwitz-Birkenau"

What could this helpless old Jewish woman with those worn out hungry little children do but follow instructions to undress and take a bath. Wouldn't you do likewise under those circumstances?

and caught sight of Bram and Joey.

I had not expected to see them again.

Bram told me that father and Lajos were close by, behind me. I made my way back, slowing down, and saw them. A deep sob broke out of me.

I returned to the living.

Quickly father grabbed my one hand and Lajos the other. Together we continued the race around the pit of death.

I wondered how much longer we could go on like this. Are we to die here in this unbelievable dance? We were all thinking the same thoughts. Bram, wild and panting, expressed them this way: "If we are to die, let us take revenge. I have a razor for just this moment. I will jump the Nazi and slash his throat. I will then slash my wrist and hand you quickly the blade. You jump the next bastard and kill him, and you might as well take your own life. But make sure you have someone to pass on the blade to." Mad words, and yet, under the circumstances, reasonable enough. I came to feel that the push to the pit could not be stopped.

Tibi quickly lined up behind me and Joey, Bram's little brother, hardly fifteen, just looked and listened.

Yet, inexplicably, the whirl of men did stop. I heard the raucous voices of Kapos and SS men yelling, "Back to the barracks! On the double! Everyone back to the barracks."

Swinging their whips and barking like wild dogs, they yelled over and over, "Back to the barracks! Everyone back to their barracks!" For those who remained alive, those vicious voices were a sound of wonder, voices from heaven. We ran to the barracks, with our guards following close behind.

What was it—that cruel, unbelievable nightmare of flames and panic, of running and dying? Why did they inflict that upon us, immediately after our arrival? Was it a weeding-out process to select the strong? Was it a way to kill some, to thin our ranks? Was it to frighten us with an indelible vision of hell so that all thought of resistance would be forever suppressed? Or was it just an aberration of a demented mind?

117

After a brief rest in the barracks, we were ordered to assemble outside with our shoes and belts in hand. Still naked, we marched into a nearby barracks where barbers were waiting. They shaved off all our hair so that we looked like peeled onions. From there, we were marched to a shower room. By now we were alerted to the use of the showers. I watched the exit of the building, to see if those who entered would come out alive. A sigh of relief hit me as the first batch came running from the building still holding onto their shoes and belts.

Our final stop was a clothing storeroom. There each received a pair of pants, a shirt, a jacket and a cap, all striped and made of the same cloth. "This is to be your prison uniform for the summer," the Kapo of the storeroom explained. "This is the only set of clothes you'll get. Anyone caught misusing it will be flogged. The shirt is to be worn at all times...even in your sleep."

That didn't bother me since I was accustomed to sleeping in my shirt at home, but the striped blue and white garment disturbed me. We all looked alike. For the first time, I experienced a world with no class distinction. Rich and poor, young and old, shared the same fate as in no way before. I hardly recognized my father. Lajos couldn't tell me apart from the others.

The constant calling of names was ever present. One could not recognize another. Friends would pass you by. It was a nightmare.

By this time it was dawn and a heavy fog hung overhead. My sleep on the ground outside the storehouse had been a deep one, but interrupted by cries too loud to be ignored, cries from the elderly, the sick, our women and children—all hysterically calling for help. We began to talk among ourselves, wondering what to do. How should we respond? We knew where they were headed, but we were forced to deny ourselves the truth if we were to survive.

Some insisted that we should have fought when we were taken off the train, before we were separated. But hope was on the side of submission, and besides, they were armed and we were not. There was no question that any resistance would have met with instant death.

The end of the war seemed close, and our best course was to hang on, and hope for liberation and for the end of the war.

We lay resting on the ground together, with Lajos and father, protecting one another.

The order to assemble was heard and we formed a ragged row, five abreast, clinging to one another. We had not eaten in days, and the effort of walking and standing became a burden. It made us weak and constantly tired.

In the distance, toward the railway tracks, we once again saw long columns of women and children walking toward the blazing chimneys. There were hundreds of them quietly humming and chanting. The column neared our barracks. Separated only by strands of barbed wire, I could see them. I saw my mother for the first time since we had been separated the evening before. I saw Tibi's mother too. I couldn't believe my eyes when suddenly I recognized Etu and Magda. But I quickly turned my head in another direction. It must not be them, I kept telling myself. "Look..." I told my father. He pulled me away. He was speechless. "On second thought," I said to myself, "that could not have been my mother. That lady had a little baby in her arms. She just resembled mother, and there are many girls that look like Etu and Magda." I made peace with myself; I had seen it all wrong.

Hate grew within us as we watched again and again our women and children walk by screaming for help. Our souls seemed to shrivel as the fires burned.

Our suffering was palpable. It grew enormously from one minute to the next.

Heavy rains began to fall. We stood there for hours, in the pouring rain. We were driven out to be tortured. We huddled against each other for protection and warmth. Many could not stand the torture. The charged wire fence beckoned dumbly. Some stared at it longingly, transfixed, fascinated by the solution it offered. Then one man broke. He ran to the wires and dashed himself against them. A crackle and sparkle and his suffering

119

The interior section of one of the five gas chambers at Auschwitz-Birkenau. Note the pipes and shower heads above. We will never really know what transpired at this last station. Some of the SS guards assigned to the ("Sondercommando") disposal squads gave reports after their capture and interrogation as to how many so willingly marched into the chambers because in essence they

120

believed that they were going to take a shower, but others who resisted in vain were pulled aside and shot. There are no photographs of the millions of mothers who were ordered to undress their children to take that "last shower". We are spared that agony. We will never know what happened inside the gas chambers. We can only guess.

ended. In the long hours that followed, the lure of the silent, waiting executioner proved too great for many.

"They're dead," Tibi murmured, looking at the quiet bodies along the fence. He said again, "They're well off now." He made a sudden move toward the wires. It took all of my strength to pull him back...I saved him from suicide.

Our pleas for food and cover were unanswered and our casualty list grew longer. Finally the rains stopped, and we were driven into the barracks. In the center aisle of our quarters was a large barrel of soup. "Food! Food!" many exclaimed. The Kapos rushed in with ladles in one hand and whips in the other shouting to form a single line. We couldn't believe that we were to be fed, after all we'd been through.

The sun began to shine and the warm air penetrated our soaken bodies. There was a sigh of relief.

It was in the afternoon of our first day in Birkenau, when a group of prison officials stepped into our barracks to officially welcome us. "You've completed the first phase of the process," one of them said. "From here, you'll be assigned to different labor camps. Some of you will remain here for camp detail."

I felt a shiver when he spoke of remaining here. I looked around and wondered who those might be. "No, no," I said to myself, "we must not remain here." I would rather have died than lived to see those long columns go by, constantly screaming for help. "This must be hell," I kept saying. "Where is our God?"

A desk was placed by the doorway and the dignitaries, one by one, began seating themselves behind it. Subordinates produced pencils and paper, and the officials began to write down personal information on each prisoner. Beyond the doorway of the barracks huge columns were forming. "We must be going somewhere," I assumed. "Why would they line us up in such an orderly fashion?"

Soon we were marching on an open road. The pace was increased until we found ourselves running faster and faster. The Kapos alongside would not let up. They drove us like a herd of cattle. We ran on and on, breathless and frightened, passing through countless rows of barracks.

Surrounded by an endless string of barbed wire, we finally reached our destination. We stopped. We couldn't believe our ears. There was light music in the background. A band was striking up a march! I thought music had left my life when I left home. At first I thought I was hearing things, but it was music, and it kept getting louder.

As we approached the entrance, a huge iron gate appeared, and above, a sign. It read, in large Gothic letters, *"Arbeit Macht Frei."* Work will make you free. Could it be? Was this the work camp we had heard about in the brickyard? Were we really going to avoid our journey through the chimneys? I began to feel at ease; a ray of hope entered my body.

Next to the first sign was another: "Auschwitz." We had heard of it by now, but we had not been told it was a labor camp. I looked and listened. There were no laborers to be seen. From here, I concluded we would be reassigned to different sub-camps.

Auschwitz No. 1, as it was called, was to be our final destination. It was the graveyard of four millon human beings, of which ninety per cent were Jews, and a million little children. And the music played on.

Once through the huge iron gates, we could see brick barracks. They were two story structures, but there was hardly a prisoner in them. "Where is everyone?" we began to ask. "Is this to be our permanent home?" There were no answers. We guessed.

Suddenly the windows from a number of barracks opened. The prisoners were greeting us; old-timers we were told, but they looked young. They were eight, ten and twelve year olds. "We were misled," many began to say. "You see, they don't send the young through the chimneys."

"There," said a neighbor standing by me, "We've nothing to fear."

A few moments went by and bread was hurled from the windows. Bread! Chunks of black bread, like manna from heaven, began to shower us. Everybody was excited. We hadn't tasted bread for days.

A fight broke out over the chunks of bread. We began snatching and kicking, gouging at each other, and rolling on the ground. I jumped high in the air, above the crush of people, and managed to catch a few chunks of the precious bread. I found Lajos and offered him a piece. Father, too, shared in the feast. We sat around gobbling chunks of black bread. Then Kapos stepped between us and put a stop to the whole affair.

There was no defying a Kapo, we soon learned. They were the ruling class in the death camp. They hit us indiscriminately. They were outright murderers. The heavy boot of a Kapo often smashed the skull of an inmate in broad view. There wasn't anything one could do, but obey, yield, submit to the Kapo, or fall dead before him. We soon discovered that there was a deal between the Kapos at Auschwitz and the SS. For every prisoner he killed, the Kapo was to receive a reward of an extra ration of bread—perhaps some marmalade, or a cigarette or two.

We learned to duck, to avoid a Kapo. Everyone pushed to the rear at head count. I never dared to look into the eyes of a Kapo. I learned to stay clear of them. There were some Jewish Kapos as well, we soon learned. But they were in a precarious position. They were not murderers. Themselves doomed, they looked for a way to help to organize for survival. A Jewish Kapo often pretended to be mean and vicious to his fellow prisoners, only to try to save himself from the gas chambers. Strange, was it not?

Once again, we were put through the showers and given clean prison clothes. It was an odd feeling; only hours earlier in Birkenau we had been put through the same process. "What could this mean?" I wondered.

Finally, we were driven to our barracks to find them warm and cozy. There were bunks with straw sacks to serve as a mattress, and blankets too. It was a neat environment. Bunks, covered with blankets...I couldn't believe my eyes. This must be an illusion...a dream. My first night in Auschwitz was spent in a bed under blankets, in a heated room. It seemed a strange beginning.

The next morning we were aroused by the Kapos. They rushed in with clubs and routed us out into the chilled morning air. There we stood, shivering, while a head count was conducted by the SS. It was a thorough count; not a single person was missing. Even the dead were counted. It lasted for hours. It seemed that they were afraid to lose us, but we discovered that while fortified and electrified, Auschwitz was vulnerable to escape. As we soon learned, two inmates of Auschwitz had escaped just prior to our arrival. A Slovakian Jew named Rosenberg and his buddy broke out. They made it, we were told. Otherwise, he and his friend Alfred would have been brought back to Auschwitz for public hanging. I was sure they would tell our friends on the outside about Auschwitz. But they had escaped on April the 7th, and here we were, toward the end of May, when the gas chambers were hard at work. The chimneys were belching a fierce reddish flame. "They must not have made it," I thought, "Otherwise, help would have come long ago." Again I was dreaming.

The head count ended, and for the rest of the day we were assigned to various tasks around the camp. Thus ended the first day in Auschwitz.

The following day I was not assigned to camp detail. Instead, I was ordered to return to the barracks and remain there. I wondered why. I didn't dare ask. I stood there looking through the window at the activity all around me. The inmates of this part of the camp were circulating freely and talking to each other, seemingly unconcerned with other, more weighty matters. I watched for a while and then, summoning my courage, left the barracks and walked among them.

The occasional Kapo or SS man whom I confronted while walking, did not bother me as long as I saluted. I noticed that there was freedom of movement in this area of the camp. It was a new experience. I discovered a rudimentary marketplace where inmates were trading loaves of bread for shoes, tobacco, sweaters and gold. The entire atmosphere seemed unusual; it was unreal.

By Bread Alone

The following day, still unassigned, I began to make the rounds of the neighborhood, exploring the possibilities for "organizing"—snatching from warehouses or storerooms within the camp.

I became aware of trucks heading toward the supply rooms. They were army vehicles driven by prisoners. Alongside sat an SS man, calm and unperturbed about the flock of prisoners that followed. I noticed too, that the trucks headed to the kitchen were followed the most. No wonder—they were loaded with bread— loaves of bread fresh from the bakery, each resembling a block of clay but spreading a heavenly scent. I was floating in the clouds...away from Auschwitz.

Suddenly, a Russian prisoner took a dash, followed by another and then another. *"Davaj! Davaj, Tovarish!"* they kept calling. "Give me! Give me, my friend!" They followed the truck, calling to their buddies, "Throw me a loaf!"

I was stunned. Every plea was answered. Bread, in single loaves, were flying one after another. Then it quickly dawned on me. Why can't I, like the others, demand a loaf? After all, we looked alike, I thought; how could they possibly tell us apart?

I gathered strength and courage and began to follow the truck. I had hardly let out my first syllable when a loaf of bread came flying toward me. I caught it and headed back to my barracks. On my way, I stopped at the marketplace, only to discover that Lajos had traded away his husky pair of shoes for a loaf of bread! I was saddened, since I knew that after bread, shoes were the next necessity for survival. I could not reverse his decision. I urged him to trade my loaf of bread for another pair of shoes. It was no use; he wouldn't listen. He just went on his way, contented, not worrying about the next day.

I headed back to the barracks. There I found Bram and Tibi. They were struck by the sight. They looked at my feet. They seemed surprised by the sight of me. A loaf of bread under my arm, and still my own shoes. "What gives?" they asked. "How did you get that?" pointing to the loaf of bread. I revealed to them my secret and we decided to go out together the next day.

It was a bright and sunny day. Tibi, Bram and I formed a team of organizers. "We'll share alike," we promised. I briefed them and led them to the area of the kitchen and supply room. Soon the trucks began rolling by. One by one, we followed and got a loaf each. We decided to follow the rest of the organizers to the supply room. On our way, we discovered a storeroom for onions, and nearby, a warehouse where sweaters were flying from every direction. We joined the crowd and just kept following them.

The onions were well secured. They were stored in a basement, locked away. But from the surface, I could see them. The fence around the onions was merely slats with spacing between them. I quickly designed a pole with a nail at the end and decided to snatch them one by one. I filled my pockets with onions. Tibi and Bram did too. Fully loaded, we returned to our barracks to share our loot.

I discovered that both Lajos and father had been assigned to a work detail outside the camp. I waited for the band to stop playing, so I could go with them as they returned. I found Lajos squatting on the ground, breathless and worn out from a full day's detail and torment. I hardly recognized him. He must have lost ten pounds in that one day. I wanted to change places with him and he saw in my eyes that I cared. I gave him part of my bread and onions. Together we went in search of father. We found him close by. I went up to him and tapped him gently on the shoulder. Surprised, he rose to his feet and threw his arms around me and Lajos at the same time, as if trying to shield us from the flames that were in sight. Lajos and I led him away from the others to the back of the barracks. Slowly he regained his composure and began to talk to us. There was pain in every syllable as he spoke.

"I have done you wrong," he began. "I never should have stopped you from fleeing into the forests or joining the partisans." We tried to reassure him, but it was to no avail.

"This is a place of impending death," he went on. "It waits for all, and it will get all of us in the end." He went on and on. His words offered no hope. We did not understand his utter despondency until it became clear that he had been on a special detail where he could see the corpses as they were being disposed of after gassing. He was obsessed with communicating his feelings, wanting at the same time to make us understand what we must do.

"There's only one way for us to survive," he said. "We must stay apart, each in a different location, each away from the other. At least one of us will live to tell what they've done to us, to our children, and to our people."

Lajos and I tried to remonstrate, but he continued without hearing us. "If we remain together, in one place, there'll be agony for us—to feel each other's sufferings, to witness each other's pain and experience each other's hunger and starvation."

I will never forget his face as he spoke. I looked deep into his clear and convincing eyes. Memories of my growing up flooded my mind; our meager home, our friends, our aunts and uncles, grandparents, and all. But father stood taller than everyone. He was the commanding figure in our home. I respected and feared him at times, but now I realized it was a deep love that I always felt for him. My perception of him gained a new maturity; I began to understand the wisdom and sheer courage in what he was asking us to do.

"In this place of death and evil, it's better for us to stay apart." He raised his hand to still my look of protest and puzzlement.

"I know, I know," he went on. "You want to stay with me. You think you'll be able to take care of me, bring me bread and protect me. But it won't be like that. There'll be no help and no protection. There will be only suffering. Don't you see, my sons? If we're apart, I won't see your suffering and you won't see mine. And to see that would be the greatest suffering of all."

Over and over, in the months that followed, I was to hear his words ringing in my ears. Over and over, I saw his prophecy fulfilled. Often during our roll calls at camp I found myself standing behind Pinchus and his son Lief. I envied them; they were together. Then one day Lief fell on the ground, unable to stand any longer, and an SS trooper stepped up and beat him on the head.

Pinchus begged the guard not to kill him. "It's my son," he pleaded. "You can't kill him—it's my son." The SS turned viciously on Pinchus and beat him too. Both were sent to the gas chambers in the next selection.

In the camp, suicide was very common, but it could complicate as well. It was much easier if a buddy helped. It was a Sunday, a day of rest—but not for Zalman, the youthful Pole. Zalman was found hanging, not a rare event at Auschwitz. He knew he was destined for the gas chambers. He was bruised from beatings by the Kapos. He was tortured with hunger. He knew he would be pulled out of the lineup in the morning and sent to the gas chambers. I heard him beg his bunkmate to assist in the suicide. He wanted to hang himself, but Zalman had neither the stamina nor the strength to tie the rope and noose and go through with all the macabre details. His friend refused. All night long he begged and cried and pleaded for mercy, till finally the assistance he needed was given. His assistant—his friend, his bunkmate, his "buddy"—was his father.

I was still listening to my father's voice. I began to realize that he was giving his last will and testament. He was giving us all of his wisdom and courage. Then came his final words—the hardest yet, the most courageous and dreadful of all.

"Your mother and sisters are..." He paused a moment, unable to go on. "And you must not torture your minds about their fate. Yes, yes. Look! There!" And he pointed to the flaming chimneys. The vision of mother, Etu and Magda being burned alive made me feel faint. My head began to spin. I wouldn't accept it. I wanted to run, but where? I started to rise, but father laid a restraining hand on me.

"And it'll happen to us, too," he added quietly. Then more firmly he said, "But if we stay apart, at least one of us will live to tell."

129

And with that, we fell into silence. As I was about to leave, I wanted to share my onions, bread and most of all a sweater to keep him free from the shivering cold, but to my surprise, he refused it all. There was no way to convince him to slip on a sweater or take a piece of bread, since he insisted we needed it more than he.

The following day, we were issued pieces of paper with numbers printed on them. The number on my slip was A-4685. This was to be my prison number, and I soon found it tattooed deep into the skin of my left forearm. For days my arm was painful and swollen and the poisonous ink, which penetrated all my layers of skin, left me feverish for days. We were told not to rub it out. It could not be erased. From that day on I was but a number, not a human being, but simply a number, A-4685.

A feeling of terror came over me as I looked, for the first time, at my indelible number. I was no longer human. I could not feel myself. I became one of the herd, branded and marked forever. The indelible and poisonous ink had hardly sunk into my vein when I ran to tell my brother and father to take note of my new number. I wanted them to know, in case they looked for me later.

I rushed to meet father, but he was no longer there. "He has been shipped out," I was told. I wouldn't believe them, and ran from one barracks to the next trying to find him. "I must tell him my number. How will he ever find me?" I cried. My sobbing became uncontrollable. I felt beaten. In the midst of it all, I ran into Tibi who, like myself, was looking for his father to tell him of his number. He looked at me and broke the terrifying news. "Both of our fathers were shipped early this morning to a coal mine in Jaworzna!" The name stuck in my mind. I kept repeating it a dozen times. Jaworzna! Jaworzna! Jaworzna!

I ran to Lajos feeling totally distraught, barely able to tell what I had heard. For the first time in Auschwitz, he consoled me. He said, "It may be strange to say at a time like this, but we have been lucky. We've been together until now. Let's take that as good fortune. At least we had some time together." He embraced me in a big brotherly way and urged me to remember father's words of survival. I was to remember. In fact, it stuck like glue.

"But how do I survive, alone in an inferno?" I asked. No one beyond knew any longer where we were. They gave up on us. We were written off, I felt. Why had the Allies not bombed this factory of death? It was visible from the skies, wide open. Certainly the Russians, who were across the Vistula River only a short distance from here, could have disrupted the operation of mass extermination.

I kept asking myself over and over, "How can I survive?" Then a hidden part of me began to react. I must not believe what I heard. I'd have to blot out what I saw. Those flaming chimneys were something else; I wouldn't care what others tell me about them. I began to hear my father's voice: "Let's stay apart—each for himself, each in a different location—at least one of us can live to tell." Then another voice countered: "But why me? Why should I be the one to survive, and what will happen if I do survive while they don't?" I began to tear myself to bits until I finally gave up. The struggle over who should live and who should die was too much for me. Somebody else was supposed to be deciding that anyway, and so I went about my business.

I gave Lajos half of my previously "organized" loaf of bread. As it turned out, we spent our last day together. The next day I couldn't find him. A week later, I discovered that he too had been shipped on a transport to the coal mines...to Jaworzna.

Weeks passed with the same routine of rising and tedious waiting—the unbearable head counts. Many newcomers were shipped to other camps and many more arrived. I watched them come and go. I began to fear the long presence near the crematoria. Day after day I was hoping to be shipped.

Finally, after six weeks at Auschwitz, the time came. We were restricted to our barracks, which was the first sign that something was about to happen. "But what?" I began to wonder. After all, selection for the gas chambers likewise was started with restriction to barracks. But then the instinct for survival took hold. I began to refresh my memory and fill it with hope. I felt sure that this would be a transport to a labor camp. After all, why keep us alive for so long so close to the gas chambers if they wanted us dead?

Numbers were called and one by one we filed out of the barracks. With Bram, Joey, and Meyer too—we had consecutive numbers, mine the highest—I was grouped in an area isolated from the rest, and later marched to a line of trucks. Before mounting the truck, a tall, slim-looking officer in his thirties stepped forth and gave us a speech. "You men are hand-picked by me. You'll be transported to a new camp. You'll be well treated if you work hard. You'll be well fed if you obey. Anyone who gets out of line will be dealt with swiftly and severely. Attempted escapes will not be tolerated. We shoot first and then ask questions."

We didn't know, at first, that this officer was in charge of the entire Auschwitz III complex, Monowitz, (also known as the Industrial Complex), with thirty slave labor sub-camps. He was no small fry, as we learned after. SS Hauptsturmfuhrer Heinrich Schwarz: from 1941 to the end of 1943 he managed the employment section of the region, and was chosen by Hitler to be the master of millions of slaves. Later he was a commandant of Natsweiler concentration camp. Then, at the end of the war, he fled, only to be captured by the French liberating forces. He was tried, convicted, and sentenced to death by hanging. The sentence was carried out. In 1944, when I saw him, he was in charge of the entire Monowitz area, a big undertaking.

He told us that the new sub-camp, Gleiwitz, was in its growing stage and was to be a model camp. We listened intently and with some joy. I couldn't believe it, that we'd be promised a good life for good behavior. I looked at him with some trust.

I was at the tail end of the truck as we mounted. I could see the battle-dressed storm troopers behind us, their weapons in ready position. I was frightened when the convoy began to roll, but I was leaving Auschwitz-Birkenau alive.

CHAPTER FIVE
"In The Shadow Of Auschwitz"

The canvas above made strange sounds as the convoy began to roll faster and faster. I watched the route to memorize every inch, every curve. The scattered houses that were visible seemed to be deserted, totally abandoned. Not a soul in sight. I was frightened, yet excited to be leaving the tall fierce chimneys and the awesome stench they produced. The roads were barren and there wasn't any pasture around, not a cow in sight, nor a bird to be heard. It was a haunted road which stretched for miles with only a few curves and barbed wire strung from beginning to end.

There were warning signs posted throughout every meter saying "*ACHTUNG*—Concentration Camp"—"Stop, do not go beyond." I wondered why all those signs when there wasn't a soul around—no one to be seen. I looked and listened as I leaned against the tailgate. Suddenly, I heard machine gun fire, followed by the rapid sound of a burpgun. I straightened my neck to look and then I saw them. They were prisoners of war in bunches. Russians, from the far reaches of Mongolia. They were bunched in small groups of about ten each, lined up against a pile of rocks and then machine gunned to death.

It was a short ride and we arrived at what appeared to be an unfinished concentration camp. There were prisoners, old-timers, waiting at the gate, and a band to welcome us too. I was happy to dismount into what looked like a labor camp. There were a number of wooden barracks outside the fence, while only a few of them visible on the inside. We lined up in columns of five. There again I saw the familiar sign, *"Arbeit Macht Frei"*—Work Makes You Free.

After a thorough head count and examination, the chief Kapo quickly emerged and took charge. Hours of drilling followed to the tune of German marching songs. It was like soldiering; I couldn't believe it. We marched to the left, to the right, to the rear and finally forward, across into what looked like a hastily built ramp which served as a gate. As I crossed the gate I could see to my right railroad tracks leading into and out of the camp. This was Nazi-occupied Poland, in one of the largest industrial regions of the area. Countless slaves of all nationalities were gathered here. It seemed as if all of occupied Europe were drained into it. There were no chimneys in sight. For once I was relieved.

Once again we were met by the camp commandant. This time, he extended his official welcome to the Gleiwitz Concentration Camp. Briskly he made an about-face and handed his command over to the elder Kapo in charge of admissions. The green triangle on his lapel clearly identified him. I knew from Auschwitz the meaning of his insignia. Kapo Peter was one of the vicious criminals of the Auschwitz hierarchy. He was a convicted murderer and a professional killer whose services were well utilized. Swift and deadly were his lashes. Mean and cruel were his motives. He too gave us a little speech. "You dogs," as he referred to us, "will never get out of here alive. I am going to murder everyone who gets out of line. You did not come to a resort, this is not a boys' camp. The chimneys are but a short ride from here and I promise...you'll never get out of here alive." He was convincing.

Standing but a few feet away, I could tell that Peter meant what he said. His hands and feet were in constant motion, beating and kicking everyone without rhyme or reason. I watched his actions and in the midst I suddenly felt his full fist between my eyes. I fell to the ground. He was about to step all over me when I suddenly rose to my feet and quickly disappeared behind the rows.

As we were admitted to our barracks, the camp clerk handed each of us two slips of cloth. Our tattoo numbers had already been stenciled on them. Needle and thread were distributed and we sat in the field to sew our labels. I was assigned to barracks number five.

The bunks were triple decked and each contained two blankets and a pillow. I chose a bottom bunk; the center went to Bram, and Joey took the top. There was hardly time for a breather when another Kapo emerged. He entered the barracks from the special quarters reserved for the barracks' elder and his orderly. They were both neatly dressed. Their clothes were tailored to their feminine shape, with matching caps slanted to the side for glamour. Kapo Petzol introduced himself, and so did his orderly. "Meisel, that's my name," he shouted violently.

I could tell from his I.D. that Petzol was not an ordinary barracks elder. His purple triangle insignia, pointed upward, indicated that he was a dangerous criminal, a man who had committed a murderous homosexual act in a crime of passion. He was sentenced to die long before the Nazis took power, but was liberated to wield power over us. It was a strange twist of fate.

His helper was no ordinary prisoner either. A Jew from Belgium, no more than twelve—a rare sight in a death camp. Meisel was one of the early arrivers to Auschwitz, and lived through years of horror, escaped countless selections and was saved from the gas chambers by perverted Kapos. I could tell that he was no longer human. He spoke like a brute, a barbarian who always carried a whip.

"Any son-of-a-bitch I catch loafing, stealing or lagging will be flogged; twenty-five lashes," he yelled. I could not picture him so mean, but this gentle-looking little brute soon proved it. Dov, an elderly Jew, standing beside him raised his hand to quiz. "We don't ask questions here, you swine," shouted Meisel. He swung his whip, knocking Dov to the ground and stomped on him until his voice faded into silence.

With Meisel in command we quickly learned the art of bed

making. It was past midnight when we were finally permitted to go to sleep.

The next day we were put to work building the camp. More barracks were needed and added latrines had to be dug. I was assigned to the outside, on the rockpile. Picks and shovels and wheelbarrows were handed out. We were lined up at the main gate; the SS guards with their rifles and the Kapos with their whips were waiting. Beyond, I could see a huge mountainous pile of rocks. Without a moment's delay, the Kapos drove us to it. With pick in hand, I cracked the rocks to smithereens and then shoveled them into a wheelbarrow as we worked in teams.

In the afternoon I was switched to the wheelbarrow team, pushing tons of rocks through rough terrain into the camp. Even though I felt exhausted, there was nothing I could do but keep up. The tenth time around the wooden wheel of my wheelbarrow collapsed. The SS guard behind me burst out laughing as I dropped to the ground. I began to shiver; I couldn't understand his reaction. I froze from fear. Then I heard him speak to his fellow SS man in near perfect Hungarian. I couldn't believe my ears. I must be dreaming, but then he continued and I listened. I detected a slight accent as he was saying out loud, "The sons-of-a-bitches ought to supply them with better tools, don't you think?"

His buddy responded by nodding his head. I was eager and anxious to get in this conversation, but I was afraid to talk. Then I rose and asked him where he'd learned to speak Hungarian so well. He responded in kind, and that shocked me more.

"I am from Bosnia," he said, "a Yugoslavian Magyar. I joined the German SS instead of those dumb Magyars. I thought I would be fighting the Russians, but instead I wound up in this death trap."

I felt relieved that he was telling me all this and happy when he told me his name. "Call me Pista," he said. Then it dawned on me that Pista was looking ahead into the future. He was convinced that the Nazis were through. For him the war was over and he wanted me on his side. Suddenly I felt I was human once again.

He ordered me to leave the collapsed wheelbarrow and marched me back to my barracks. As I was about to leave, Pista reached into his pack and handed me a small piece of his bread.

A few days went by and the entire camp was divided into groups; work gangs. I was asigned to *group twenty-five.* We were to repair freight cars; the bombed-out ones, we were told. The Kapo in charge briefed us. Kapo Newman, a political prisoner of German origin, took the whole day to tell us that we would be working inside the freight yard, and so on. "You will be guarded by civilian workers of the shop. The work will be hard and I will be around to check on you. There will be no mingling with civilians. You are forbidden to talk to them and they, too, know that they are not permitted to talk to you. Should they be caught violating the rules, Auschwitz will be their destination."

The mornings began with the usual head count, but this time only long enough to verify those present. Quickly we were lined up in our respective work gangs and marched through the city of Gleiwitz. It was a grand feeling, for the first time in weeks to see local inhabitants go about their daily work. I saw countless men and women on their bicycles and in their work clothes, heading to their place of work. For the first time I saw children, too, roaming around the streets in their school clothes. There was a human element in the air as we marched through the city's narrow cobblestone streets. It was a good feeling to see people, ordinary people, in the city streets. For a brief moment I forgot there were guards around.

We arrived at the railroad yard. It was huge. The miles of railway tracks within resembled a railroad station with high ceilings and heavy beams for support. People of all kinds were pouring in, in small groups. Russian, Ukrainian, Polish, Belgium, German and French laborers scattered to their stations, awaiting the new arrivals. We were to work with them, as they were our supervisors and we were their new helpers.

The yard was hardly filled when we began to work. It seemed like the entire place had been idle for years due to lack of help.

There were not enough workers to fill every station. I soon learned that the manpower was drained from here to the fronts for combat, and that we were to take their place.

With twelve other prisoners, I was led to station twenty-five. An old German, a civilian worker, was already waiting to receive us. In a low tone he set out to greet us. "My name is Wagner, Hans Wagner. I'll be in charge of you and will be responsible for your work. As you can see from the wreckage of those freight cars, the work will be hard. Every one of them has to be repaired and put back into service. My job's to show you how the work is done, and since all of you are machinists, I'll expect you to do it the right way."

He reached into his pocket for a match to light his pipe as he was talking, and then let out in anger, "You must be better fed if you are to perform hard labor. I have no food for all. I'll have to demand that your commandant feed you properly. You can't perform here without food. You need strength to straighten those beams. Doesn't he understand ... that stupid idiot!"

He seemed angrier than all. Hans, it seemed, was unaware that he was talking to a condemned bunch. I listened in wonderment. I found myself assigned directly to Hans as his helper, and he began showing me around taking me to the scattered toolbench where tools of all sorts were piled on top of one another, totally uncared for. I began to clear the bench, placing every wrench and socket in its place. Soon Hans walked over, puffing on his pipe, looking through his thick glasses, and pretending that I wasn't around. I noticed he wanted me to work by myself. I stopped to look at him, and then in a fatherly way he asked, "How old are you, lad?"

"Seventeen," I replied.

"Why are you in a concentration camp? You seem too young to be here. Where is your home? Do your mother and father know where you are?" He was asking me questions I could not comprehend. I was lost for words. Doesn't he know what is going on around, I thought?

I shook my head and pointed to my insignia. "I am a Jew. Don't you know what they do to Jews?"

138

He moved closer to examine my insignia and then placed his rough and heavy hand upon my shoulder, quietly mumbling, "God. God. God in heaven."

At about nine the sirens blew. It was to be our coffee break, but for prisoners there was no coffee, only a brief rest period. I watched the laborers sip on their coffee and nibble on chunks of bread. Hans called me to his side and handed me half of his coffee with a thin slice of buttered bread. The sweetness of the coffee uplifted me immensely, and the care with which it was offered gave me new hope for life. He was to be my friend, and I felt, through him, that all would be well again.

That evening, soon after we arrived, Commandant Schwarz announced he would need volunteers for extra detail around the camp. There was a need for gravel and rocks to fill the swamp near the camp. I volunteered, since extra soup was promised in return. I was glad to go and so were many others. David and Willie joined the group. Pista was there too; he was one of the guards assigned to this special detail. I was glad to see him along. I felt safe with him around. The work was not as heavy, I felt, and after two hours the call to gather all tools came. There was excitement when the huge kettle filled with hot steaming soup appeared. We were ordered to line up. Everyone received a big share ... a three-quarter full bowl, filled with beets and potatoes. It was invigorating. The kettle was nearly empty when another arrived. It was an unbelievable sight. We were getting more than promised. It just couldn't be true. It wasn't, as we soon discovered.

Following behind the kettle Kapo Peter emerged, visibly drunk. He placed himself in front of the group and began to lecture on life in the concentration camp, on extra detail and on soup. "You're lucky to be rewarded. I wasn't treated like this," he said " ... ever. You bastards are lucky to be still alive. Don't you know that this is Auschwitz, and no Jew survived as long as you have here? I've been around for ten years, and I have never known prisoners to be rewarded with anything other than a flogging and a rope around the neck. And you want extra soup ... ha!"

139

His voice became louder and louder as he spoke. He was beside himself and he kept repeating the same hateful theme, over and over. He fell against the blockwall which separated the camp from the SS barracks. I thought he passed out. He was dead drunk. He screamed and screamed, "You want more soup, extra soup ...ha! You swine; you cursed Jew dogs."

There was malice in every move he made and in every syllable he spoke. I was frightened, scared and shaken by this mad killer. Then he reached for the kettle, grabbing it by its handle and flipping it, spilling its contents on the ground. There were beets and potatoes all over. They looked delicious and appetizing. In seconds, a wild fight broke out, one on top of another, grappling for a beet or a potato. We were fighting over it like animals, no longer human. Survival of the fittest was the only rule.

It was the morning of August 11th. A heavy fog hung close to the ground and the daily roll call showed eleven missing. The guards were quickly reinforced. All around the barbed wire fence machine guns were set up in rapid succession, and another count taken. A thorough search began. German shepherds, well trained to sniff out a hiding prisoner, were everywhere. For hours the search went on while a detachment of SS stood by with their heavy machine guns at their sides trained at us ... ready for the kill.

Finally, in a rage rarely to be seen, Commandant Schwarz appeared. In a burst of fury he shouted, "The swine will not get far. From now on, for everyone who escapes, I will hang ten by the neck! Did you all hear me?"

The shouts of *"Yavol! Yavol!* Yes! Yes!" were loud and clear.

Bram, David and Willie began to explain, to elaborate that if one of us from Munkacs escaped, all from that region might be executed. "We must not talk or think of escape any longer," said Bram.

"I'll think what I want, and I'll talk about it too," replied Willie angrily.

"But they'll gun us down if they find out," snapped David.

I was at a loss. "I'll sure miss dreaming about it," I said dejectedly.

"Don't worry," said Willie. "We'll not only talk about it, but even plan it. You see, those guys who escaped planned it day and night, otherwise they would have been caught."

"I'll bet," said David, "that they were helped by the OST workers." These were forced laborers, non-German civilians drafted by the Nazis. They were permitted some freedom to move around town.

Bram nodded. "The Poles help the Polish, the Russians and the Ukrainians help theirs. Who the hell will help us?"

We went around and around until we understood that no matter what we did here, there wouldn't be anyone out there to help us. We stood in awe, wondering how the escape was planned and carried out. Our hopes were high that the escapees would get word to the Allies, who would then hurry up our liberation. Nine Poles and two Russians were missing.

Schwarz was mad. It was visible in every move he made and in every syllable he spoke. He executed a snappy about-face and stomped away.

In the evening, when we returned from work, we found new orders posted all over the barracks. They were brief and concise: "Each prisoner is responsible for the others. One for all and all for one." We began to digest it slowly.

Coupled with the new orders, a watchman was placed at the doors. No one was permitted to the latrines without signing the register. We were not to go in groups either. One had to wait for the other to return. There was panic. Prisoners were lined up, but many couldn't wait. The barracks began to smell like the latrine. All night long the moans and groans were loud and the agony drove us mad.

The following day we were hastily lined up for roll call and were quickly surrounded by another detachment of SS, more heavily armed. Machine guns were all over the place, loaded and manned. Two trucks roared into the camp. When the canvas was rolled up, two well-constructed, wooden gallows were revealed. They were placed within the semi-circle formed by the two thousand of us

141

wearing the blue and white striped prisoners' garb. There was no mistaking the intent of the well-trained, "Death's-Head" detachment of SS troopers who guarded us.

Two handcuffed prisoners, Ivan and Fedor, were brought forward, two of the eleven who had escaped, we were told. Their faces were bruised and their limbs swollen. Each prisoner was escorted by two SS guards and a Kapo. "Swiftly, swiftly," the prisoners were ordered. "Get to it—let's go," yelled the Kapos. They were led up the stairs of the gallows and made to face the crowd.

The swaying noose was placed around their necks by Kapos Fritz and Peter, and the Commandant took his place on a specially built platform centered toward the prisoners, who faced the victims to be hanged.

With a haughty, military manner, he read the death sentence, none of which remains in my mind except for the final words: "Death by hanging." And then the traps were sprung, and the two dropped, swinging into space.

With his last breath Ivan shouted, "Long live Stalin!"

And Fedor, as he was about to be choked to death, screamed "Tell the world what they have done to us! Don't forget to tell." Suddenly his voice broke.

Both Kapos, Fritz and Peter, served as execution assistants. They placed the noose around the prisoners' necks, and then tied their feet, too. In their lust for strangulation and an eagerness to have a hand in putting an end to the condemned, the ruthless Kapos slapped the hanging prisoners and threw themselves upon the corpses as they were struggling to die. It was a moment of joy for both to have taken part in this event.

I stood close to the gallows and I could see clearly the life drain from the faces of Ivan and Fedor. Their necks broken, their tongues hanging from their mouths, their bodies swaying from side to side, all of us watched as they died a violent but heroic death.

I could not eat my meager rations of bread that evening.

NO. LA 3029

Since 1878

BERLITZ TRANSLATION SERVICE
A DIVISION OF
THE BERLITZ SCHOOLS
OF LANGUAGES
OF AMERICA, INC.
3345 WILSHIRE BOULEVARD
LOS ANGELES, CALIFORNIA 90010
TEL (213) 380 1144

-333-

W e a p o n s - SS
Garrison Headquarters K.L.Auschwitz III   Monowitz, August 18,1944.
File No. KL 14 k 1/8/.44./Schw.-Mi.

Subject: Abatement of various deficiencies in the individual labor camps.

To all Officers in charge of Camps and Squadrons
K.L. Auschwitz III.

During my last inspection visits at a number of labor camps I found a series of deficiencies for the immediate elimination of which I am holding each Officer in charge responsible. Above all, I am pointing out for the last time that any and all instructions,orders from Headquarters as well as circulars must be carried out without delay completely. Unfortunately, I found that especially all of the instructions regarding camp security, daily supervision, double checking, and investigations pertaining to possible escape preparationsaand the like, have in some cases either not been followed at all or only in parts. Despite my order, for instance, in Gleiwitz I, under similar conditions like once before in Eintrachtshuette, an underground tunnel was dug, through which 11 Russians escaped. I shall have this case as well any similar cases in the future submitted to the SS-Court and I shall suggest due punishment of the guilty person, whether camp worker or camp commander.

In many instances, night watch duties performed in certain blocks by prisoners proved to be illusive because they allowed very frequently a very large number of prisoners go to the restrooms at the same time without registering their numbers or implement strict controls otherwise. Double checking of blocks, as ordered frequently, for the purpose of completeness of count, was also not done conscientious-ly. Further, prisoners were found not having numbers on their pants and jackets and the red stripes were barely visible on their civilian clothes. It is the most urgent task of all camp commanders to recognize such deficiencies and have them eliminated as quickly as possible. In this connection I am also explicitly pointing out that the white coats of the Physicians and those of the Barbers are to have such numbers and that they are to be especially made recognizable by the color stripes. In addition, one of the supervisors brought to my attention that some prisoners, who showed a significant reduction in their labor output and who had been reprimanded sveral times by their supervisors, had not been reported by their respective officers in charge of camps and squadrons, however, they had even covered for them. This is an impossible situation. I am emphasizing hereby once more that each Commandant is also responsible for the work output and that it is of course, his job to see that each and every prisoner contributes his utmost to War production.

The Camp Commander:
signed S c h w a r z
Chief company Commander of SS.

This is a true copy
(signed) Orlich
Assistant Company Commander.

By Bread Alone

Since 1878

No. LA 3029

BERLITZ TRANSLATION SERVICE
A DIVISION OF
THE BERLITZ SCHOOLS
OF LANGUAGES
OF AMERICA, INC.
3345 WILSHIRE BOULEVARD
LOS ANGELES, CALIFORNIA 90010
TEL (213) 380-1144

Headquarters
Concentration Camp Auschwitz III

Monowitz, September 2,1944

File: K.L.14 3/Schw.-Aw.

175 331

Type of custody	Nationa-lity	Personal data of culprit:
Political	Jew	First and last names: Nijman BIERMAN

born: 11.12 1914, at Amsterdam

Facts:(when,where,what,how?)

He has grossly infringed upon his duties
while having been on night watch patrol
in block 4 of the labor camp Gleiwitz I
aiding and abetting the escape of 11
Russian protective custodians.

ORDER INFLICTING PUNISHMENT!

According to the penal code for concentrations camps and by virtue of
the authority vested in me to excercise disciplinary punishment, I am
punishing after due examination the culprit as follows:

Penalty for breach of peace:

.....Forewarning under threat of penalty

.....hours forced´labor during off-time under supervision of SS-Adjutant.....

To write private letters or to receive such shall be prohibited for.....weeks

No lunch to be served while working fulltime on ..../......../.......

To sleep only on bare wooden planks after his daily labor, in a cell,

during following nights....

PUNISHMENT GIVEN:
Step I or II   Step III (Sol.conf.)
given from....to... from....to....

(Solitary)confinement:

Step III may be applied as solitary
or single, or as further intensification
of step II for days in a row.

Step I medium	II stricter	III strict
up to 3 days	to 42 ds	to 3days
Wooden planks		Without any facility to lay down or to sit down
cell w. window	dark cell	

144

AUTHORS' COMMANDANT AND SS GUARDS

MOLL, Otto

Neither could anyone else. I saw my own inner torment reflected in the faces of every prisoner I encountered.

The bodies hung loosely all evening as a display for all to see, for all to take note of. Standing in the shadow of the gallows, the dangling men, and the Kapos' lust for murder—everything burned itself into my mind. For a moment I felt old, beaten and dead.

The escape was a success; nine of the eleven had made it. They were on their way to join their partisan fellows, if not already in the woods, to fight alongside their comrades.

Then a change took place. All the Jews were confined to the barracks while the Poles, Ukrainians and Russian prisoners were ordered to assemble for roll call. We began to wonder: why all this shifting, screening and segregating? Rumors began to fly that Schwarz had decided to get even. All of the Poles, Ukrainians and Russians were going to Auschwitz—to the gas chambers.

Without the non-Jewish prisoners, our work load steadily increased. Almost a week went by, and we were greeted by a new commandant, an SS officer named *Oberscharfuhrer* Otto Moll. His first words were, "There will be great changes in this camp." As he stood before us, we had no way of knowing what kind of commandant he would be.

There was a weakness in his face. Perhaps it was compassion. Perhaps here, at last, was a man who would recognize our suffering and increase our food ration. He might even stop the daily floggings and restrain the Kapos from their indiscriminate torture and killing. There was nothing in our past experience to justify such speculation, but we were eager to hope. No one seemed to know anything about him, and rumors were rampant.

Moll had been in Auschwitz since 1941, and had steadily risen in rank, recognition and responsibility throughout his years there. No one, even among the SS, remained in Auschwitz for four years without possessing unique talents and abilities, and knowing how to use them to the fullest. The road to *Oberscharfuhrer* had been paved with the ashes of burnt corpses.

146

THE MOLL PLAN

OTTO MOLL IN HIS
SUNDAY DRESS

DEMOLISHED GAS CHAMBERS AT BIRKENAU.

SITE OF GLEIWITZ 1 CONCENTRATION CAMP

PICTURE TAKEN BY AUTHOR IN 1967

"SONDERCOMMANDO" WORK DETAIL

147

ENTRANCE TO THE GAS CHAMBERS

These ovens were designed and built by highly specialized Germans who knew that they would be used for mass extermination. These ovens were used at Auschwitz-Birkenau and Buchenwald.

Ruins of gas chambers at Birkenau.

1967—The site upon which Gleiwitz was located from 1943-
Jan. 18, 1945, when the camp was evacuated and destroyed
by the Nazi guards. Survivor Mel Mermelstein took picture in
1967.

Ruins of gas chambers at Birkenau.

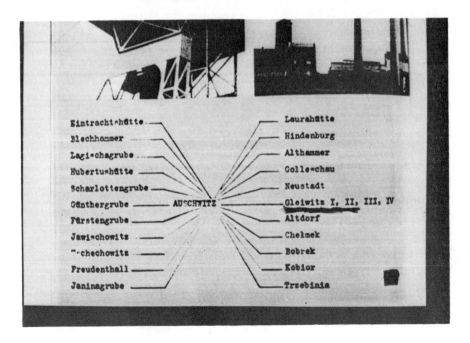

From a supervisor of agricultural workers, he was promoted to head of the prisoners' penal company. Then he was considered hardened enough to be in charge of cremating the first corpses. The Birkenau crematorium was not ready yet, so Moll had corpses cremated in pits near Bunkers 1 and 2. For his superb management of this and similar activities, Hitler awarded him the German War Cross of Merit, First Class—with Swords, as an extra pat on the back. When, in March 1944 the new branch of Auschwitz was established, Gleiwitz Sub-camp I, it was Otto Moll who was honored by being named its first commandant. Had we known that, we would have known all.

In May of 1944, Rudolf Hoess, who had the overall responsibility for the extermination of the Jews of Hungary, recalled Moll to Auschwitz and elevated him to the post of Chief of the Crematorium at Birkenau. You couldn't expect to go any higher than that. When the crematorium was going full blast and the ovens were unable to consume the thousands of corpses fast enough, he devised open pits and a system of efficient burning to handle the overflow. He hadn't received the War Cross medal for nothing.

He was remembered, too, for a selection of twenty beautiful women from a transport that had just arrived. He had them undress and stand naked facing him in a single row. He then shot all of them, one by one, in full view of witnesses. It was a special honor and reward he reserved for himself as bearer of one of the Fuhrer's most respected decorations.

Twenty-five and thirty years later, charges against Otto Moll for his naked brutality were recited in courtrooms where similar members of the SS were charged with crimes against humanity, the destruction of the Jews. In January 1974, a war crimes court in Frankfurt heard testimony that a transport which arrived from Hungary loaded with Jewish children, ages eight to fourteen, was driven to Moll's open pits and the children, four hundred of them, were forced to jump into the flames. The witness at this 1974 trial testified that Moll gave the order, and it was Moll who stood by to make sure that it was carried out. This is the one beast I remember, with clarity and certainty, above all the other beasts. On May 28, 1946, Moll was executed on the gallows he had used to hang his own victims, something none of us could have predicted for Moll while we were still his prisoners.

Moll took a personal interest in the overall operation of our slave labor camp, and he stood by to see that every detail was carried out to his satisfaction. Little time was wasted in dividing us into two groups, a day and a night shift. The two shifts were totally separated from one another, with each shift working twelve grueling hours without pause, without a break to rest tired bodies and tortured minds. The irony of it all; the civilian workers had their lunch while all of us slave laborers continued with our work. Our ration of bread was cut, from a sixth of a loaf twice daily, to a quarter of a loaf once a day. Extra details, too, were forced upon us as soon as we returned to camp. Moll saw to that, as well.

I grew weaker and weaker as the days passed, and I could feel a deep apathy coming over me. "How long can I last?" I asked myself. I quickly fell by the wayside. It seemed that there would be no return for me; I had become what in the concentration camps were called a *musselman,* one who has lost the will to live. The others looked upon me as finished.

My buddies began to pity me, which was a sign that I was too far gone. Bram warned me, "You'll be in the next selection if you don't shape up." Willie warned me, too.

The following morning, while in the washroom, Bram, Willie and David grabbed hold of me, forced my shirt off my back and shoved my head under the cold water faucet to revive me, to try and shock me back to the living.

"You're gonna have to get with it," exclaimed David.

"You're gonna end up in the gas chamber if you don't," Bram warned me as well.

"Pretend you're a soldier," Willie kept ordering me. I was bombarded from all sides. "You're a soldier, do you understand? A soldier, a soldier. Just repeat these orders and rap them out

153

sharp and clear. Your commander means business. Wash up!
Chin up! Take deep breaths! Walk straight! Keep your head high!
Keep clean, neat and wash up! Don't feel hungry. You don't need
any food. Keep working; keep clear eyes; work steadily; wash up;
keep your head up—up—up!'' It was easy for them to say, but it
was I who was suffering and dying. It was I who was trying not to
become a *musselman* and get sent to the ovens.

I tried. In my fevered state I repeated the orders to myself, and
it really sounded as if another voice were talking, giving me
commands that I must obey. And sometimes I did. But the signs
were still there. I was still a *musselman*.

As cold weather set in, we were promised heavier clothing and
overcoats too. But the Nazis weren't about to pass out coats to
those who wouldn't need them. It was Sunday, a day of rest, but
this time it was set aside for a special selection, a weeding out
process. We stood naked, outdoors in freezing weather, in a single
line to be examined by the SS doctor. I was prepared for the
inevitable. I knew from past selections that a *musselman* or even a
near *musselman* would be weeded out and sent to Auschwitz to
the gas chamber. I froze with fear as the doctor looked at me
steadily. I tried to find the eyes behind his thick glasses, but
couldn't. I was shivering and weak-kneed.

"How do you feel?" he asked in a brusque manner.

I felt I was not in control enough to dissemble. I took a chance
on the truth. Maybe he has a son at home, I prayed, and to him I
heard myself saying, "I am not well enough to go on, Doctor."

He looked at me for a moment and then said, "You are too
young, and can still work. *Loss, loss!*" he ordered. "Hurry,
hurry! *Mach schnell!*" He shoved me to the side, and I went to
receive my winter clothing.

I was jolted back to life. Then a struggle entered my mind, and
the reasons I was saved haunted me. Why would the doctor not
heed my plea? I wondered. I did not want to suffer any longer. I
wanted an end to my endless pangs of hunger, to the misery and
cold, and to the helplessness. But most of all, I felt that I was

robbed of my last meal. Someone, somehow, somewhere had convinced me that I would receive a last meal before entering the gas chambers. I was sure of that, and I was ready to die for it. A last "good" meal—how I wished for that! A last meal, and here the doctor denied it to me. I was at odds; they wouldn't let me live, nor would they let me die. I was struggling with myself for days.

The following Monday morning at roll call I collapsed. Bram and Joey were standing by my side. They quickly took hold of me until the roll call was over. Then they helped me to the barracks elder. But Otto Moll, dressed in his warm SS clothing and highly polished boots, spotted us and rushed over to see what was happening. I could see his broad shoulders in front of me as I was propped up by Bram and Joey. I soon straightened out and was about to report that I was well enough for work when he lashed out, hitting me with his fist in the pit of my stomach, shouting and ranting to take me back to the barracks. I quickly regained consciousness and ran to report to the camp clinic.

The *Krankenbau,* or clinic, was merely another barracks where privileged prisoners would go for a rest. The ordinary prisoner had little chance to survive in there. I longed to go there. All longed to go there, especially after a selection. I dreamed of a rest to regain my strength. The *K.B.* was the ideal place for it. You were left alone once you were there. There was no roll call in the *K.B.,* and there was no work either. But, then you gambled with your life by merely reporting sick. I went to the *K.B.* I took a chance.

The sun was shining brightly that morning when a tall figure in a white gown stepped out of the barracks to examine me. He was the camp doctor, a Jew from Holland. His male nurse, Jan, also a Jew from Holland, stood by. He, too, was dressed in white garb, with a thermometer in his right hand, waiting for his first patient of the day. I stepped forward and raised my left arm to take my temperature. A minute went by and Jan announced the result. He reported loud and clear . . . "A-4685 has no fever, doctor." I had no fever. I could not understand.

I began to wonder what would happen now, since I had no fever. Would I be sent to my barracks for a rest? I waited outside. Then I became anxious. Every second that passed I thought: "Will this be my day of all days to be left alone in peace, to myself? Or will it be the gas chambers?" I could only guess.

In the meantime, my appetite vanished; my hunger pangs were no more. An hour went by and I was still standing and waiting. Finally the doctor came slowly over to me and began to examine my eyes; he checked my heartbeat, as well. Then, in a rage, he burst out: "You dirty swine. You gold brick. Report for work! There's nothing wrong with you! You have no fever. On the double, report to the Kapo. Get to work, you dog!"

I ran as fast as I could and was assigned to the latrine detail. I helped clean the pits that served as our latrines. I was handed a pail with a long handle and driven to the huge pit, overflowing with remains. The smell all around was unbearable. Soon it was lunch time. The soup kettle arrived at the scene. We stank from head to toe; there wasn't time to wash. We lined up in a single column for the heavenly soup. The usual shoving and pushing took place. No one wanted to be first. No one wanted to receive the watery part of the soup from the top. Herman, the midget Kapo, got into the act and began to drive us to stay in line. My time arrived; I faced the server and rolled up my sleeve to show him my tattoo number so I could receive my portion of soup. I was struck with the ladle and driven off. I didn't know I had to have a meal ticket, so I reported to the Kapo in charge. Kapo Fritz was no ordinary Kapo. He was chosen to stay in camp to be in charge of camp detail. He was never allowed to leave the camp. Fritz was a mass killer and had been condemned to die long before.

Without listening to my reasoning, he punched me flat in the face. I fell to the ground and froze as the vicious killer Fritz began to kick me, and continued until he tired. There wasn't anything I could do but to wait for his fury to subside. Then I got to my feet and ran to the nearest hide-out, the latrine.

In the afternoon we resumed cleaning the pits. All the work was done on the double. Each time a bucket was filled we carried it to the rear of an empty lot and spread it over a larger area, there to be used as fertilizer. We had no break, so many of us would sneak into the latrine to rest and hide. Killer Fritz, leather thongs in hand, often rushed in only to find us around the faucet. We ran all at once, pushing and shoving through the narrow door to escape the wrath of the killer, but in the end Fritz always managed to capture the last one out. Simon, the shoemaker, was caught. Fritz had beaten Simon mercilessly and chased him into the pit filled with manure. He was left there to drown. We were not allowed to rescue Simon. Simon had to die.

It was now late in the evening and the band was playing the usual march. The prisoners were returning to camp. I could see Bram, Willie, Meyer and David coming to a halt. Everyone was ordered to line up for roll call. I joined them quickly, and once again became a part of my group. The fall season was coming to a close and the weather was getting colder.

The canteen was still in existence. The coupons we'd received a month before were still valid, so I decided to cash them in. Two months of coupons could be used for two cigarettes or a package of harsh tobacco that looked and tasted like wood chips. I settled for two cigarettes, hoping to trade them for bread, but there wasn't any bread for trade. I waited for another time. Days went by, and I couldn't hold back any longer. I wanted to smoke them, but I wanted bread—bread alone.

There were no traders to be found for a full week. Everyone ate their bread to the last crumb. One morning, as I walked dejectedly to the washroom, I spotted Pista. He was on guard at one of the exits. I waved, and he acknowledged my greeting.

"I've got two cigarettes," I said to him in Hungarian. "I want bread for it," I told him.

He looked to the left and to the right to make sure that no one was a witness to the deal; Pista hinted that I leave the cigarettes in the corner on the floor. I saw him reach into his cargo pack, pull out a chunk of bread and place it nearby for me to fetch. He walked to his post, looking in the opposite direction as I snatched up the bread. I picked it up and ran quickly into the washroom.

In minutes I was in possession of my life. Bread from an SS man was not the same as ours. It had the ingredients and taste of homebaked bread, with yeast and salt for taste. Ours was black, heavy and tasteless. It was mixed with sawdust, or so we were told. I sat on the toilet wondering what to do, and how to handle my chunk of bread. Five or ten minutes went by and I still hadn't eaten my bread. I had it hidden under my armpits, covered with my jacket. I walked back to the station, holding onto my newly acquired chunk of bread and cuddling it in my arms so as not to lose a crumb. Bread crumbs are precious. They could keep you going in a make-believe world. The taste of a crumb felt like a meal; time and again it was like at home tasting the fresh bread and rolls mother used to bake in the oven.

I broke a small piece off and began eating it and looked to the sides as I was walking, holding onto my bread with one hand and placing the other over my mouth. No one must find out that I had just acquired bread. No one must know that I had eaten. I must not let even my closest fellow prisoner know that I had extra bread on me, otherwise I would have a sleepless night fearing an attack by a fellow inmate. I might be killed for a piece of bread except for a few crumbs in my pockets. Those crumbs kept me going for days.

The change in commandants soon proved to be in our disfavor. Daily, more and more joined the ranks of the *musselmen,* Meyer, Chaim and Itzak, too. They were all too close to me. They all had been healthy, at least by concentration camp standards, only weeks before, but now they became lethargic...human vegetables. I know how they felt. Everyone kept away from a *musselman* to avoid falling into the same pit. It was a contagious disease. There was nothing one could do but stay away from a *musselman*. The gas chambers were no myth to a *musselman*; they were a reality, something they had come to accept.

Moll ordered those who could not work at full capacity to be weeded out. They were placed in open trucks and driven to Auschwitz to the gas chambers. They took Chaim, and Itzak, too. Meyer survived, he was not chosen for Auschwitz.

The month of December arrived, and with it came the cold freezing weather, but we still were forced to march to and from work barefoot. There were some protests lodged on our behalf. They came from the townspeople, we were told, who watched us march by everyday. They were grim as they looked and watched, seeming to feel sorry for us, at least that's how I pictured them. At the freight yard Wagner told me that the Gleiwitz authorities also had filed a protest with the camp commandant at Auschwitz headquarters. Regional Commandant Schwarz responded quickly in a letter to the mayor. He said there was a war on, and the Germans must conserve shoes and leather. "I am concerned," he wrote "but there is nothing I can do to help."

Wagner mumbled and grumbled, and all I could hear were the words "War, war, war, war!" His reverie ended, as always with "God in heaven!"

Irena, a frail Polish civilian slavegirl, was part of our team. She and Wagner were friends and often communicated in the course of their work. She was a switch operator and her job was to move the wrecked, bombed-out and worn-out freight cars from one track to another.

She was a frequent visitor to our area and often waved to me. She wasn't a beauty, but then I couldn't tell, as she always looked the same with her monkey suit, heavy work boots and work gloves day after day. Her heavy-rimmed glasses always slipped down, making her look like an old maid, and yet she wasn't more than eighteen. I often waved back to acknowledge her greeting. We communicated in sign language. With my crow bar or sledge hammer in hand, I jumped as she passed by me, and on many occasions I'd watch her jump off at my station. She would pause for a few seconds to see that all was clear, and then move cautiously under a boxcar with a can of soup and a slice of bread.

"It's for you," she would signal as she walked by me.

I ran to fetch the can of soup and consumed it rapidly, leaving the empty in the spot that Irena placed it. I was hungry, starving, and Irena knew it. She was like an angel from heaven and she was aware of the chances she took by helping the *Katzetnicks,* as the camp inmates were called. Irena gambled with her life; she cast her dice and she lost. Around Christmas time Irena was caught by the Nazis in a scheme. She was accused of being involved in an attempted escape; she was brutally beaten by a special SS killing squad and shot against the wall in Block 11, at Auschwitz.

The long and torturous night shifts reduced me once again to a near *musselman.* Wagner was aware of my condition and allowed me to hide periodically through the night in the boxcars. The brief naps helped me regain my health, and so I chanced it and repeated it night after night. One night, however, Wagner told me he'd be away for a few hours. He had to attend a Nazi Workers Party Meeting. Wagner, while a member of the Nazi Workers Party, was not like any Nazi I'd seen. He cared, he was human, but insisted he could not change the situation all by himself. If the war were to end, he kept repeating, normalcy and common humanity would return. I always disagreed with Wagner on that, and told him that I had nothing to do with the war. I was still asleep in the boxcar when I heard a loud knock on the huge slider. The door slid open and I suddenly felt a hard object against the side of my ribs. I jumped to my feet and wanted to run. It was pitch black inside the car and I couldn't tell who it was, but I soon found out. I was relieved when I discovered it was Kapo Newman. Kapo Newman was not a bad Kapo. There weren't many like him. He was a political prisoner of German origin. A refined individual who hardly lifted a hand to hurt a fellow inmate. He was well known to all as the only human Kapo in the camp, a rare sight in a concentration camp.

"What're you doing here?" he asked, in a toned down voice. "Don't you know that you're committing sabotage? You'll hang for this if I report you." He didn't sound like Newman, the Kapo we knew, but it quickly dawned on me he wouldn't be a Kapo unless he at least sounded tough. I began to plead with him to let me go this one time, and told him that Wagner let me rest. I pleaded and cried, "You can check with him." Newman wouldn't heed and he was prepared to take me to the administrative department. He was ready to hand me over to Kapo Peter. That would be my death sentence, irreversible without a doubt. I was getting ready to jump out of the boxcar and there I saw Wagner returning from his meeting. I quickly called on Wagner and he briskly walked over. He began to argue with Newman and told him that it was his fault, that he was at a party meeting. "I gave him permission to rest while I was gone. He didn't get a break during his regular rest period." Wagner stood tall and reasoned with Newman as I stared at him steadily, paralyzed and over-whelmed by the contemplation of my fate.

Newman's eyes shifted, and to my relief he turned to me, advising, "If I catch you once again, even as much as loafing, I will assign you to the penal commando, a sure death sentence by exhaustion and hard labor."

With cold freezing weather and reduced rations, many of us took to "organizing." Every night the storerooms were broken into. The "perpetrators" were caught and brought to the square for punishment at the next roll call. Twenty-five lashes for everyone caught.

One evening at roll call, eight "looters" were called up to receive their punishment. Kapos Peter and Fritz stood by with the whip in hand anxious to mete out the punishment. Their numbers were called aloud, one after another, for all to hear and see. A-4684 was last among them. It was Meyer, I could tell. Reduced to a near *musselman* Meyer couldn't hear his number the first time. Once again his number was called, even louder and angrier, but Meyer did not respond. I began to shiver, since my number followed his. One never knew whom they would pick next for a scapegoat. I was frightened. I began to shield myself, but then I saw him, hunched and reduced to skin and bone, stepping forth to receive his twenty-five lashes. There were cries for mercy and help, but not from Meyer: he was far too gone. He no longer felt

161

pain. He had lost his senses. He was a *musselman*.

The flogged were left in the center square until they regained consciousness and dragged themselves back to their barracks.

At roll call the following day the Commandant issued an order that henceforth anyone looting or breaking into a storeroom or a warehouse would be shot. The threat, grim though it was, did not stop the looting. The choice was to die of starvation or of execution. There was no choice.

Misery, death and destruction were the daily portion of our lives, and in the midst of it all, Commandant Moll announced the formation of a theater troupe for our amusement. The first performance was called for a Sunday and everyone was expected to attend. But when the time came, only the commandant, his SS entourage, the Kapos and the camp elder appeared at the hall. The rest were too exhausted to make the effort and remained in the barracks.

This enraged Commandant Moll who ordered everyone out of the barracks and into the theater. Soon wild Kapos charged in with clubs, swinging at random. They rushed into all the barracks, ranting and screaming, "Out, all out! Everyone to the theater." They drove us to the rear of the camp where the hastily improvised theater was set up. A group of SS were already inside the theater waiting for the show to start.

Packed so tightly we could hardly move, we were first ordered to rise in salutation to the SS and our Commandant. Otto Moll, in a holiday mood, welcomed us in jest; he asked, "Would all rather sit and watch the theater, or be moving rocks?"

Loud voices shouting "Theater, theater, no rocks!" were heard. Thus he ordered the show to begin.

There was a dancer, a comedian and a clown too, all very much appreciated by Moll and his henchmen, the Kapos, but not by us, who were starved for food and rest. For us it was outright torture. Our response to the theater was not to Otto Moll's liking either. We did not applaud, nor did he hear any expression of joy or appreciation. How could we, when there was no zest or joy left in us? We were no longer human. When the show ended Moll angrily ordered us all out, and as we were shoving each other through the door, there were all the Kapos lined up to take a swing at us as we ran to our barracks.

So ended the artistic experiment. From then on our Sundays were devoted to hauling rocks from one side of the camp to the other, with Moll himself, in the forefront leading the column, whip in hand, constantly reminding us of the theatrical experience of the first Sunday.

The Christmas holidays approached. Rumors spread that we would receive an extra ration of bread—a Christmas gift. The war news, constantly worsening for the Nazis, gave us new hope. Bram and Willie fed us a stream of good news.

Willie, the fabulous adventurer, took chances by quoting the newspapers out loud. "It'll soon be over," he repeated to everyone. "We shall be free before long. The Red army is but a stone's throw away from here. The Nazis are on the run. They're through, kaput."

In Yiddish, in Hungarian, and in German the good news spread through the camp. There was a re-awakening for all.

Some of the Kapos, and SS guards too, must have begun to believe the news because they suddenly seemed to ease up on their punishments. Then we were told that the gas chambers at Auschwitz were no longer operating, and the selections stopped. But our rations did not increase, nor did our work lessen. And most of all, Otto Moll was still in our midst. The day of Christmas arrived, and to our disbelief we received an extra portion of bread. I clutched it with both hands and wept for joy. We even received a small piece of margarine for a spread; it was truly a feast. The joy of Christmas was all around.

We were promised a day of leisure, a day of rest for Christmas; we couldn't ask for anything more. There was even music in the background, soft Christmas carols in German, and a glittering tree with all the Christmas trimmings in front of each barracks. There was an extra special huge Christmas tree in front of Otto Moll's quarters, and there was a lively Christmas party in progress only a few yards from our barracks. All the SS, with the exception of the guards, were having a good time enjoying and celebrating

Christmas Eve. Suddenly out of the clear, Moll appeared in the middle of the night. I couldn't understand what was wrong. Why were we driven out in the cold, just as we were promised a restful day?

Moll had a weird look on his face, apparently drunk, dead drunk. He was ranting and shouting. "No more selections, no more gasings! You are overjoyed ... you think the war is over ... you think of yourselves as the victors ... No! No! No!" he screamed. "There will be no rest for you dogs. You will be hauling rocks the whole night, and tomorrow, too. This is not your holiday." He went on and on until he collapsed in the middle of the field. The Kapos took charge and picked up where Moll left off. Then at dawn, finally, we were allowed to drag ourselves, one by one, back into the barracks.

That night there appeared before me a vision of food, delicious food, appetizing and tantalizing. By merely closing my eyes I saw various dishes. Even when I opened my eyes, the plates were still there before me. They floated on the clouds and in the air, and the odors were sharp as the picture. In my mind I began sorting and laying out a banquet. There were *Gefilte* fish, soups, *chulint,* dishes of potatoes heavy with gravy, *kugel* and sponge cake. Everything was beautifully prepared in mother's way, appearing in just the right order, as at a Sabbath feast. When I reached out to touch them, so strong was the vision that they were there; and yet they were not there. They did not fade, mirage-like, but my hands simply went through them.

I began to weep, "God, God, please God, before I die couldn't I have one last meal; like this one, but a real one—a real one?" I swallowed tears mixed with growing indigestion. What had I done? What had any of us done to be punished so severely with the ceaseless, bottomless hunger? I wailed and I pleaded. "I will die happy, God, if you just give me enough to eat, just once." I prayed and cried and prayed, and something strange happened. Just before I awoke from my sleep, exhausted, and in the last echoes of weakening sobs, all of my hunger vanished, and for that brief moment I was completely satisfied and at ease.

With the passing of the holiday, changes began to take place in the camp. First, some of the SS guards were replaced by Wermacht—regular army—soldiers, most of whom had been drafted. Then many civilians were sent to the front. This last move convinced us that the German armies were weakening and that our chances for survival were improving.

The increasingly frequent air-raids were another good sign, but we realized, too, that some of us could be killed by bombs that were intended for our enemies. At the railway, an air-raid was a signal for the civilian workers to disappear — to underground shelters, we presumed — while we were herded into a corner of the factory on the ground floor. So great was our fatigue that we discounted the danger of life and welcomed the air-raids as a chance for an unscheduled rest.

As the new year, 1945, arrived we began to hear word of Russian advances in the East which brought them near to the site of our camp. Our hopes of liberation began to rise, but were soon dashed when, on the 17th of January, it was announced that we would be moving westward ... on foot, we were told.

The announcement was made official by the Kapos. They said that we would be issued food and clothing rations for the move. In the meantime the opportunity to "organize" was too great to resist. Everyone rushed toward the warehouse; I followed and when I got there it was in chaos. Prisoners were throwing bread and sugar out of the windows of the storerooms. I caught three loaves of bread and ran to the barracks, hiding two in my pack and quietly eating the third. It was almost as if God had answered my prayers for enough to fill my stomach. Suddenly it was heaven. There was no fear of your bread being stolen, or that the Kapos would strike you. There was a sudden atmosphere of ease, jubilation. I returned with a calm to my barracks to rest, until I remembered that I had to have gloves and a shawl for the journey. So I returned to the warehouse and found gloves, a sweater and even an extra blanket.

At dawn the whole camp, two thousand in all, was lined up in groups and then columns of three for the march. The order to move came on a bitter, cold morning. Bram, Joey, Meyer, David, Willie and I each inspecting the other's packs. With broad smiles, we adjusted our blankets around us. A last head count was made, we were issued another loaf of bread, and then we awaited the arrival of the Camp Commandant and his force of SS troopers.

Snow began to fall as we stood there. Bram lectured us as we waited, warning that it would be a tough journey and that we were to pretend that we were soldiers. "Walk straight. Let your hands swing freely at your side. Remember the soldiering lessons from back home, this is the time to use them. Shoulders back, and keep your heads high and straight, and breathe freely." He was moving around like a lieutenant advising his troops. His past experience as a soldier came in handy now.

"Don't look behind you. Always look to the front, always ahead, straight ahead. I know it's tough, but you've got to do all you can to just keep moving. We don't have enough strength to help others who are faltering," he continued. "It'll just get you a bullet in the neck. These bastards shoot first and ask questions later. We've gotten this far—we've just got to make it! Look, the Russians are on our heels, and their tanks will be eating up the kilometers a lot faster than us." His voice grew to a pitch; he wanted us all to survive. "Please keep your minds on number one. Please listen to me, all of you, we've got to make it. We must prove it to ourselves that if we made it this far, we shall make it home."

My ears buzzed and my eyes glazed. I didn't know what to say.

He wasn't too happy with some of the enervated responses, "For God's sake," he kept shouting, "don't fall behind. Stick together, all of you. Do you hear me? Stick together. There's got to be an end to this. It can't go on much longer, and I want to see you alive at the end. Don't let them have the victory, boys. Somebody has to live. Don't you see that?"

Heavily armed and well-dressed soldiers arrived. The troops took up their stations on both sides of our lines, while a sizable number brought up the rear. As I looked behind, I saw the infirmary, with numerous sick patients inside; I couldn't help wondering what their fate would be.

It was time for us to leave, and Commandant Moll stood before us. "All of those who cannot walk, drop out now." he commanded, and "Anyone who shows weakness on the road will be shot. Do not be foolish enough to try to escape. You'll be shot on the spot." He was brief and to the point. Then he gave the order we had been waiting for — "Move out! . . . Forward March!!!"

By Bread Alone

ELECTRIFIED BARB WIRE FENCE AT AUSCHWITZ.

CHAPTER SIX
"Evacuation"

With arms linked together we passed under the giant archway into the open space beyond, leaving behind the barbed wire fences of Gleiwitz. We marched, singing, past the open gates, and for the first time since our imprisonment we felt a genuine taste of freedom.

As the day progressed we became accustomed to the open roads, and by midday we began to like it. The march soon picked up speed.

We passed through the small towns and villages, covering many kilometers. Here and there a few women and occasionally a man watched us as we passed by. Some spectators went to the extent of quizzing the SS guards about where we were headed. The evening rolled by fast, and we arrived at a civilian labor camp. There we were received and assigned to wooden barracks and ordered to remain indoors. The camp seemed deserted with only a few women attending the mess hall. They treated us to coffee and a biscuit. From the disarray of the camp we could tell that they, too, were on the move. Their men had already left, transferred to the interior of Germany, and the few women left behind would soon follow, too.

In the morning it was coffee again, and after a thorough head count we were commanded to march. The road was deserted. We passed numerous groups of prisoners of war still in their green uniforms. But they were heading in the opposite direction from us. We waved and greeted each other in several different languages. There was no clear pattern to the process, because they didn't know where they were going and we knew even less than they did.

Some in my group began to fall behind, tiring under the rapid pace, while others were hoping to be ignored by the guards and try to make a run for it. But soon Moll ordered stragglers shot, and within minutes the order was obeyed. Rapid machine gun firing became louder and louder; as I looked back, I saw numerous SS busy finishing off the fallen prisoners, some with their bayonets and others with their rifle butts. I quickly stepped up my pace and abandoned the idea of escape. In minutes I found myself running to catch up and close the ranks. I heard constant shooting as I ran, and it felt like the SS were shooting at me, too.

As the last shots sounded in my ears, a weary old-looking man, huffing and puffing, moved alongside me. His weary voice muttered, "Please help me, please help me. They'll shoot me, too. I can't keep up. Please let me hang on."

I forgot Bram's advice and told him to cling to my arm and increase his pace. Together we made it to the next steep hill, but as we dragged ourselves downward, he stumbled and fell to the ground, pulling me down with him. I sprang to my feet and tried to pull him up, off the ground. An SS man quickly rushed over, his rifle drawn and pointing.

"Please, please don't shoot," I cried. "Don't shoot. I can walk." I began to run and rejoined my group. Ten seconds later I heard a shot. He finished off the old man. "God," I thought, "how could I leave him like that?" And then, unbidden, another voice sobbed silently at me: "What would you do if that old man were your father?"

"Look," I struggled with the challenge, "I'm just an ordinary youth. Am I a prophet or a philosopher? How can I be expected to face such heavy life-and-death questions? You want me to be able to fight my natural instinct for self-preservation? You want me bone-tired, hungry, abused, hounded, threatened by death at every turn—you want me to be the conscience of the world? Where is the world, anyway? Why don't the good people come and save me? You want me to take care of everybody here? Am I my brother's keeper?''

But these last words trapped me, for I saw them come out of the mouth of our Rabbi, and I saw him shaking aside all excuses. I knew he was waiting for me to answer the question myself. For, seeing me hesitate, he seared the answer into my soul with a question of his own, his question that had been my question all along: "And are you your *father's* keeper? What would you do if that man were your father?"

And so, keeping up with the hurrying men, I continued on a road that led me away from the dead man whose life had but a few moments ago leaned hotly on my shoulder. I didn't know what new trials were ahead for me on that road. Pounded from the outside by monstrous taskmasters, racked from the inside by an aware and feeling soul, I felt my youth slip away from me and knew that the question would never go away.

The weather grew worse. Snow began to fall hard and the winds increased in force. We marched until late that evening, when the commandant selected a barn in which to sleep. We were warned again that if anyone tried to escape, the entire group would be shot.

On the third day of our journey, many of us began to show that we lacked the strength to go on. Our shoes began to wear out. Many marched barefoot, but no one could last long that way, for the snow and the cold took a quick toll.

Liebel the Glazier, as we knew him, lost the wooden part of his shoes and was forced to march that way. The SS guards amused themselves watching Liebel until he collapsed. They pulled him to the wayside to be shot.

Our group became smaller and smaller as we marched along. The snow was getting deeper and deeper. Suddenly rumors began to spread that the march would soon end, and so it did. We were driven till midnight when we entered a forest. A light in the distance played hide-and-seek as we walked deeper and deeper among the trees. Then, through the gloom, we came upon tall, concrete walls. A light shone over the inevitable sign: *"Lager Blechammer,"* it said—Concentration Camp Blechammer— and below it, *"Arbeit Macht Frei."*

It was a relief knowing that we had finally arrived, but we found the camp in the midst of its own evacuation. Rumors began to spread that the Nazis were retreating and the Russians were advancing rapidly. Exhausted though I was, I went from barracks to barracks seeking information. Camp discipline broke down. There were no more Kapos to be seen. More and more prisoners, inmates of Blechammer, broke through the concrete walls and took to the open roads. I became weary and had no strength left and when I reached the nearest bunk I fell asleep.

That night I had a dream. I dreamed that Lajos was on his way to meet me and together we would look for my father. My father was alive, I dreamed, and well too. I saw him clearly in my dream but couldn't talk to him. He seemed too distant to hear me. I was heard yelling and calling for my father. It was all a dream, but in my dream he was alive.

I awoke the next morning and saw inmates in their striped uniforms walking in and out of camp without interference. They were free to go as they wished. I couldn't understand that. A truck pulled up to the main gate. The driver got out quickly and dumped his load. He was an SS man. It was bread that he dumped. I couldn't believe my eyes. This must be a trick, I felt. It's a hoax the SS man is playing on me. Why is he bringing us bread? The heap was getting bigger and bigger and the inmates began to gather closer and closer. The SS man, finishing his job of unloading, pulled away, disappearing into the forest. And then I saw it. A squad of the elite SS emerged from the outskirts of the camp. They watched the inmates gather around the mountain of bread, and then they opened fire, rapid fire. I ran into the nearest barracks and hid under a bunk.

Suddenly there was silence—not a sound to be heard. There was no crying or moaning. They were all dead, piled up on top of each other, covering the heap of bread soaking it with their blood. "The staff of life," I thought bitterly as I stared at the horrible spectacle—people sprawled like squashed ants on an ant hill. I shuddered and hid my face.

I retreated toward the rear of the camp, where I found a group of newly arrived men from Camp Jaworzna. Knowing that father had been sent there, I began to inquire about him. Many had known him, but no one could tell me if he was here or still alive. Then someone told me that Lajos had come here with the new group. I despaired of seeing him again, but set off at once on a feverish search, making my way laboriously through each barracks. I caught at least a glimpse of every face, most marked with hopelessness and branded with past pains. I peered at people lying face down on their bunks, trying to see each face in the groups of men huddled together for comfort. I pushed my way in and out of the camp through masses of men milling about outdoors, pushed myself beyond endurance. I grew more and more desperate as each cluster of humanity, each heaving formless wave of people, rushed past my eyes and washed across me, as if I were the prow of a ship in a heavy sea, leaving a crusty scum of hurt upon me. I saw no sign of the one face I longed to see, the one face that could heal my disintegrating soul. A hand reached out and grabbed and stopped me, as if it knew I was drowning in the storm. It was Bram!

"I've found you! I've been hunting for you high and low. We've got to join the group moving out of here right now. They're going to shoot everyone who remains behind," he said.

Another decision. What if Lajos *is* here? What if he doesn't leave? But Bram would hear none of it. "He isn't here. I've looked everywhere. Besides, he can take care of himself." And he swept me into the group.

Moving along once again, I noticed Pista nearby. He was assigned to be our SS guard. He handed me his cargo pack, to

173

carry for him. I was relieved and felt safe with Pista at my side. He let me reach into his cargo pack to take some bread for the journey.

"This might be a long march," Pista warned.

We marched all day, and as night came, we were again put up for the night. I was assigned to a barn with Pista as a guard. As we waited outside to be led into the barn, Pista came up to me whispering, "The Russians are on our heels. If they keep up their advances, you'll be free by the morning, and will end up shooting the 'beast' Moll."

Then he turned to me again and said quizzingly, "You wouldn't let them shoot me, would you, if we were captured by the Russians?"

"No, I would shield you as you have shielded me," I answered. Thus I entered into a secret agreement with an SS man.

I was confronted with the disturbing matter of "the good Nazi." Pista, the volunteer SS man, befriended and shielded me. I wondered why. Was it because it was already late in the war, and he may have seen the handwriting on the wall? Was it possible that he was just conniving, that I was to be put into a position of power over a Nazi? That was inconceivable.

I was frightened with my conscience, but my gratitude was natural and my need was great to find a friendly voice among my many overlords.

Feeling all that hatred, I yearned to forgive as well. Forgiveness and mercy were the central traits of the Jewish Bible, and the tradition I had been taught at home.

I saw it all, the good and the bad. The SS were a force of hundreds of thousands and had solid support from the military establishment at large. Countless reports, some from the SS commanders themselves, tell us that in the few instances where the local population did not cooperate in the roundup and extermination of Jews, the operation was slower, more difficult and incomplete. But in the Eastern Nazi-occupied countries cooperation was always wholehearted and often surpassed in zeal that of the SS. The planning, transport and execution apparatus of the Nazis was enormous and terribly efficient, and the numbers of innocent, helpless men in the organization were very small. Yet in the last months of the war we were inundated by a flood of "good Germans." Suddenly everyone who had been against us turned against Hitler and his war, even insisting that they had been against Hitler all along. Suddenly no one knew the meaning of "the final solution," no one believed that Jews were killed.

In the morning, under a light snowfall, we continued our march. My wooden shoes began, at long last, to fall apart. I pointed it out to Pista.

"You must find a pair of shoes at once, or you'll be shot. Yank a pair off one of the dead bodies lying by the side of the road—and do it quickly!" he said.

The idea repelled me, but Pista meant what he said. He'd watch over me in the process and would prevent his fellow guardsman from interfering. The snow was falling harder and harder, and I felt that unless I began to take heed of Pista, I would soon have to fall to the wayside and be shot.

There were hundreds of corpses lying on the side of the road, and I could have my pick of their shoes, if I only had the courage to pull them off. My conscience was splitting. How could I do this? How could I rob my fellow inmate of his possession—his shoes? I learned at Auschwitz that your shoes are your most prized possession. Life and death depended upon your shoes.

But my mind worked quickly, and I came to terms with it. My life would be spared if I had a useable pair of shoes. Those by the wayside needed them no longer. I was alive. Those by the wayside covered with a thick layer of snow and frozen to a cake of ice were no longer alive. I must act quickly or I too would turn to a chunk of ice. My father's voice was dictating: "Survive, you must survive, so you can tell what they have done to us."

The first time around, I was unsuccessful in removing the pair of shoes. They were frozen solid to the feet of the corpse. I struggled for awhile, but then I had to give up and try again.

175

Pista told me to look for a pair of low shoes, and finally I found one which slipped off the feet of the corpse easily enough. I guess the corpse was not yet frozen. He must just have been shot. I carried my newly acquired shoes under my arm until nightfall, when we again settled into a barn.

It was strange. We were prisoners, and yet, we were out in the world. We passed ordinary people, moving about freely by cart or on foot. They wore no prison garb. They were well fed and their eyes were clear and unhaunted. They seemed like creatures from another world, and we must have seemed even more bizarre to them.

As we were entering the barn, a somewhat stooped, grey-haired man stood by, perhaps a farmer, but obviously free; one of the strange ones from the world I had forgotten. He stared at me as if wanting to rescue me. "Who are you and where do you come from?" His voice was tinged with pity and wonder.

Overhearing the old man, the SS quickly turned and hissed at him, *"Diese sind Juden."* Was a further explanation necessary? "These are Jews, and that should tell you everything, my countryman, and squelch your misdirected pity."

Yes, I thought, we are Jews; we are Jews, and the lesson was clearer to me than to the old man. I fought its corroding implications, but it was constantly forced upon me. I was sure we were the good and they were the evil; but then, why were they the master and we the slaves? All they had to say was "These are Jews," and they could get away with anything. Why was it like that? I kept wondering.

Our home for the night was a huge, unlit barn. As our eyes became accustomed to the darkness, we discovered several cows. Some rushed over and began to milk them, while others waited for the pail to fill. They managed to fill one pail and then another, but no one drank any of the life-giving milk that night. We were far removed from the normalcy required to conserve and share. Argument quickly escalated to struggle, and all the milk in the pails was spilled to the ground. I felt a pain as I saw the pool of white milk spread out and sink into the dirt. Memories of home and another world, a world of milk and bread with butter and sugar sprinkled on it came to mind. Tears welled up within me. I moved to the other end of the barn. I still had my newly acquired shoes. I had to put them on before they were snatched. There was no string in them, so I bound them with a length of wire that I found hanging on the wall.

When morning came, the roll call disclosed that some of the men were missing. Joshua and Chelm had escaped during the night. Mojse and Yankel were missing, too. I remembered Moll's warning, and feared for our lives. Moll was quick and decisive. He ordered the hay stacks that dotted the barnyard set afire. Within minutes, the missing prisoners came running out of their flaming hiding places. Like flaming torches, they ran, screaming pitiously. It didn't matter. They were gunned down indiscriminately and without ceremony.

Day followed day as we marched on and on without food or proper clothing. For water, we ate the snow off the ground. I noticed our group continued to grow smaller and smaller. We had been on the road for two weeks and there was no end in sight.

Our numbers declined from two thousand to less than two hundred. Hershel, the watchmaker, was no longer around, and neither was Willie. He must have remained at Blechammer, but not Hershel. He was shot. I saw him lying face up on the side of the road, half covered with his blanket, and half nude. His eyes were still open. I wondered if he could see me as I passed by. He looked content, and I wondered again if he wasn't better off. My head quickly turned for a last glimpse at my friend the watchmaker. I looked at him for a second and then I thought: I must not think that way if I'm to survive, so I jerked my head to the front and kept on marching and marching. Survival, survival, I must survive!

At night a miracle took place. We entered another barn and I discovered carrots and potatoes deep inside a pit. It was a storage pit.

"Come and see," I exclaimed.

Like madmen they ran...stuffing carrots and potatoes inside their pockets and shirts. I tied both my pants at the bottom with strips of my blanket and stuffed both my legs with carrots, potatoes and onions too.

The next day, in the late afternoon, we passed through a small village. It must have been a Sunday, around dinner time, as I saw entire families gathered at the windows and staring at us. I suddenly sensed that there was not hostility but sympathy coming my way. The people, surprised and shocked by the sudden appearance of a long line of shuffling, hungry-looking prisoners, had been moved to pity. To my amazement, I heard many shouts of greetings, too. Soon there were others who joined in. Even more startling was that some of us answered back, and there was an exchange of waving, greeting and shouting...an interchange and communication between human beings that we had long forgotten still existed in this small village of Manstein.

Our guards were getting fidgety, and began hurrying us on, when a rain of bread fell all about us. I could see women and children running to their tables for the bread bins and hurling rolls and pieces of bread and half loaves and whole loaves at us. An amazing sight! I forgot for the moment that I was a prisoner, condemned by the Nazis because I was a Jew. I felt human again.

More important than the pieces of bread we snatched, was the unexpected surge of hope within us. There could be concern for us after all, I thought. Perhaps we were so alone, cast out and neglected, because people didn't know or see. History didn't bear that feeling out. There was more knowing and less caring than people would like to admit.

But the people of that small village had at least opened their windows to us, and nothing detracted from what was, for us, a glorious moment at the time. In a face-to-face, people-to-people experience there had been a shower of bread that carried the rain of compassion.

Our guards saw the situation growing out of control. Furiously the SS pointed their rifles at the civilians and hollered, "These are

Jews. You will be shot if you don't stop throwing bread at them."
Quickly, the civilians pulled their heads from the windows and
disappeared from sight. The heavens had shut their gates, and the
gentle rain had ceased.

In the evening, we arrived at a deserted castle. We passed a
stream and I dipped a tin in it for water. Scholtz, the SS guard,
saw me and grabbed the can of water from my hand and threw it
away. He threatened to shoot me if I got out of line again.

Once in the castle, we were permitted to move around freely,
but again warned not to go outside. Shortly after the warning,
Gershon, the tailor, was found outside. He tried to escape. He was
shot. His body, dripping with blood from his head and hands, was
left hanging on the terrace as a reminder to those tempted to
escape.

Three weeks had gone by and still no end in sight—especially
when I realized that Otto Moll was still with us, supervising and
directing the march. He was here, I thought, to make sure that we
didn't fall into Russian hands. We heard that he had personally
shot many Jews...eighteen thousand was the number! He carried
it out single-handed. He was known to the SS as "the man of
action." Now we were his charges, and he wasn't about to spoil
his record. To add to the challenge, many of his SS, sensing their
precarious position, were deserting into the forests, leaving him
short-handed for the number of prisoners he had to lead and
control. There were but a handful of SS guards left now. Mohr,
Schuller and Ilisch were gone. Scholtz, Lumnitzer and Bauer were
not to be seen either. Pista was still with us but he would disappear before long he told me. Moll ruled with an iron fist, and on
many occasions rerouted the columns onto smaller roads,
sometimes even into small paths, to avoid the advancing Russians.

Hungry, weary and filled with fear, we marched on and on. We
reached a huge forest where once again a camp was visible.
Through the heavy slush and snow we marched toward the camp.
I lost my shoes in the mud, but managed the final mile barefoot.
After twenty-one days of marching, two hundred survivors out of

the two thousand who had started out, arrived at the Gross-Rosen Concentration camp.

Gross-Rosen was situated on a mountain, knee-deep in mud. We were driven into barracks without windows or roofs. They had been bombed we were told. There wasn't a dry spot in the area, so I went about looking for rocks to fill the puddles. Instead, I found a board and placed it over the mud. I covered myself with my blanket, or what was left of it, and fell asleep.

In the middle of the night, Kapos appeared. They woke us..."On the double," they shouted. "Soup...soup...line up for the soup! *Loss . . . loss . . . on the double . . . hot soup!*"

This must be a very unique camp, I thought. Why bother in the middle of the night...I wondered. All had lined up for soup. To our surprise, everyone received a three-quarter loaf of bread, a chunk of wurst and margarine too. I had a feast.

Added to all of this, Otto Moll had disappeared. I no longer felt the shadow of Auschwitz, with him gone. I was never to see him again.

At dawn, we were once again lined up and driven to the railroad tracks. Long lines of cattle cars stretched from one end to the other. Packed like a herd of cattle, I began to wonder what it was all about. Where to this time? Hours went by and we were still not moving. Crammed against each other, with no room to sit...panic struck.

The smell of bread was the triggering mechanism. Clawing each other we fought for a bite of bread, each for himself, one against the other. The beast of man was at work. I quickly ate my small chunk of bread and thus was left alone.

Many had been crushed to death in the fight, and soon I found there was more room...enough even to sit. I sat on a corpse for the whole journey. I could not tell who he was, but his soul was before me the whole time.

CHAPTER SEVEN
"By Bread Alone"

The trip lasted three days and two nights, during which time we received neither food nor water. Though these were open freight cars, without roofs, the smell of the bodies lying on the floor was quite strong—especially now that the transport had come to a halt. But while we were moving they had much been a part of us.

We arrived at a large camp that lay sprawled out before us under a layer of slush and mud, and were ordered to dismount. Prior to disembarking, we were told to toss the corpses to the side and line up to be counted, along with the dead.

There were no bands to welcome us as at Auschwitz or Gleiwitz, but there were many strange prisoners on hand, like dignitaries, awaiting us at the rail sidings. We couldn't understand this type of welcome. "Where are the SS?" I wondered, "and what about those mean Kapos?" This place puzzled me, and in a feeble-minded way, I began to inquire as to where we were. What kind of camp was this?—Buchenwald, we were told. This is Buchenwald. Soon we were welcomed by a somewhat cultured prison elder, well dressed and well fed. He told us that soon we would be cared for.

In the midst of shoving, pushing and killing one another in the open cattle cars, many had lost their shoes, and our clothing was torn to shreds. My shoes, my third pair since the outset of the march, had been stolen in a brawl, when someone thought that I harbored two loaves of bread under my arm. Instead of shoes, on

181

my feet were strips of blanket. At last the Kapos and prison elders took notice and began the process of admitting us into the camp. We were stripped naked and our bodies searched for tools or potential weapons; then we were sent for delousing and a bath.

I received clean clothes and wooden clogs. My tattoo number was no longer any use except as a record of the past. We were issued new numbers of Buchenwald registry on pieces of cloth, and told to sew them on our striped jackets and trousers. As I waited to receive my new number, which was 130508, one of the elder inmates began interrogating me. He was interested in the details of our march, how long it had taken and how many of us were shot along the way.

Suddenly I found myself behind what looked like an office, next to the camp secretary filling out all sorts of forms and documents. My name, nationality, previous prison number, as well as home address were emphasized. He made out a *Haftlingspersonalbogen des KL Buchenwald* (prison personnel history card), *Arbeitskarte des KL Buchenwald* (work card), *Nummernkarte des KL Buchenwald* (prison number card), *Schreibstugenkarte des KL Buchenwald* (barracks card), *Haftlingspersonalkarte des KL Buchenwald* (prison personnel card), *Revierkarte des KL Buchenwald* (hospital record), and the documents, which certified me as a Jewish, non-Orthodox political prisoner.

What I couldn't have known at the time was that this man was one of a large group of political activists—socialist and communist prisoners who had banded into a large and efficient underground organization within the camp society. They were able to give aid to the ill and save the dying, and at the same time prepare themselves for the day of resistance and liberation. In the years that followed I revisited Buchenwald, as I had a compulsive wish to see the place in which I had been liberated. It was the liberation process of my imprisonment which set the stage of my new life. Thus I walked through the camp and was able to better understand the full impact and horror of this huge apparatus for imprisonment, death and destruction. It was here that Ilse Koch, the Bitch of Buchenwald, as she was referred to, vented her sadistic cruelties, and the SS doctors conducted medical experiments on inmates to develop new strains of vaccines for the IG Farben trust. The human guinea pigs inevitably died. The careful German records show that 238,980 inmates were admitted to Buchenwald, and almost all of them were used as slave labor for German industry. It was here that the SS actually hired out the prisoners to the industrial trusts, and made huge fortunes from their labor—over 60 million marks profit in 1944 alone.

Standing at the crematorium and other sites of horror (hangings, torture, the special Nazi execution of shooting through the neck), it was with an indescribable flood of painful memory that I conjured up the vision of Buchenwald concentration camp in 1945: the strange faces, the hugeness of the place and the starving, emaciated crowds of prisoners milling about. I remember clearly that then, as now, the division of Buchenwald into two camps was quite marked.

As I took my first walk through the camp on that cold February day of 1945, I listened and questioned. I learned that the main camp was occupied mostly by political prisoners of different nationalities. The "Little Camp," as it was known, was an isolation place for the condemned, the hopeless. It was also a special breeding place for disease, hunger, misery, and sheer death.

At first I was assigned to the hastily constructed infirmary, called the Revere Block, because I was stricken with typhus. The barracks had shelf-like bunks, each of which held five inmates. They were victims of all sorts of disease, indiscriminately crammed into those shelves, and made to stay there, and ordered out only to be counted. Day after day I lay on my back on the hard surface of the shelves without any cover, without any heat, using my clogs as pillows—just dying away slowly.

The daily ration, distributed once, always in the morning, consisted of a quarter loaf of black bread and some kind of

Haftlingspersonalbogen des KL Buchenwald.

Konzentrationslager _____ Art der Haft: _____ Gef.-Nr.: *130508*

Name und Vorname: *Mermelstein Mór*

geb.: *25.IX.1926* zu: *Munkács Kom. Bereg Ungarn*

Wohnort: *Oroszveg 272, Kom. Bereg*

Beruf: *Maschinenschlosser*   Rel.: *mos.*

Staatsangehörigkeit: *Ungarn*   Stand: *ledig*

Name der Eltern: Vater: *Selester Hermann M.*   Rasse: *Jude*

Mutter: *Fany geb. Klein*

Wohnort: *Oroszveg 272. w.o. ist ausgesiedelt*

Name der Ehefrau: _____ Rasse: _____

Wohnort: _____

Kinder: _____ Alleiniger Ernährer der Familie oder der Eltern: _____

Vorbildung: _____   *10.2.45 KL Gr Rosen*

Militärdienstzeit: *Mermelstein Mór* ___ von — bis _____

Kriegsdienstzeit: _____ von — bis _____

Grösse: _____ Gestalt: _____ Gesicht: _____ Augen: _____

Nase: *10.2.45* Mund: _____ Ohren: _____ Zähne: _____

Haare: _____ Sprache: _____

_____ Gebrechen: _____

Schreibstugenkarte des KL Buchenwald.

Polit. *130508 Mermelstein Mor*
Ung
Jude
geb. 25. 9. 26 *Munkács*
maschineuschlosser

10. 2. 45   GROSS-ROSEN

Arbeitskarte des KL Buchenwald.

Copy of original document pertaining to author's personal records: Note: (Konzentrationslager) Concentration Camp, Buchenwald. Date of birth, prison number, etc.

Revierkarte des KL Buchenwald.

Kol. Ungar-Jude	Name:	Vorname:	25.9.23
Rio.			Kunkscs
B.V.	*130508*	*Mermelstein*	*Mor*
Jude			

| | 1 0. Feb. 1945 | | Einlieferungsgewicht | |
| Geburtsort: | Einlieferung: | Größe: | (bekleidet) kg: | Entlassung: |

Krankengeschichte und Einlieferungsbefund	Krankmeldungen		
	Tag	Kr. B. Nr.	Befund
Schlosser			

Krankmeldungen		
Tag	Kr. B. Nr.	Befund

Besondere Vorkommnisse		Revieraufnahme	
Tag	Befund	Einlieferungstag	Entlassungstag
	3x IV U n. i. Schlag		

Körpergewicht							
Monat	kg	Monat	kg	Monat	kg	Monat	k

Revierkarte des KL Buchenwald

Hospital record showing that author was inflicted with typhus.

185

By Bread Alone

Copy of original transport list. Note that a group of prisoners had arrived in Buchenwald on the 10th of February 1945 from the death camp of Gross-Rosen. Note: One of the prisoners among the transport was the author, Mermelstein, Mor - Born 25 September 1926 - Munkacs. A machinist by trade, prison tatoo number A-4685, also to left of column the new Buchenwald Prison Number 130508.

186

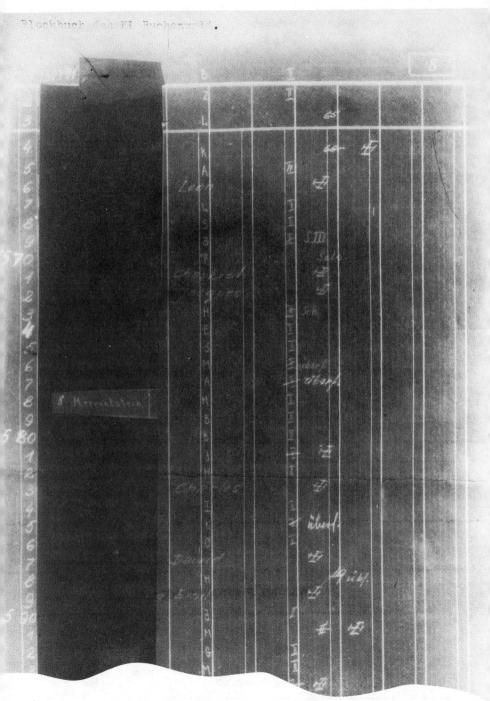

Buchenwald Barrack Roster: Note author in Section 8.

Copy of original transfer list dated 24 February 1945. 833 Prisoners transferred to Barracks Number 56 from the main camp at Buchenwald to the section known as "The Little Camp". "The Little Camp" was the death section where prisoners were dumped to die. They were mainly "musselmen", no longer of any use for slave labor and most were infested with lice and disease such as typhus. Note the author, Mermelstein, M#8 among transport.

BUCHENWALD "LITTLE CAMP."

Buchenwald was divided into two main sections.

1) The upper level which was on top of a hill surrounded by a forest of trees. Most of the occupants were political prisoners and a great many of German origin. There were also many P.O.W.'s, primarily Russian, Scandinavian and other European nationals. There were few Jews at the main camp of Buchenwald.

2) "The Little Camp" was located on the lower level of the hill and it housed mainly the sick, the dying and those known as "musselmen", no longer containing any life in them. The little camp was the death section of Buchenwald and most of the inmates were Jews. The author was one of the occupants for two months from where he was liberated April 11, 1945. See documents on pages 184 through 188.

By Bread Alone

Some just made it and others didn't.

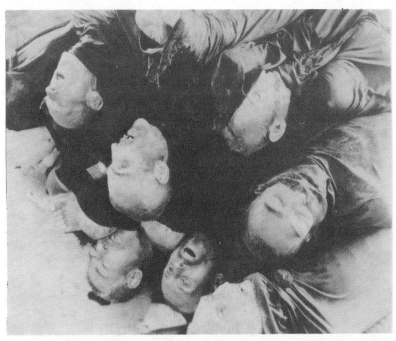

"Executed Prisoners."

PRISON GARB

Concentration Camp Slave Laborers Daily Ration: watery soup, imitation tea or coffee, a small piece of bread, and from time to time an extra allowance of margarine and a thin slice of imitation salami.

imitation coffee or tea. Each day, with outstretched hand, we received the long-awaited piece of bread and the sip of coffee or tea. No sooner had it been eaten, than I began to long for the next day's ration. The vicious torture from hunger was total. There wasn't anything to occupy the mind, so bread was the only wish, the only thing we could think of, the only thing we could talk about, the only thing we could dream about. It was by bread and by bread alone that we hoped to survive. I was transferred to the "Little Camp" and it was a frightening and horrible place, always mud-ridden, cold and windy. The barracks had previously been used as horse stables; they each had stalls for 28 horses and each was packed with about two thousand prisoners. With the sudden influx of prisoners fleeing westward from the advancing Russians, Buchenwald became grossly overcrowded.

Two large tents were set up within the camp, and there were sometimes as many as six thousand prisoners jammed into it. Disease was rampant, hacking and coughing was constantly heard. I discovered that I was in Barracks #56, designated for those dying from typhus. The pushcarts were ever around, constantly busy shuttling the dead to the nearby crematoria. The ovens could not consume the dead fast enough, and the corpses piled up at each barracks awaiting their turn to be consumed to ashes.

I heard there were nightly gatherings at the back of the barracks for Jewish evening services. I collected my strength and joined them in the evening prayers; suddenly I recognized a familiar face, someone I thought I knew. Perhaps a cousin, an uncle, or a friend from home.

"You look familiar to me," I said.

"So do you," he replied.

But I could see that he was uncertain. I could feel his eyes take me in, and I wondered why he looked me up and down so intently. It was eerie. This old man was a walking skeleton. Perhaps what I felt was an aura of death about him. And then it struck me that he was looking at me in much the same way. It was my awareness that I, too, was a walking skeleton; ill for weeks with typhoid, dragging myself about, with nothing to eat but bread and water. The pity in the old man's eyes told me more fully than any mirror could just what I looked like.

"I am the son of *Hersh-Ber* Bernard Mermelstein," I told him. "From Munkacs. You know . . . Munkacs."

He looked at me with a start. "Don't you remember me? I'm your father's friend, the son of Shimshe the wine maker. *Oi, nebech!*" he added, "Oh what a pity!" He went on to elaborate, to tell me about my father, as he looked at me.

"What a pity," I echoed in wonderment. "What do you mean? Why are you expressing sorrow for my father? Why are you letting it dangle there before me unadorned, undesignated as a subject or object?"

"You don't know?" he asked cautiously.

"What! What! What don't I know?" I demanded.

His pale features turned whiter, and he began to walk away from me. Then I knew him.

"You're Shimshe Friedman's son!" I cried. The appellation came to me just as I heard it at home. I pulled him by the shoulder and literally spun him to me; he was so slight. He looked at me, concerned. My question could contain itself no longer. "Where is my father?" I demanded to know.

But I knew before he could answer. It was visible in his eyes, in the sudden sagging of his body, and in the hesitancy with which he answered me.

"I thought you knew. It happened during December...December 18th...I remember the date exactly, because it was the last day of Channukah. The evening before we had no longer been able to "organize" enough wax to light the eight candles. It didn't seem to matter anymore. Nobody had any hope left the Maccabees would rise again, that the strong would once more be given into the hands of the weak. The light in your father's eyes had been growing dimmer and dimmer, but that night it seemed to flare up again. Maybe in honor of Channukah...maybe a

194

remembrance of his hopes for you. In the morning he simply did not wake up.''

Shimshe's shoulders straightened up a bit. The old man was moved by the moment, and sensed the significance of his mission—to tell the son the worth of his father. "Your father was a hard worker. He worked hard, extremely hard. He tried to stay out of trouble by working himself to death. Of course he smoked alot, and used to trade his meager food ration for cigarettes. Then one morning, he simply didn't wake up. The effort proved too much for him. Your father, your father, your poor father.''

My eyes swam. Shimshe took me by the shoulder, and with his hands wiped away the tears. "Moishele. Yes, Moishele, your father called you. Be proud, Moishele, that he was your father.'' Then he concluded by urging me, "Don't give up hope, have faith, my son.''

I was too overcome to clamber to my shelf that night, and slept on the floor beside those who had died during the day. For me, my father was among them.

Morning came and I looked for someone to turn to. I walked from one barracks to another until I found Elijah, a frail, bent youngster from Sighet. The other was Berry, who was from Munkacs. Berry Spitz and I had played on the same soccer team. I remembered him as the left striker and I the right striker. We played well as a team. I couldn't believe my eyes when I saw Berry lying near death inside the rack. I wanted to help him, but what could I do? He told me about many of our friends who were with him at the coal mines in Jaworzna. "You remember my father?" I asked. He didn't hear me, so I asked him again, "Don't you remember him?" He looked at me strangely, understanding that I spoke of him in the past tense.

"How did you find out?" he wanted to know.

Elijah listened in silence, his eyes brimming with tears. As he realized that I had just heard of my father's death, he began to cry softly. I learned that he was crying not only in sympathy for me, but for the loss of his father too.

Elijah was a sensitive boy, with a strong nose and haunting eyes. There was pain and suffering in his eyes. Elijah cried for his father every time I saw him thereafter.

I discovered through Berry that Lajos, too, had been in Jaworzna, working in the coal mines side by side with father. I began to envy Lajos, but then a fearful thought hit me. I remembered the words father had spoken in Auschwitz. "But if we stay together, we shall see each other's sufferings, and that would be the greatest suffering of all." How they must have suffered together, I thought. But Berry didn't know what happened to Lajos. After a lengthy talk and some tears, I returned to my barracks.

That night, as the inmates gathered for evening prayers, I joined them, this time as a mourner saying Kaddish, the Hebrew prayer for the dead, for my father. It was a prayer for peace on earth, a peace, I presumed, that would be hastened because of the merits of my father's deeds. Tears rolled down my cheeks, as the words I heard from others came to my lips for the first time.

"May He who makes peace on high make peace for us and all Israel." It seemed a prayer hopeless of fulfillment, and yet I finished the Kaddish with a feeling of relief.

The next day I began to seek out someone who knew something about the rest of my family, but to no avail. Later in the day, I walked to the gate that separated the "Little Camp" from the main camp and began to inquire of the by-passers about Lajos. No one had heard of him and I couldn't find anyone who would have known him. I crouched by the fence and just watched the inmates go by. Then I thought I saw Bram. I let out a yell, and he knew it was me before he saw me. He bounded toward the gate demanding where I'd been. Why wasn't I in the main camp with them?

"You're in the morgue, don't you know?" he said.

"It doesn't matter," I replied. "There's little hope left in me. My father's dead, and I haven't heard anything of Lajos. If only there was some news about him, I could have more will to live."

But Bram was not prepared to accept this. "You must collect your strength and hold onto your courage. The end is near. I can smell it. We have come a long way, and we have fought hard to survive, and we will survive! Don't give these bastards the satisfaction of taking your life now."

He reached across and took my hand. He pressed it firmly with both of his. "It'll soon be over," he repeated. "In a matter of days now, we'll be free again."

With Bram's words in my ears, I began to collect my thoughts as I walked back to the barracks. What had we been doing there in the "Little Camp"? ... no work details, no supervision, no duties of any kind. It was death just waiting for us it seemed. The change was unnerving and debilitating. And every day more and more corpses were hauled away.

Our only function was to line up, day after day, in front of our barracks, only to be counted as dead or still alive. Hour after hour we stood in line to be carefully counted, again and again. Slowly I realized *that* that was precisely what we were doing there ... being counted, to see how many of us had died. *WE WERE IN THE DEATH SECTION.* And the books had been kept with compulsive efficiency, and the records in perfect order to the end.

Endlessly, we continued to spend our days lying on our racks, lice-ridden, shivering with cold, starved for a bite of food, and crushed with bitterness and grief. Then the weather changed, and with the change came the sun with its warming rays. We were permitted to spend most of the day outdoors. The warmth of sun was a healing balm that I never expected to feel again. There were those who felt well enough to lay out in the sun and remove their lice-infested prison garments. I removed mine and spent most of the sunny days outside the barracks sunbathing, coupled with lice picking.

"Piled up before burning."

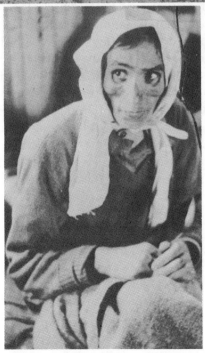

And then a new sound took over our lives, one which promised more than it threatened: the scream of air-raid sirens. At every warning we would quickly be driven into the barracks. The alarms were pleasant sounds to us, and we waited for them each day. As the days passed, the raids became more frequent and lasted for longer periods of time. Soon they took place at night as well as by day. The planes appeared and disappeared, and we knew they were Allied planes. Occasionally they flew low and the pilots would see us and wave.

All of this gave us new hope, and some began to think once again of living; but many were too far gone, and continued to die of disease and starvation. We talked for hours of the possibility of liberation, of our families, and the homes we had long since left. This made it possible for us to ignore, or at least forget for a while, the dreadful reality of the concentration camp in which we were trapped.

We talked and dreamed of our past constantly. It was those dreams and illusions that kept breath in us. Ben, the dreamer of Galicia (a region of Poland), sat on the ground next to me. He was describing in minute detail his favorite Sabbath dish, a common topic of discussion. He was licking his fingers and wiping his mouth as he described the *chulint* and the delicious stuffing it contained. He built himself up to a feverish pitch, and then suddenly took a deep breath and fell to the side with his eyes and mouth wide open. I was startled. As often as I had seen death, I had never learned to accept it calmly. I rushed to Ben's side and tried to revive him. It was no use. He was better off now, I heard others remark. First I bristled at this, but then I began to realize they were right.

Two men with a pushcart rushed over to where he lay, grabbed his arms and legs, and dragged him off to the pile of the dead in front of the barracks.

March went by. The war news was favorable to us and we heard rumors that the Americans were advancing rapidly. Americans! Strange. All these months we had waited for the Russians to free us. Somehow it seemed better this way. The Russians conjured up visions that were mixed with fears for Jews. Somehow the Americans would make us freer. Allied planes continued to fly low over our heads, almost if they had been assigned to guard us. Because the raids in the area were more frequent and longer, we were no longer permitted to leave the barracks.

Each day our food ration was cut and many times not distributed at all. It was a clear, sunny day so I decided to sneak out of the barracks, and joined a small group of inmates nearby who had a small fire going. Elijah was among them. I went to pick grass, and scrounged a small tin cup. I filled my cup with grass and I added water and salt and put the can on the fire to cook.

The green delicacy had only begun to stew when an air-raid siren went off. It was fierce, planes flying all over, and soon we recognized them as American planes. I poured the water from the can, rushed into the barracks, and together with Elijah ate the grass raw. As bombs exploded not far away from the camp, we calmly chomped and chomped at the sweet green nourishment.

With April came the clear echoes of liberation. On the fourth of the month, we gratefully enjoyed hearing a new word— evacuation. Rumors spread that the entire camp would be evacuated, but no one was sure what our destination might be.

The main camp began first. I could hear the shouted commands, screams and constant shooting as the guards mustered all their resources to get the 50,000 prisoners in the main camp to line up for evacuation. Within days the camp looked virtually empty. It seemed to be going smoothly as the inmates yielded to the evacuation, but then many began to resist by hiding in the Little Camp. Suddenly the typhus barracks and all of the Little Camp became the most sought out hiding place. It was safest because none from the main camp, in particular the SS, would dare enter the area for fear of catching the contagious disease. In the meantime, a turmoil broke out, and no one knew what would happen from one minute to the next, so I took advantage of the situation and crossed into the main section of the camp. There I found barracks totally empty except for some abandoned packages. I couldn't believe my eyes when I saw clearly marked Red Cross packages filled with sugar, cocoa, and candy. I was furious to find that only a short distance from us, my fellow prisoners were feasting on Red Cross packages while we were dying by the thousands from hunger, starvation, torture and disease. I soon learned that those in the main part of the camp were political prisoners, and many were of German nationality. I filled my stomach with some of the goodies and packed my pockets full. I then moved back to my old barracks and shared the food with Berry. He was rejuvenated when he tasted the sweetness of the sugar, cocoa and candy. It was a miracle for him and a return to life for both of us. I felt assured that Berry would make it, and I was confident that I would also be able to survive.

On April 8, 1945, the evacuation of the Little Camp began. Berry and I were now determined not to leave, being convinced that this would ultimately lead to death. Evacuation conjured up an image of a death march, with the exhausted shot or falling dead by the wayside. It seemed more advisable to take our chances in the camp and hope for a quick liberation, than to risk again the horrors of the road, and death in the gutter.

The next morning, after our daily rations were distributed, the SS arrived at the Little Camp. They had never been visible in this part of Buchenwald before. Why were they here, to fetch and drive us typhus-ridden, dying prisoners out? Why couldn't they just finish us off? Why all that trouble to evacuate near-dead prisoners? Nevertheless, we were systematically ordered out of the barracks, driven into line and made to march toward the main gate on top of the hill a short distance away.

At first we refused to go, but then we had no choice, as we were threatened and then beaten. In the end we had no alternative but to move slowly toward the gates. Those who tried to hide in the barracks were quickly removed, shot and placed outside near the heaps of dead who had died of disease. As we started up the hill, we were interrupted by the siren, sounding an air raid. The sirens blew fiercely and the planes were clearly visible as they flew in over our camp and we were once more driven back to our barracks until the raid was over. But then we were lined up again to start our journey as the Allied planes flew away. The air-raid sirens were a pleasant sound, and I prayed for them to last.

I soon discovered that among us in the Little Camp was a large segment of political prisoners from above, hiding under the barracks to avoid evacuation. I now became certain why everyone was so reluctant to go through the gates. Remaining in camp increased the probability of survival, and beyond the gates was sure death.

The camp was now largely in control of the political, socialist prisoners, who had been building an underground organization and resistance network for some time. They were the ones who succeeded in making a deal with the SS guards to obtain large quantities of weapons for the expected take-over. In exchange, they offered vague promises of shielding the SS or letting them escape from Allied prosecution and the prisoners' revenge.

Realizing their position in the face of the rapidly advancing Allied armies, the SS were afraid to carry out any more executions within the camp itself. But in the forests outside the camp it was a different story. Once they got the prisoners beyond the main gate at the top of the hill, they had no hesitancy in gunning them down.

For hours each day, I maintained a solid position. I held steady by backtracking. As I walked closer to the gate I dropped to the ground and pretended to be dead. I was driven harder and harder until I reached the main gate and was determined to die there, rather than leave. Once again I dropped to the ground near the main portals where several SS men were in command. One of them fired his pistol, but I was lifted to my feet by fellow inmates who encouraged me to join them in the evacuation.

As I reached the gate, I was asked to give my number. Since I was a prisoner with two numbers, I asked the recorder which one he wanted. I rolled up my sleeve, and he remarked cynically,

"That will do, since you are not going anywhere from here but to the pits." At first I did not get the gist of what he said, but it soon hit me as I began to hear the machine gun fire in the background.

I looked deep into the recorder's eyes, begging for advice. "Where shall I go?" I kept asking. "Where is my group?"

I saw but a few near-skeleton, half-dead prisoners lined up a few yards from the clerk. I also noticed that he was not eager to expedite the evacuation process, so I asked him what to do next. He shrugged his shoulders, motioning to hold still. Seeing that he did not care whether I joined the group, I decided to move slowly back through the gate into the camp. Just then the sirens sounded once again, and the order came through to return to the barracks.

As I scampered down the hill, I yelled for Berry, running all the way shouting till I could breathe no longer and my lungs were in pain. Finally I saw him rushing toward me with open arms. His eyes were filled with tears, and for a moment, I feared that something had happened. But to my amazement, they were tears of joy.

"Listen," he said. "if we are not evacuated or killed today, by tomorrow we will be free. They are close, very close."

With our hands on each other's shoulders we ran downhill the rest of the way to the barracks, to await our liberation.

Morning arrived and all was quiet—too quiet for us to believe. It was April 11th. The usual roll call had been omitted, and we began to hope. We were ordered to remain in our barracks. The rations were not distributed, but later in the morning, the barracks elder asked for a few volunteers to haul the kettle of soup and other rations. Berry was there, so the two of us volunteered, and with a few others marched to the kitchen where we picked up several barrels of soup and coffee.

As I was dragging the barrel of coffee, my eyes focused on a crate of marmalade on the shoulders of a fellow inmate just in front of me. I asked him to drop the marmalade "accidentally." He obliged, and everyone quickly dropped whatever he was carrying, and we all pounced on the marmalade. I filled my tin can with marmalade, shoved it into my pocket, and joined the rest in cleaning the marmalade from the ground. We lifted our barrels and slowly headed toward the barracks.

We filled our stomachs with the thin soup and watery coffee. Then we were told to stay in the barracks and remain still and orderly. Soon a well-dressed and obviously well-fed inmate entered. "Men," he said, "you must be very quiet, not a whisper or a sound. I bring you good news, we may soon be liberated." The words were spoken with authority, but they sounded strange and unreal and somehow sent a chill down my spine. Once more the door of hope opened for me.

Then events moved quickly. First we were told that an Allied plane had dropped a message that read: "Hold on; the Allies will soon be in the camp to liberate you."

The message was stuffed in a loaf of bread, and I felt that the bread itself was the message. The fact that they even thought of using a loaf of bread to communicate with us was both natural and intriguing. Bread was heavy enough to serve as a good missile, and would land where aimed. But it was a soft and non-explosive one that carried both the energy and promise of life within it. Bread would certainly be picked up and not neglected, and it would certainly be broken to reveal the note.

For me it seemed an inspiration that a loaf of bread from the skies—manna from heaven—should proclaim our imminent liberation. Bread had been the staple of our diet. If I had bread, I could survive.

"Man cannot live by bread alone," the Bible says, meaning that spiritual food is also necessary for sustenance. But for me, the first struggle was to preserve a body in which the spirit could live. Contrary to Biblical teaching, I found over and over that I could live "by bread alone." The gift of bread, from our Allies who had finally destroyed the Nazis, told me that there were people who understood our suffering and our need. They were coming to help us, which in the first place meant to feed us—bread. There would be bread!

Next, rumors swept the camp that the majority of the SS had left, and that only a handful of guards remained. Then another rumor was heard: dynamite had been planted throughout the entire camp, and as soon as the order was issued from Weimar, the camp would be blown to bits.

Indeed, it seemed more than plausible that the Nazis would want to destroy as much of their handiwork as possible, together with the living witnesses against them. We heard rumors that the order did come through, and the fuse was lit, but the dynamite failed to go off.

Again, there was talk of a deal between the SS guards, the camp commandant of Buchenwald, and the political leaders of the prisoners. We didn't know the details of the plot or how it was thwarted, but for hours the sinking feeling persisted, that in spite of all our hopes and the nearness of rescue, our end would be to die after all in one grand explosion, a final act of Nazi sadism.

The last few hours before liberation passed before me as in a dream. Actually, it seemed as if I was watching a gigantic scene in a movie. I was one of the actors, with the outcome—which was my survival—far from certain. My world had turned upside-down. People were actually fighting to rescue me. The SS were running out of the camp. To me, it seemed as if they were fleeing from me. I had beaten them! My father's wish was being fulfilled. I was alive and safe, and they were scurrying into the woods.

"Father! Father! Come look! They are running; the Nazis are running!" I exulted. "Did you ever think we'd live to see it?" My exuberance was smothered in hysteria, and brought my father back to my side, watching, smiling and nodding his head in satisfaction. "They are running, Father. They are afraid of us. They know that if we tell what they did, they will be smashed by heavy boots. They will be burned in ovens, and their flaming bodies dragged to Hell, where they will burn forever and ever and ever!"

Was my father frowning slightly at my explosive hatred and vengeance?

Mordeche de Tzadik reit of'n ferd,
Homen, haroshe likt in der erd!

The Purim ditty, a milder victory chant, came to my lips from a childhood memory.

Mordechai, the righteous, rides high on the horse,
And groveling is Haman, the villain, of course.

It seemed just the right accompaniment for the scene. The victory of the Jews, saved from their enemies who were paying for their cruelties. But even in jubilation, I knew that the excesses of these Hamans were beyond atonement.

The reality of the liberation itself seemed more of a developing process rather than an act. I watched, fascinated, as medical prisoners dressed in white moved out in the open, forming an SOS signal for the low flying Allied planes. Their call was soon answered. Allied planes flew low over the heads of the fleeing SS men, firing at them. The planes repeated their passes several times, and then flew over the tower in which two SS guards were manning a heavy caliber machine gun. As long as they were there, any movement in camp was extremely dangerous.

The planes continued to fly over our heads, firing at large groups of fleeing SS troopers. Many prisoners were frightened by the sounds of rifle and machine gun fire and began to pray.

Looking around, I saw Shimshe, the winemaker, lying on the ground. He was frightened. In a whisper he was reciting a prayer . . . *"Shma yisroel adonoi aloheinu adonoi echod* — Hear Oh Israel, the Lord is one." I joined with him and prayed too. I lifted my head and saw smoke coming out of the Allied planes as the machine guns blazed away.

Tension grew as the two SS men stayed at their post and continued to dominate the camp ominously with their fearsome weapons. Then the action shifted to the right of the barracks near a forest, where a large group of SS troopers suddenly appeared on the run. The Allied planes spotted them and opened fire until they disappeared from sight among the trees. They had either escaped or were dead.

By Bread Alone

Nazi Camp Ex-Prisoners Still Dying From Effects

BY M. E. WALTER
Managing Editor of the Houston Chronicle

PARIS, April 28. (AP)—Prisoners left in the notorious German labor camp of Buchenwald are still dying at the rate of 15 a day although it has been two weeks since the American Army opened the camp.

When captured the camp had a population of about 20,000. Those able to be taken away were removed so that only about 6000 were there when a party of editors visited the place. The prisoners were sick and starving, most of them past saving.

The camp is a place of unbelievable degradation and filth although Army officers and prisoners say much has been done since the Americans arrived to clean it up.

Germans Avoid Hardship

In contrast to the starvation and filth at Buchenwald is the cultural center of Weimar which adjoins the camp. The town suffered some bombing damage, but is spick and span except for rubble around the buildings hit. Well-fed, well-dressed Germans go about their business, paying little attention to American occupation forces.

"We certainly have attracted little attention," remarked an American colonel. "Certainly not as much as a circus would have caused."

The natives are aloof and dignified. They comply with rules and regulations readily. Whether they were merely indifferent to conditions in the camp during the many years it was operated or ignorant of them is debated by officers in town. Certainly there is no evidence visible that any of them feel any guilt or responsibility.

No Conquered Attitude

As one editor remarked, "They certainly look less like conquered people than any conquered people could possibly look."

But perhaps their placidity will suffer a shock if the town is turned over to the Russians for permanent occupation.

Obviously in the short time given editors for inspecting the camp there was little opportunity to weigh evidence and decide on the reliability and credibility of witnesses. Horror stories by the score are told.

Liberated prisoners at Buchenwald April, 1945. This picture was taken by the U.S. Signal Corp. five days after the camp was liberated on the 16th of April 1945. Some have slightly recuperated by then but others were still dying of typhus and dysentery. Right after this photo was taken all were moved up the hill to permanent barracks where first aid stations and hospitals were set up by the Americans. Note encircled liberated prisoner . . . the author "By Bread Alone", Mor (Mel) Mermelstein.

208

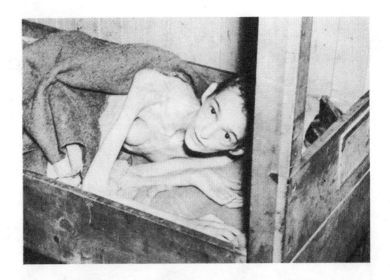

Prisoners as they were liberated 1945.

BUCHENWALD: Too late to be revived. April 11, 1945.

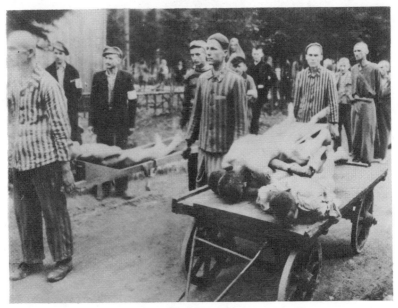

"Liberated Prisoners 1945"

211

Liberated prisoners waiting for Allied
help and assistance, 1945.

A SMALL BOY STROLLS DOWN A ROAD LINED
WITH DEAD BODIES NEAR CAMP AT BELSEN

The British soldiers liberated "Bergen-Belsen" one of the infamous death camps in Nazi Germany and this is what they found. In most death camps as well as concentration camps when the Allies finally arrived to liberate us, they discovered that they found more dead prisoners than alive ones and so mass graves had to be dug to give them a common burial. There are mass burial sites in every concentration and death camp throughout Europe which are a part of the memorials.

Los Angeles Times

Europe's Peace Hailed by Millions

Many of World's Cities Celebrate; Tokyo Determined to Carry On

BY THE ASSOCIATED PRESS

The great bells of St. Peter's Basilica rang out over Rome yesterday soon after the Associated Press report that peace had come to Europe while several Allied capitals proclaimed VE holidays for today and Tokyo announced continuation of "this sacred war."

Many of the world's cities went wild at the news, and even neutral capitals were bedecked with flags and filled with celebrating crowds.

Germans Quick to Renounce Nazi Principles

BY CLIFTON DANIEL
New York Times Correspondent

LONDON, May 7.—Having surrendered unconditionally, the skeleton German government of Grand-Adm. Karl Doenitz turned immediately to postwar problems today, and, if the words of its Foreign Minister can be believed, renounced Nazi principles and began a campaign to regain Germany's eventual independence.

Now that the Allies are in position to dictate Germany's future the government appears to have been converted rather quickly to ideas of justice, international law and respect for treaties.

Announced Surrender

Broadcasting from Flensburg, Foreign Minister Count Lutz Schwerin von Krosigk was the first to announce at 2 o'clock that Adm. Doenitz had ordered the unconditional surrender of all the German forces.

He acknowledged that due to a "collapse of all physical and material forces" Germany had succumbed and repeated that Germany had continued to fight as long as she had, only to save as many men as possible from the Red army.

"No one," he added, "must be under any illusions about the severity of the terms to be imposed upon the German people by our enemies."

215

By Bread Alone

Slaughter of 4,000,000 in Nazi Camp Disclosed

Russian Commission Reveals 'Most Horrible Crime Against Peoples of Europe' in Poland

MOSCOW, May 7. (Æ)—More than 4,000,000 persons were put to death by the Nazis in the "most horrible crime against the peoples of Europe" at the Oswiecim concentration camp in Poland, an official report of the extraordinary State Commission declared today.

(This was the first official Soviet report on the number of persons killed at Oswiecim. On April 11, Dr. Bela Fabian, president of the dissolved Hungarian independent democratic party, in an interview near Erfurt, Germany, accused the Germans of killing 5,000,000 Jews at Oswiecim, from which he himself narrowly escaped.)

The committee report said the dead included citizens of Russia, Poland, France, Belgium, Holland, Czechoslovakia, Romania, Hungary, Yugoslavia and "other countries" and that they had been killed by various means, including torture, poison, gas and cremation.

The committee stated that Oswiecim surpassed anything heretofore disclosed as perpetrated by the Nazis against the people of Europe.

Medical experts and scientists from France, Poland, Czechoslovakia and Yugoslavia participated with the Russians in the inquiry, conducted in February and March.

The report was made on the basis of the questioning of persons who escaped from the horror camp and from captured German documents. Other evidence included crematory stoves and gas chambers.

Children Infected

As part of the camp's routine German doctors had carried out systematic experiments on living men, women and children, which included sterilization and castration. Children were infected with typhus, cancer and malaria, the report added, and the reaction of young children to certain poisons was "observed" by the Nazi medical men.

The report said investigators found the most extensively and elaborately equipped Nazi death laboratories yet. Gas chambers where thousands lost their lives had signs above the doors reading "special baths" "disinfection point," or simply "entrance to baths."

Himmler Blamed.

The investigating committee placed the full blame on Heinrich Himmler, declaring him the organizer of the camp in 1939 for the special purpose of wiping out citizens of occupied Europe.

The report said the camp occupied a large territory around Oswiecim, 31 miles east of Krakow, embracing the small camps of Aushwitz, Birkenau, Monowitze, Goleshau, Yvaishowitz, Niedachs, Blekhammer and others.

216

MONDAY, MAY 14, 1945 · Los Angeles Times

6,200,000 Jewish Deaths Laid to Nazis

Welfare Group Says One 'Mein Kampf' Plan Carried Out

BY PAUL GHALI
Chicago Daily News Foreign Service

BERN, May 13.—At least one point in Adolf Hitler's "Mein Kampf" program has been carried out thoroughly—the bestial extermination of European Jews.

Of the total of 8,000,000 Jews living in Germany and German-occupied countries before the war, 6,200,000 have died from either execution, cruel treatment or starvation, according to latest figures compiled by Jewish welfare organizations here.

In Germany, where the great majority of European Jews had been concentrated, only 500,000 are alive today—and the word "alive" is a mere figure of speech.

Frail Executed

The slavery of the able-bodied and the execution of the frail continued until the beginning of 1944, by which time the Nazis had reached the saturation point of their cruelty. More than 5,000,000 Jews had been liquidated and the remaining ones were no longer regarded as a "problem," as Hitler saw it.

Rudolph Kastner, a Budapest lawyer who since April, 1944, has devoted his time to rescuing his fellows of Jewish faith from the Nazi grip, told how he "bought" 30,000 Jews from the Nazi S.S. member, Kurt Becher.

Millions Imprisoned

First came the period of "extermination" proper, from the time of the declaration of war on Russia until the end of 1942. Millions of Jews were taken to the camps at Auschwitz, Maidenek and Tremblinka, which boasted the most modern gas execution chambers and crematories. The S.S. hordes invading Russia were, simultaneously instructed to shoot all Russian Jews wherever they were encountered.

By the end of 1942, however, Germany felt the need for foreign labor and the remaining able-bodied Jews were sent to work camps. The women, old men and children all disappeared into the gas chambers.

Dealt With Gestapo

Becher was sent to Budapest "to detect everything in Hungary which might be useful to German economy." He bargained Hungarian Jews, then in the hands of the Budapest Gestapo, against money or jewels and promises of more money and jewels.

Thirty thousand Jews were deported in this manner from Hungary and the S.S. promised that they would be allowed to leave for Switzerland. Only 10,-000, however, finally arrived here.

As for the others, they were kept in Austria, though not ill treated.

Grand Mufti Charged

One of the individuals mainly responsible for the extermination of Jews, Kastner said, was the Grand Mufti of Jerusalem, who, incidentally, since he was expelled from Switzerland a week ago, has not been heard of. Amin El Husseini had fought the Jews in Palestine.

In Germany, he finally had the opportunity to realize his life dream: suppression of Jewish emigration to Palestine. With no Jews left in Europe, there would be no more emigrants to the Holy Land. That was his scheme.

Copyright 1945. Chicago Daily News. Inc.

217

Soon after, I saw two inmates with rifles in their hands crawling toward the guard tower. A shouted order went up to the two SS men to give up and lay down their arms. One of them pulled a white handkerchief from his pocket, tied it on the end of a stick and waved it in the air. That simple sign marked the end of Nazi power in Buchenwald!

With the tower post empty, the men slowly began to file from their barracks. I looked out to see and to my surprise, I saw flags of various nationalities hanging from each barracks. The political prisoners had made the flags already. They had expected to be liberated.

There was no Jewish flag in sight. I noticed that soon. To make a flag ready, one would have had to believe the liberation was coming. That was possible for the others, but not for the Jews. Jewish suffering and degradation were absolute. The massacre of Jews was ruthless and unceasing. The idea of liberation and survival was but a myth to every Jew. For the Jewish partisans and underground fighters there was no hope, there was a spirit to defend, but not for us. Even as we hoped to be liberated we could not help but think of it as a dream.

There were other reasons for the lack of a Jewish flag in Buchenwald on that day. None of the armies converging on the camp, and on all the camps in Nazi Germany, was marching under a Jewish flag. Their flags were foreign to us. The other inmates could identify at least with the Russian flag, for they had countries and homes to go back to. Where would we go? Back to the lands of ancestral anti-Semitism?

Where would we go? There was no Israel to go to, at least not yet. We could not look upon ourselves as a nation. Only the Nazis had recognized us as such, but only for the purpose of total extermination. But now Buchenwald was in the midst of being liberated and the Nazi plan to exterminate all Jews had failed, though not by very much.

"We're free! We're liberated! The Americans are here!" These words were shouted in many tongues and dialects—Czech, Polish,

French, Russian, Yiddish, Hungarian, and German. It was a day of rejoicing, a day of deliverance and, above all, a day of triumph, but not for us, not for the Jews.

On April 11, 1945, at 2:30 p.m., misery, torture, starvation and death were to come to an end in Buchenwald. That was a moment to remember! We were told the moment to treasure forever and ever.

"Freedom" is a powerful word; its value is immeasurable. But to the Jewish inmates of Buchenwald, the liberation and the freedom were meaningless. While we were free to go, to pass through the gates, we were not free of the barriers of pain, disease and death. No, no, we were not free to go. I was not free to go. I was afraid of what the future would reveal and what it might bring. I could not face it, and there wasn't any help in sight to ease my struggle and pain.

As I stepped from the door of the barracks, I looked to the right and to the left at the stacks of dead bodies piled against the building. I was unmoved by the sight. I was numb, without feelings. I walked away and soon found myself in a group amongst prisoners who were celebrating their liberation. They were political prisoners, but not Jews. I wanted so much to join the group, to share in their spirit, but I couldn't do it. I was a Jew and I did not belong. I was not liberated. No one came to free the Jews; strange as it may have seemed, I was still a prisoner.

At four in the afternoon I gathered my strength and followed a crowd headed in the direction of the SS barracks to look for food and clothing. There I found a piece of dry bread, a leather jacket and a pair of matching trousers. I wandered into the basement where I was confronted by a pile of boots and German military shoes. I climbed to the top of the pile and sat there mechanically trying on boots and shoes. I felt that I had found a refuge, a place to weather the turmoil of screaming and shouting and people running about out there, not knowing what to do with their first hours of freedom. Here I had no choices to make, except to find a pair of shoes that fit. That seemed just enough for my mind to handle.

219

Finally, a pair of shoes fit me perfectly. As I was putting them on, the sound of rifle fire jarred me out of my reverie. I slid down the pile of shoes and hid behind it. When the firing ceased I went outdoors to see what had happened. As I stepped into the sunshine, a voice shouted to me in Russian, "Stop—Halt, halt or I'll shoot!" A soldier appeared, weapon in hand. He wore the same leather uniform as the one I had on. He approached me threateningly.

"Who are you?" he demanded.

"An inmate," I responded quickly.

"What are you doing here?" he snarled as he looked at the pile of shoes.

"Throw your bag over to me, I want to see what's in it." I did so, also rolling up my sleeve so that he could see the tattoo mark on my arm. He handed the bag back to me with a warning.

"Don't you know that the SS are still in Weimar? Many are hiding in this camp. Go to your barracks and stay there until it is safe."

On the way back I passed a potato field where I stopped long enough to fill my bag with potatoes. When I arrived at the barracks, I found Berry and Elijah, they had built a small fire, and I placed the potatoes in a pail of water and watched as they cooked. When they were done, each of us ate a few potatoes to stifle our hunger pangs.

Slowly the sun set and the moon rose but even with the stars in the sky, they could not dissipate the darkness of Buchenwald. Many continued to die from neglect and diseases which were taking a toll that even "liberation" could not reverse.

With the Allies came richly cooked food that was distributed to all. As soon as the food reached the barracks, the inmates with their unclean plates, pushed to get a share of the richly cooked soup. The potatoes I ate had quelled my hunger pains, and thus I could resist the temptation of gorging myself on the greasy and heavy foods. Berry became ill, very ill. I didn't think he would make it. I thought he was going to die as his body rejected the sudden intake of fat. I busied myself by helping serve the food to the ill and dying. They were too weak to get out of their bunks to feed themselves. I warned them to eat slowly and as little as possible. There was no help yet for us. I was panicky ... I thought we would all die.

The morning of April 12th saw more American soldiers in camp. A ray of hope entered into our barracks at the Little Camp. The GI's looked shocked and saddened at the sights they encountered in this section of Buchenwald. I saw tears in their eyes, too. I felt their anger ... I felt their guilt. They were beside themselves. They looked beaten. They wanted to get even ... they wanted revenge. They could not stand it. They had to leave.

At headquarters, the Americans insisted that the German civilians be brought to the area to see with their own eyes what had taken place at Buchenwald. The Germans from nearby towns and villages were dragged in to witness for themselves the atrocities committed by their masters. They ordered town and village leaders of nearby communities and public officials to come and witness the brutalities. They demanded to know by what authority they allowed or acquiesced or participated in the mass destruction of humans. The good burghers claimed shock, and were dismayed that they were being accused.

The civilians claimed that they had known of Buchenwald only as a detention camp, a political prison camp. They insisted that they had not known it was a mass murder factory. The civilian leadership said that they were not aware of the extent to which murder had been carried out in the camp. The captured SS and camp leaders insisted that it was their duty, not their will, to participate in the mass murder programs. After all, they said, they were soldiers, and as soldiers they were forced to carry out orders.

They came to view the scene, some under duress and others of their own initiative. Women and the young wept, shaken by the horrible sights of the dead stacked in heaps next to every barracks. They saw the ashes, too, of those already cremated in a huge pile next to the ovens. Although they lived within sight and sound of the camp, they still insisted they were unaware that such things had taken place.

As they were led around the camp I could see them bow their heads as if in prayer. They were visibly shaken and it was obvious to me that they expressed sorrow and anger. I began to quiz myself. What was it all about? I was at a loss. Who was to blame? There was no one who would take the responsibility for this genocide, this cold-blooded murder. It was maddening; I had to blame someone ... that someone was me. I had no choice; I had to blame myself, because I survived.

The war was at its height and we were told that it would soon end. Along with that news came "the death of a great American leader." I never knew much about Roosevelt until one evening around the 15th of April when the elder of our barracks entered the hall and in a quiet voice said, "I bring you sad news. A great leader passed away. He was greatly responsible for our liberation, and who of all men should have lived to see the end of this war." Thus I learned that Franklin D. Roosevelt died less than a month before Germany surrendered. Even the mighty, I thought, cannot always have their wishes fulfilled or see the fruits of their labors. We grieved for Roosevelt that day at Buchenwald.

...As years passed I was to have second thoughts about Roosevelt. I couldn't understand it. It was a mystery. F.D.R., the man with a great heart, who led America out of the Depression, the aristocrat who was able to reach the common man, the statesman who saw the evils and dangers of Hitler and the generous leader who helped the Allies in their darkest hour. He was idolized by the poor and the minorities throughout the free world. The Jews renamed leading thoroughfares in their neighborhoods in honor and respect. I was at a loss to learn that he also denied entrance to a ship named the "St. Louis," the ocean liner filled with European Jews expelled from Nazi Germany. I could not understand why, together with Churchill and Stalin, they couldn't spare a squadron of Allied bombers to destroy the railway lines leading to the crematoria and gas chambers at

Auschwitz-Birkenau, Buchenwald, Bergen-Belsen, Maidanek, Treblinka, Sobibor.

Then on April 16th around noon time, a group of dignitaries appeared at my barracks. I was shocked to see so many civilians and soldiers around. I wondered what they had come for, and why they were looking at us with such curiosity. After all, it had been nearly a week since we were liberated. Didn't they know who we were? Then an order was given for us to file into the racks again. I couldn't understand that, but I wasn't about to disobey such an order. I rushed to the top of the rack, attempting to conceal myself from these people whom I knew nothing about. Then the flash of a light bulb went off and I quickly reacted by looking up to see what had taken place.

It was a minor event and yet it loomed quite large later in my life. I later discovered the photographer was a Private Miller from the U.S. Special Services, who wanted a photo of the liberated prisoners of Buchenwald so he could properly capture and record on film what we looked like. On that day I was still in Barracks 56, but soon after I was removed to the permanent quarantine quarters for treatment of malnutrition and disease. I had typhus.

That photograph turned out to be one of the most widely circulated and published portraits of the camps. It had been blown up and exhibited all over the United States and Europe. It is included in the exhibit at Buchenwald. In addition, it was soon reprinted in newspapers throughout the world for all to read and for all to learn. It appeared in the *Los Angeles Times,* the *New York Times,* the *Chicago Tribune* as well as the *San Francisco Chronicle.*

I was surprised to see my own face looking back at me from the upper right-hand corner of the bunks at Buchenwald. Our deep eyes, full of pain and suffering and sickness and fatigue, were already telling the tales of which we could not put into words. Faces, faces, gaunt faces and ribs protruding where flesh should be. And yet, all of us in that photo were alive that day. Slowly, ever so slowly, I began to accept the fact that the portrait bore witness to: *I had survived.*

By Bread Alone

Fat, husky S.S. women remove bodies of victims from trucks and throw them into a common grave.

These bodies were found stacked inside Buchenwald Concentration Camp at war's end.

The weather became more and more beautiful as the month of May arrived. As was the custom, the first day of May was a day for celebration. Everyone was urged to join in the festivities of May Day throughout the camp. Hitler was hanged in effigy, and Stalin was hailed for his accomplishments and greatness. There were scores of loudspeakers to be heard constantly, and when the event came to an end, some of the Russians, Ukrainians and others continued to celebrate far into the night.

The days passed and my health improved. My weight was restored to normal, and I was growing taller. The day finally arrived when it became safe for many to return to their homeland. However, the news from Czechoslovakia was not good, and many Czechs decided to remain at the camp. The few who did leave for home soon returned, when they discovered that their homes and families had been destroyed. Buchenwald would have to be the starting point for a new life.

I began to take walks that led me into the nearby village. From time to time I would see a farmer, a little girl, or an old woman. But for the most part, the village seemed deserted. The few people I encountered seemed to be afraid of me. I wondered why, but I soon discovered that they were afraid of all of us ... they thought we wanted revenge.

On my way back from the village I passed by an elderly lady. "Good morning," I said to her and I was surprised that she returned my greeting warmly. I felt at ease and appreciative. I stopped to talk, and she invited me to her home.

As I entered the house I noticed a blond little girl clutching her mother's hand as if afraid. I greeted them warmly, trying to ease the tension and fear that must have existed in the house. It was strange for me to grasp the situation, because I wasn't their persecutor, nor were they mine. The war wasn't over yet and they were still afraid. The table was set and I was invited to sit and eat with them. Then I began to understand why they were afraid. They needed my forgiveness, but I wasn't ready to forgive. It was too much for me to cope with, so I returned to camp, never to see the Mullers again.

225

By the time I returned to camp, it was late in the evening. I lay on my bed and my thoughts were of home, my mother, Etu, Magda and Lajos. My hopes of finding them were high, very high, because all of them were of working age, strong of mind and body, and in vigorous health when I last saw them. I was anxiously awaiting the day when it would be safe to return home.

At last the war came to an end. The Nazis surrendered unconditionally and we were all free to go home!

Concentration camp survivors on their way home.

CHAPTER EIGHT
"The Wanderer"

Preparations for the journey home began. Civilian clothing was issued and credentials prepared. Weeks passed, and then the day arrived when I was ordered to line up with a group of Czechs to be transported home. Dressed like a civilian again with papers in hand, I took a last look at the long rows of barracks. Then walking slowly down the road to the waiting trucks marked "U.S. Army," I found myself alone. There was no one beside me ... not Bram or Joey or any of my friends. As I was sitting in the truck my mind began to wonder ... will I ever see them again? Where could they be?

After a short briefing, the convoy began to move. It sped through German towns and villages until it reached the Czech border. Once out of Germany, the convoy slowed, and we were welcomed by the inhabitants of each small village. They threw us flowers and shouted slogans, "Long live the heroes. Hail to the fighters of Czechoslovakia. Long live freedom!" They scrambled onto the trucks to shake our hands. Youthful girls with rosy cheeks hugged and kissed us. Flowers were pinned on the banners that hung from the side of the truck bearing the one-word, dramatic legend: "BUCHENWALD." The people streamed behind the trucks as we moved slowly through each village. It felt good to be alive again—at least for the moment.

As the day neared its end, we stopped for dinner in a small clearing. The soldiers spread out their canned rations and distributed portions to each of us. In addition, they shared their chocolates, cigarettes, and chewing gum, which was a rare and valuable commodity at the time.

After this brief stop, we knew our liberators much better. They were a happy lot, always "horsing around" and "kidding" one another. They started singing and urged us to sing and be happy, too. They kept repeating to us over and over, "The war's over and you're going home. The Nazis are *kaput,* dead. We defeated the bastards."

Filled with encouragement, the military convoy began to roll again. The convoy picked up speed, omitting the welcoming stops at every town and village. It was nearly dark when we pulled into the city of Pilsen, the home of the finest beer in the world. We were taken to the hotel where spectators had gathered awaiting our arrival. Most of them were searching for a missing father, brother or other kin. Some were fortunate; others turned away to await the arrival of the next convoy.

As I moved through the crowd, I heard sobs of despair and turned around to see a maiden of about sixteen with tears streaming down her cheeks. Tears were not uncommon these days, but the sobs that accompanied her tears were almost unbearable.

I approached her and asked, "Can I help?"

"No, no," she replied, still sobbing.

I stood by her side, waiting.

The sobs ceased and she looked as if she needed a friend.

"What happened?" I asked.

"My boyfriend, he's dead!" she replied. "He was killed by the Nazis just before Buchenwald was liberated."

"Are you sure?" I asked.

"Yes," she said, tears beginning to fill her eyes again. "As the convoy arrived and I was yelling his name, some man came to me and told me what happened. He was with him—just before liberation. The Nazis shot him, shot him in the head."

With some measure of hiding her sorrow, she disappeared into the crowd.

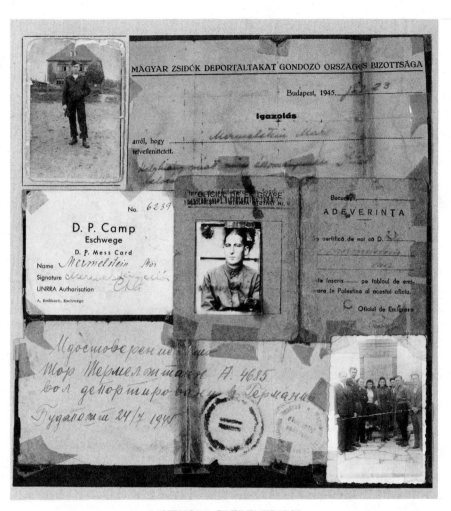

"AUTHORS CREDENTIALS"

By Bread Alone

In any war, in this war no doubt there have been and no doubt on both sides-numbers of brutalities and atrocities. They must have seemed terrible enough to those against whom they were committed. I do not excuse or belittle them. But they were casual, unorganized, individual acts. We are dealing here with something entirely different. With systematic, wholesale, consistent action, taken as a matter of deliberate calculation-calculation at the highest level . . . There is one group to which the method of annihilation was applied on a scale so immense that it is my duty to refer separately to the evidence. I mean the extermination of the Jews. If there were no other crime against these men, this one alone, in which all of them were implicated, would suffice. History holds no parallel to these horrors. Sir Hartley Shawcross. British Chief Prosecutor at Nuremberg

231

By Bread Alone

in command at Bergen-Belsen

Josef Kramer

rese

Lieutenant-Colonel Rudolf Höss,
Commandant of Auschwitz

Adolf Hitler

Heinrich Himmler. His obsession with
the superiority of the Germanic 'race'

Ernst Kaltenbrunner

Dr Mengele

Captured women overseers at "Bergen-Belsen". Some were brought to justice but most escaped or set free by Allied Tribunial.

Hungarian Fascist Leaders charged with War Crimes and Crimes Against Humanity. From Left to Right: Ministers Gera, Remenyi, State Secy., Endre, Premiers Bardossy, Imredy, Szalasi.

We were assigned rooms in a hotel, with baths and hot running water. After I cleaned up and ate, I went for a walk to see for myself the newfound freedom and brightness of my homeland. The city was crowded with American GI's, most of them puffing away on cigarettes. Desperate men, too dignified to ask them for cigarettes, would follow the GI's around, not at all ashamed to pick the cigarette butts as soon as they were dropped on the pavement.

The more I watched the civilian population, the more convinced I became that Czechoslovakia, under Nazi rule, had been no less than an immense concentration camp. The people I saw looked poor and undernourished. Our lot had been infinitely worse, yet each person I encountered was the measure of his pain. Not all the suffering, I realized, was in the concentration camps.

In the morning, I received meal tickets and railroad fare for the journey eastward. I joined several young men from our liberated camps who were heading toward the railway station and boarded the train. We were joined by girls as well, who were also returning home. The feminine company was a fresh breeze. Together we sang and celebrated. I was feeling human again.

Our train was halted at several points, and we were forced to abandon it in its tracks. The beastly looking twisted tracks still lay scattered on the side of the railway bed. The result of the endless Allied bombing raids was evident throughout this region. "How will it be as we go deeper and deeper into our homeland?" I thought to myself. We hiked for miles along the roadbed, and then came to another train on which we were to continue our journey. It seemed that I would never arrive. My destination was in doubt; home was endless miles away.

Waiting for the next train to move, I heard a loud voice from a distance calling my name. I looked out and saw Bram and Joey! I scampered out of the window and we hugged and kissed each other. I heard Bram's voice yell, "I told you we'd live through it." It was a moment of real joy.

Quickly, I gathered my belongings and joined them for the rest of the journey.

Finally after days of hopping, dragging and switching trains, we arrived in Budapest. The city was alive. Gypsy music was all around. I began to wonder why Budapest, like other cities in Europe, was not leveled by Allied bombings. Why weren't the Magyar tormentors forced to pay for their crimes of genocide? Where were those who helped the Nazis all those years? Why weren't they held accountable? Had the Allies forgotten so soon the existence of Auschwitz-Birkenau and Buchenwald?

Dejectedly, I went looking around the streets of Budapest. I discovered a large, active Jewish rescue organization hard at work. I learned that their efforts were to accommodate the concentration camp victims, and help us on our way. But, they also helped us in our search for family and friends. Lists were posted on their bulletin boards, but there were few thus far listed as survivors. I began to worry and wonder, and decided to visit other reception centers in the other parts of town. Perhaps I would see a name, a hint of anyone alive. My thoughts were of Lajos, of Etu, and even little Magda, but I shattered the thought of mother.

Bram and Joey joined in my search. As we were about to turn the corner, I spotted a tall man, with a slight limp, heading in the opposite direction. I yelled out to him, "Hey, Willie Bacsi," and he quickly turned his head, and rushed toward me with full speed. We embraced and our hearts were filled with joy. He began to tell us how fortunate he was to have been liberated in Blechammer, while we were force marched in the snow and sleet. "I should've urged you to stay in Blechammer," he kept repeating. But then he described some scenes of killings at the hands of the fleeing SS murder squads. "They dumped another truck-load of bread," Willie recited, "to bring us out of our hiding places, and as they rushed to the pile they were gunned down."

He went on and on, without a pause, and then he asked us to follow him.

He took us to the finest hotel and to the best restaurant in Budapest and we couldn't believe the food that was put before us.

In the afternoon, we went for a swim, and in the evening he took us to the brightest night club in Budapest.

For days Willie kept us in high spirits, laughing and living it up. "It's all over. We've made it," Willie would announce from time to time, as if he didn't actually believe it.

The time arrived for us to board the train again for the journey eastward. Willie accompanied us to the station, where we bid him farewell. The train began to move closer and closer to the border of the Carpathians ... our home. We stopped for the night in Bratislava, the capital of Slovakia.

The following day, as I walked to the station, I noticed a familiar face. A youth my age greeted me and I returned his greeting. I suddenly realized it was Joncsi. "What are you doing here?" I asked him. I pressed him to tell me where he was coming from with his back-pack, and to my astonishment he replied, "From a concentration camp—from Buchenwald."

"Why would the Nazis imprison you?" I asked him skeptically. He knew that I was aware of his enrollment in the SS as early as 1943—when he was hardly seventeen.

"They took me away one day, during one of their roundups," he answered. "It was in May."

We spent hours reminiscing. Soon I began to believe him and sympathize with his plight. I was aware that he was running from the Russians and that his life was in danger. The Russians gave no quarter to a former SS man. We walked to an ice cream parlor where I ordered ice cream for both of us and soon we separated. It was a strange parting. I felt that I should help. I wanted to urge him not to go home to Munkacs where he was born and reared— because the Russians were there. I knew that he was terrified of them. I wanted to tell him to go to Hungary, his ancestors' national homeland.

Later, as I was waiting for my train, I noticed a group of prisoners being escorted by two Russian soldiers. Among them was Joncsi. I watched from a distance as their credentials were checked. I could see Joncsi as he was searched. I approached a

236

Russian guard and in my newly polished Russian asked, "Why are those men held prisoners?"

He replied, "These men are liars and criminals, they will be shot before dawn. They are SS swine. Have no mercy on them, my friend." The Russians weren't suffering from any compunctions. I still cared. I wanted to help save Joncsi. He had been my playmate, my friend. I grew up with him. But I could not save him. It was no use. The Russian guards wouldn't listen. They were brutal.

My train pulled in and I boarded it.

At last the train crossed the border of Slovakia into the Carpathian Mountains. The sight of the tall mountains with the beautiful trees and flowers adorning the foothills thrilled me. We continued onward, through the small mountain villages, until we arrived in the city of Munkacs.

The day was sunny and warm and the skies were crystal clear, with not a cloud in sight. I lifted my bundles and briskly stepped down from the crowded train with Bram and Joey behind me. Together we walked the streets of Munkacs. It was a strange sight. Russian soldiers were all around. Slowly, I inched my way in the direction of my home. I hesitated—dropped my bundles to the ground and sat down to reflect. I could not believe that I was home.

Eventually, I picked up my bundles and headed across town to the house I'd left behind a year before. I started toward the bridge that connects the city with the outskirts of Munkacs. I could see that the once beautiful and picturesque bridge across the rushing river Latorca, had been blown up, then crudely patched with logs to make it serviceable. I crossed the bridge and saw our house. My heart stopped and so did my feet. The suspense was too much. I watched for someone to appear, but no one did. All was quiet and there was no one in sight. My breath came harder and many questions whirled through my mind. "Where is everyone? The war had long ended. Why was it so quiet? Don't they see me? Please someone, anyone, come out!"

When I finally continued toward the house, a militia guard stopped me and asked for my identification. I showed him my papers, but he was not satisfied. He asked me to open my bags and show him what was in them. I refused and an argument began. He was about to arrest me when I heard a voice calling me. I turned and saw my uncle running toward us. When my uncle reached us, he said to the guard, "This is his home. The boy's just returning from a concentration camp."

It then became clear to me that this guard could not read , or he would have known from looking at my credentials who I was and where I had come from. He then released me to my uncle. Moshe-Aaron, my uncle, embraced me and we wept. I grabbed my suitcase and we started toward the house where I used to live. I was beginning to feel the presence of my house. My face flushed as the excitement grew within me. I was sure that when I reached the house and opened the door, Father, Mother, Etu, Lajos and Magda would all be there, as before, waiting for me. They had to be.

"Moishele, Moishele!" I heard them calling out to me. But it was my uncle who was calling, as he blocked my way.

"Moishele, stop," he was saying. "What are you doing? We're going to my house."

I couldn't understand him. "What do you mean?" I asked. "I'm going home. Everybody's there waiting for me!"

Before he had a chance to reply, I ran down the hill, rushed through the gate and into the home I had left behind over a year before.

A young woman, with a child by her side, stood there, in the middle of the main room. Startled by my sudden entrance, she gathered the child to her and asked if there was anything she could do to help me. "What are you looking for? Who are you? Do you need something?" she asked.

I was unable to speak or move. I stood, stunned, for several minutes. Finally I said, "No-no. No, thank you, I just thought someone had come home. I live here. I...I mean, I used to live here." The words coming from my mouth forced me to the understanding that none of my family would be coming home; none of them had survived the camps.

The young mother moved toward me saying, "If you wish, you may have your furniture, or whatever belongings are yours."

"No," I replied. "I don't want anything, thank you."

I turned around slowly and began to walk from the house. The woman followed me, offering me food and money for the things that belonged to me. She even suggested that she move out, so that I could have my home back again. I thanked her again, and when I convinced her that I didn't want the furniture, money or anything, she thanked me profusely, "God bless you," she said, "God bless you."

As she walked back into the house and closed the door, I moved toward the gate where my uncle was waiting for me. Shocked and with tears in my eyes, I sat down upon the grass and covered my face with my hands. My uncle placed his hand upon my head and said, "God wanted it to be so, and His judgment is holy." Slowly I lifted my head, incredulous at the words he just uttered.

"I know ... I know, Moishele. Listen, before you ask, before you question, repeat after me: 'Boruch dayen emess.'" I repeated the words that meant "Blessed is the Righteous Judge." The traditional words on learning of a death seemed harshly inappropriate. But even as I said them, a softening set in.

"Do you want me to bless God for this unbearable pain? Do you want me to call 'just' this hideous unrighteousness?" I don't recall the words I used, but my sense of being put-upon remains with me. To believe that God was anywhere to be found at Auschwitz was too much.

"Moishele, Moishele, please ..." My uncle was crying now. "Your questions *are* just, but you're not the first to ask them. 'As we bless God for the good, so must we bless Him for the evil.' Those are the words of the Talmud. They're words beyond understanding; but if we cannot say them, we cannot hope. Bitterness, yes ... but hopelessness, no. The Jewish way is to bless and to hope, and to bless and to hope, until hope and blessing surmount the pain and even the bitterness, and the living learn how to go on."

My uncle continued saying, "God is righteous. God is good. It's people who sometimes forget; who let evil rule them; who lose the sense of the image of God with themselves and become beasts of prey."

"Maybe we should translate the prayers," he said. "Blessed is the God who will judge righteously.' He does not forget. Sometimes it seems as if He needs time to assimilate everything He has seen, and to react to it and give recompense. But you'll see it, Moishele, you're young enough. You'll see. *He does not forget!*" The last words were almost a prayer, or were they an imprecation? I tried to understand, but I was impatient. "What happened to mother?"

"I'll tell you what I heard," he said. "There was a mother with many little children and an infant in her arms. She could not care for all. Your mother wanted to help. She took the babe in her arms to hold and keep her safe. The SS ordered your mother to give up the infant. She refused. She held the baby and posed as its mother. She wanted desperately to save it from the SS when they demanded it from her. She pleaded, she cried and she begged. In the end she won out; they allowed her to keep the baby. But then they took your mother, bearing the other woman's baby in her arms, and together they were led into the gas chambers."

"And the girls?" I asked quietly.

Moshe-Aaron replied sadly, "Etu and Magda went to the left. They were selected for slave labor. Seeing your mother across the way, separated all by herself, Etu could not bear it. She yelled across to mother to communicate with her. Your mother could not hear her. Etu dashed across to join your mother. And seconds later, Magda followed. The SS selecting officer at the ramp noticed them leap across. He ordered both to return to the other side.

"At first they refused, because they wanted to be by your

mother's side. But they had to obey. They had to go back. Minutes passed. Etu looked for an opening, another chance to be with your mother. Seconds later Etu once again leaped across the way to join your mother, to be with her. Followed by Magda, all three were then led to the gas chambers at Birkenau."

My mind collapsed. I could no longer stand it. I'll never know; it'll never be revealed to me, if Etu knew where she was headed. But moments later, I began to feel proud of Etu and Magda, too, who would not abandon their mother. But I did.

"Lajos?" I closed my eyes. I did not want to hear any more.

"He was shot on the road to Blechammer from Camp Jaworzna," Moshe-Aaron said, his voice barely a whisper.

I replied, broken-hearted, "I know the rest. You don't have to tell me. He died of starvation and misery in the coal mines in Jaworzna. No father, no mother, no brother, no sisters ... no one any more."

A depression such as I had never experienced before came over me. I had persisted in hope for those I loved, but it was now ended. My family had been wiped out ... exterminated. Accustomed as I was to death, to seeing people die all around me, I could not accept what had happened. I kept saying to myself, "Mother's not dead. It's all a bad dream, and soon I'll wake up." I punched myself. I banged my fists and head against the wall and I twisted my arm. But I wasn't dreaming. She was gone. No more would I see her, no more would I feel her presence, no more would I kiss her. They were all gone.

I lifted my head to the sky, a moan escaped my lips, and I cried. My uncle placed his hand under my arm, slowly lifting me and said, "Come, Moishele, come to my house."

The bitterness and frustration had left my soul spent and weary, and my body was bone-tired from the endless journey. I lifted my bag and followed my uncle. The light pack I carried upon my back felt heavy. I stopped and started, again and again, until finally we reached the place that was to be my new home.

The house was furnished with fine walnut furniture. I looked in wonder and longing at the big beds and soft pillows. In addition to my uncle, there was a cousin of his who occupied the house. I was to share one of the beds with this cousin.

At night my uncle, Moshe-Aaron, cooked for all, and when morning came he ordered fresh rolls, and butter for the rolls. Along with the fine things he gave us, he wanted us to attend the synagogue. I was squeamish about that. I wasn't sure that I had made up with God as yet, but uncle insisted.

The following Saturday morning, at the height of the Sabbath, I met with several of the men in the community who had been with father and Lajos in Jaworzna. We met in a private home which had been converted into an improvised synagogue. Since there were not enough Jews to fill the old synagogue, the few who remained felt that they would prefer a smaller, more intimate place.

When the Torah was read, I followed it closely. At the end of the reading, my name was called for the *Aliyah* as a means of giving thanks for my survival. As I walked to the *Bimah*, I again felt the sadness within me, and when I began to read the old sacred words, I burst into tears. The words were blurred, and I could no longer read them. I was about to stop when my chant continued. I had not been called to the Torah since my bar mitzvah at thirteen. But my memory had returned to me unbidden, and with tears streaming from my eyes, I continued in a trembling voice that I did not recognize as my own.

At the end of the ritual, I was asked to repeat, with one of the Talmudic scholars, the Kaddish, the prayer for the dead. I was instructed to repeat it daily for the ensuing year. I did so, and in time, after learning more of the ritual, I led the morning and evening prayers in whatever place I found myself.

A few weeks later the urge to travel came over me. I decided to look for a new way of life. In most of Europe, and in many other parts of the world, evidence of the war's destruction was all too visible. The peasants from the nearby villages who used to emerge with their crops to sell or barter were no longer to be seen in

Munkacs. The pious Jews in their Hassidic attires were not around. The Jewish population of Munkacs had been annihilated. A Jewish child or a youngster was not to be seen. The Holocaust was all around me, but I heard that in Bucharest life was more peaceful and promising, and that there were Jewish relief organizations at work there. So, one summer morning my friend and I packed our meager belongings and headed for the railway station.

Without money, but with the proper credentials essential for travel, we boarded the train and began the trip to Bucharest. We met with others like ourselves, traveling in the same direction, and we joined together as a group, sharing food and shelter from each other. We traveled as a caravan with frequent stops in hospitable villages to rest, to wash, and to hunt for food. After days on the road we finally arrived in the glittering capital of Rumania. Welcoming signs and banners in huge lettering were posted throughout the railway station. In Hebrew and Yiddish the signs advertised relief and restitution for Jewish survivors of concentration camps. We were hailed as their heroes. I felt a deep sense of relief, pride, and belonging as the Jews of Bucharest extended their welcome. It was truly a good homecoming. There was excitement in the air, of a kind I could not fully comprehend. The morning after my arrival in Bucharest, I set out on foot to look around the big and lively city. There were Russian soldiers in every street and on every corner. I looked much like a soldier myself, in my green trousers and a Russian army shirt. I was about to enter the bakery to buy fresh rolls when I noticed a patrol directly in front, motioning me to stop. They demanded to know who I was and what unit I belonged to. I was at a loss; I did not know what they meant. I began to explain that I was not a soldier and it was just a mistaken identity. The Russian guards were firm and demanded to see my credentials. I pulled out my identification card which had been given to me by relief authorities the day before. After a brief examination of my documents, I was ordered to follow them into the Command

Post. I insisted they explain why they were taking me there. Their only reply was, "Let's go, comrade, just let's go!"

The soldiers, bayonets fixed, escorted me toward the center of town to headquarters. I demanded to know why I was under arrest. "You'll find out at headquarters, you deserter," snapped one of them.

I tried to explain that I was not a deserter, nor was I Russian. I repeated that I had just been liberated from Buchenwald. I sounded strange to them—they had never heard of Buchenwald, or so it seemed. I began to plead with them.

My plea was in vain, and shortly I ended up in the Russian Military Headquarters which turned out to be an old Rumanian jailhouse. I was under arrest and placed with Russian and Ukrainian deserters awaiting hearings. A Russian private soon informed me that I would be interrogated and my story heard. The gloomy hours went by as I wondered and waited in a Rumanian jailhouse for Russian deserters. In the middle of the night, I was shoved a bowl of soup and a slice of black bread, my first food in twenty-four hours.

Those who were interrogated and found to be real deserters were led to a nearby cellar where they had to fight off the rats. From there they awaited transportation to their homeland, the Soviet Union, or to Siberia, the barren, remote and most feared part of Russia.

Weary and tired, I stretched out on a wooden plank and went to sleep, only to be awakened a short time later by a group of deserters who had just been brought in by a Red Army patrol.

Finally, my name was called.

I entered the room where an intelligence officer of the Red Army was sitting behind a table serving as his desk. He looked at me wide-eyed, demanding in a deep voice, "What are you doing in Rumania, and why are you not in your homeland?" With a slight shiver, I answered, "I am here looking for relief and a new home. You see," I told him, "the Nazis killed my whole family." I then rolled up my sleeve and showed him the tattoo number on my left forearm.

"Yes, yes," the officer replied, "I know all about that. The Nazis slaughtered our people, too. You must go back to your homeland—you are a Ukrainian," he insisted, "and your place is in the Ukrainian SSR. I will free you if you promise to go directly to your home and stay there."

I was released. I found a spot under a tree far away from the jailhouse and collected my thoughts. Then I tucked in my Russian shirt to look like an ordinary civilian and briskly made my way to the relief organization.

The following weeks I stayed close by with friends in Bucharest, waiting for restitution. When I received the meager sum, barely enough to pay my way back to Munkacs, I decided to head home again.

At the train station while waiting for the train, I was approached by members of a militant Zionist Organization who persuaded me to join them. I was rushed to the outskirts of Bucharest, to a Kibbutz where other young people were waiting for the opportunity to make the "illegal" journey to Palestine.

Soon I learned that the British, who had kept Jews out of Palestine during the war when they most needed a place for refuge from Hitler's terror, had not changed. They were brutal, and would not yield to Jewish aspirations for a home in the ancient land of Israel. The only way for the surviving Jews to get to Palestine was by means of an underground journey. It took them through forests and rivers and mountains in order to reach and cross borders in the dark of night. I also learned that the Russians and the East Europeans kept their borders sealed against them too. The French and the Italians in the West were not any different; they cooperated with Britain in making Jewish movement next to impossible. Only the Americans, in the U.S. zones of Germany and Austria, gave aid and encouragement to the Jewish refugees, but they too acted only in an unofficial manner, without the consent or the approval of Washington.

I heard rumors that the Jewish refugees were often jailed by the

British for lack of credentials and for attempting "illegal" border crossings. Yet many trekked over the snow-covered French and Italian Alps to the ports of Southern France. From there they embarked for Palestine in hired ships, frequently Greek, that were often unseaworthy and always overcrowded.

On the high seas, they faced the dangers of the British fleet, which caught many of the ships, and the Jews thus found themselves, once again, in concentration camps on Cyprus, imprisoned by their Allies, the British. This I could not understand in the fall of 1945, when I sat wondering on my bed in the Kibbutz, deciding whether or not to sign up for the next underground transport to Palestine. I simply could not accept the notion that once again I might find myself behind barbed wire, in a British concentration camp on Cyprus. I decided to go home, back to my ancestral land.

At home I found that the rapidly growing communist system was changing everything. Cooperative stores were established and people were forced to work for the Communist State. At the market places, militia raids became more frequent, and each day more and more people were rounded up for work details, a kind of forced labor. I knew some of the militia and they warned me, in time, to leave the area before an impending raid. I couldn't believe that such raids were commonplace among free people. These were our liberators, I thought, and why the Russians would behave toward us in such a brutal way was a puzzle. I didn't know what to do; I had no one to advise me. I was alone; I felt like an orphan. I was lost.

As the days passed, it became more and more difficult to move about freely. Identification and proof of holding a job became essential. It was a grim reminder of ghetto life. I wanted to run away, but where? My new-found friend, Luv, a Russian Army captain and a Jew, urged me to leave. "The establishment of a communist system in a non-communist region is tough to survive," he said. He insisted that I leave before it was too late.

"Go," he yelled, "you have no one to leave behind. I wish I could go, but I can't; they'd ship my father, mother, brothers, and sister to Siberia, into exile, if I were found missing." I dreaded leaving my homeland for good but, in January 1946, on a bitter cold night, I decided to leave, and became a refugee once again. I boarded a truck for Uzhorod, the city closest to the Slovakian border. There I was met by a "contact" who was to take me with a group across the border. Before my agreement was signed, the contact man insisted on the cash. I didn't have the money, not all that he demanded. I was a few thousand rubles short. It was not a huge amount at the time, nor was it unattainable, but I didn't have the money. What was I to do? I felt trapped and looked around at the fleeing refugees, hoping for someone to assist me. Suddenly I spotted Israel, a Hassid from Munkacs, who had brought his wife to be taken across the border too. He knew my plight and quickly offered to advance me the money. "I'll pay the difference for you. Go, go, my son ... God be with you." He handed me the money for the contact man. I was on my way for the hazardous journey.

It was getting dark, and we were loaded onto a horse-drawn wagon to begin our journey. Everyone was dressed as a peasant to conceal his identity. At the border village we left the wagon and made the rest of the journey on foot. Our guide led us across frozen fields, carefully ducking Russian border patrols.

Nearing the border, we sighted two Russian patrols with hounds. We were lying quietly in a gutter by the side of the road, when we heard rifle shots coming from the opposite direction. Prearranged? A lucky coincidence? I'll never know. But immediately, the border patrol that had been heading toward us turned around and ran in the direction of the shots. Our guide then told us to run toward a shed that was across the border, out of reach of the Russian Patrols.

My God, I thought as we dashed to the shed. Here I am running through an open field with shooting all around me. What if I'm hit? What if I'm killed after all? To survive Auschwitz and then die in my own country, shot down by the Russians! But no one was shot. We made it to the shed unharmed and hid there until it was safe to leave. I now fully realized that I had made my second escape from slavery to freedom.

When daylight came, we headed for the railway station, and then westward to the capital, Prague. There I made my way to the United Nations Relief and Rehabilitation Agency. I was provided with food and shelter, and the next day I headed north to the city of Usti Nad Labem. I finally registered as a legal resident and as a machinist.

From here I decided not to run, at least not for the moment. Though the shadow of Soviet domination of Czechoslovakia was lengthening, I remained in this picturesque city, mainly because a vast colony of survivors from various concentration camps had settled there. I felt safe, and secure too, with them around, and especially when I discovered that Bennet, Kalvin, and Steve had chosen to make their new home at Usti Nad Labem. It was getting late in the day, and I still had no place to live. I needed a bed, a roof over my head. I began knocking on doors, asking to be taken in for the night. The grocer, the tailor, and others, too, were willing to accept me, but I soon discovered that Bennet, Kalvin, and Steve were just around the corner, living in luxury in a three-room apartment, which was a rare thing to come by in a war-torn country. As I entered their home, I was warmly received by the three brothers, whom I had known well since boyhood. Bennet had been my idol, and though four years my senior, he was a great pal. Kalvin, too, was my stout buddy. We had played together at their country home in better and more peaceful times. I remembered seeing them in Buchenwald during the last days of the evacuation. We stuck together in the "Little Camp," and hid under a barracks for a whole night to avoid being sent away. I was happy to be with them and felt at home once again. I was no longer alone; I had found a family, and I became their brother. I shared a corner with Steve, who was hardly sixteen and needed a friend.

The next day, in a zestful mood, I strolled along the main streets of the town, enjoying the peaceful city, with its shops full of contented people. I soon learned that I was in the Suddettenland, a region of Czechoslovakia heavily populated with Germans, and annexed by Hitler in 1938. After the annexation, other Germans, some of the Nazis, had flocked to the area: but now, with the war over, they were moving again. The Russian conquerors would not leave them alone. They were rounded up and quickly deported. I couldn't believe my eyes when I saw them: flocks of German Nazis with yellow armbands driven to railway stations for transport to Germany. Other "Germans," though they had been born in the region and spoke the language, also were forced to leave. This was to prevent future tyrants from ever again claiming the Suddettenland for Germany. The Czechs, in cooperation with their Red Army liberators, took no chances; they wanted the Germans out. I couldn't understand their motives. Perhaps I didn't want to, because I was yearning for an understanding—maybe even brotherhood—among men. I wanted the hatred and division to stop. I couldn't stand the thought of the formerly persecuted engaging in similar acts of persecution against their fellow men. "Why must it be so?" I kept asking myself. "When will this stop?" I strolled further, and then I saw something that at first I couldn't believe. "No! No!" I yelled in the streets. It could not be. My eyes, my mind must be playing tricks. But then I saw it: rows and rows of women, the young and the elderly, heads shaven, clad in blue and white prison garb, wooden clogs on their still frostbitten feet, marching along the street, guarded by special camp guards. I ran closer to see them. I wanted to feel them, to become one of them. The guards politely shoved me aside, letting me know that the women were not to be pitied. "Have you forgotten what they did to us during the war?" yelled one of them. "We are repaying our debts to them," snapped another. Seeing these women was overwhelming, too much to cope with. I went home.

I woke up in the middle of the night in a cold sweat, troubled by my day's experience. I could sleep no longer; I had to know. I wanted someone to tell me where those wretched souls were being driven, like a herd to slaughter. I wouldn't rest until I found out. Then I discovered on the outskirts of town a well-lit area, acres and acres of grounds surrounded by barbed wire. It was a concentration camp for Germans, for former Nazis and Nazi youth leaders.

My stay in Usti Nad Labem was short. Day by day the Russian grip on Czechoslovakia grew stronger. Former Nazis and German prisoners of war were rounded up and shipped in sealed boxcars to Siberia. The trains were rolling on schedule; the railway tracks had been repaired. The Russians were running our lives; I could sense it in the homes; I could feel it as I walked through the streets. It was evident in the newspapers and on the radio. Suddenly an order was issued. All former Czech citizens from the Carpathians must return to their former homeland, their place of birth. I was faced with a dilemma. Was I to deny my birthplace and flee, or return to Munkacs and face servitude? My decision was quick and final; I chose to flee. During the night, I made my way to the railway station and boarded the first train heading west. As I arrived there, I discovered that I was not alone. Survivors of various concentration camps joined forces and decided to flee by a common route, over mountains and rivers to freedom. There I met Karen and Angel, who were also about to flee across the hills. I was amazed to learn how well the system of escape worked. We situated ourselves between the borders of Czechoslovakia and Germany, inside no-man's land, and there we waited to be escorted across to the American Zone. I discovered, too, how the Hagana and other militant Jewish organizations were sacrificing to help. They arranged our escape and guarded our route. For the first time I met with armed Palestinian Jews, who came to be with us and to lead us to freedom. I felt safe and protected.

Once across the border I made my way to the American Zone in Germany. The United Nations Relief and Rehabilitation

Organization teams were busily at work setting up Displaced Person's Camps to house and to feed the destitute. The first D.P. Camp I found was filled with fleeing survivors. I decided to move on to another and then another, until I arrived at the Esweige D.P. Camp near the German city of Kassel, where I settled among the other refugees. The following day I was officially admitted to the camp and assigned living quarters. They were meager but comfortable. My search for a new home began immediately. It could be Palestine or America, I was informed; I had to make a choice. Then I remembered a letter I received from Karen only a few weeks before, to let me know that her uncle in New York had contacted my aunt in New Jersey. I reached into my pocket and handed the letter to the pretty blonde UNRRA official. She quickly unfolded the letter and began to read it. Her eyes began to shine and then a smile informed me: "This is your ticket to the United States of America. I shall contact our office in New York and soon you will be on your way." A shiver ran through my body, and my mind, too. I could not get used to the idea that I would be leaving the continent of Europe for America. It was not what I expected; I did not believe it. I began to develop a fear of the unknown, the far away place — America! Throughout the night there was constant ringing of bells. I dreamed of seeing a huge bell I once studied about in my boyhood. It was the Liberty Bell; I saw it clearly in my dream.

The following day I looked for work outside the camp. The warehouse was in need of good workers, so I volunteered. Soon I was promoted to head the shipping and receiving department. It was a big undertaking which entailed driving into the city slaughterhouse three times a week, picking up meat rations, and ensuring that they were fairly and evenly distributed. Each week I received a bonus for my services, usually canned foods, chocolate and other delicacies, rare commodities in a Displaced Persons Camp. I decided to save up some of the goods and sell the rest, because I wanted to go on a trip. I longed to visit my friends and tell them I was going to America. I wanted to find Bennet, Kalvin, and Steve. I wanted them to know that I was leaving for America. I traveled across Germany, and finally discovered Bennet at the University of Music and Arts in Munich. He was a student there. He invited me to his room, a chamber about the size of a chicken coop. Proudly he showed me his meager supply of bread and a few grams of margarine. The poor student was amazed when I displayed the contents of my bag, which contained a veritable cornucopia of delectables for him. We feasted on my treasures and talked for hours. As it was finally time to take leave, I bid Bennet goodbye, picked up my bundle and headed for the railroad station.

It was impossible to ride through Munich and look at the devastated city without feeling a tinge of sorrow. British and American planes had wrought havoc in Munich and most of the major cities of Germany. Entire quarters had been leveled and piles of rubble were everywhere. I could smell the stench of rotting corpses where the debris had not yet been cleared away. Many buildings were windowless, with some walls blown away, and long rusting construction rods swung loosely like headless snakes from the tops of jungle trees. Here and there an apartment building had been shorn in half, revealing kitchens and bedrooms with rain-soaked furniture still intact. It was not unlike a stage set, cut away, with an air of dangling expectancy, as if a door were about to open and a brightly costumed fraulein enter, to begin her part in the play.

A dozen languages could be heard at once as I entered the crowded railroad station at Munich. It was obvious that there were displaced persons from everywhere, although Yiddish predominated. Through all the camaraderie, bargaining, laughing, and arguments, it was clear that each of the displaced persons was alone, in search of a surviving relative, or a friend. Each person was waiting for a train traveling to his own private destination, a place unknown. No one really knew what they would find when they arrived. I was weary and tired, so I found a resting place away from the crowd where I could sleep. Then I saw a group of German civil police accompanied by American M.P.'s rushing towards the railroad station. A ring was put around the station. I wondered, "What is it?" A German had been killed in revenge the day before, and a survivor of a concentration camp was blamed for his death. As a stranger in the area, I feared that I might be picked up for questioning. So I fled across the fields into town. While walking, I was stopped by an American soldier in OD's. He looked me over and I noticed him staring at my emblem with the Star of David. *"Hey bist du a Yid?"* he said. Are you a Jew? My first response was to overreact. "Why do you ask," I responded. "Do you wish to make something of it?" "Oh, no," he replied, "I am a Jew, too. An American Jew. *Shalom,*" and we shook hands.

After our handshake, Ed and I began to converse in broken Yiddish. He invited me to go with him to a beer hall. There he ordered pretzels and beer for both of us. In a short time we became good friends. He even offered me a forty-five caliber pistol for protection and invited me to his friend's house for dinner. I accepted and together we went to the house. His friends, I discovered, were displaced persons, survivors of concentration camps. I felt at home. I noticed the table was set with the traditional white candles for a special dinner. Then I noted the wine and the twisted loaves and realized that it was the Sabbath. Now I realized how many Friday evenings had gone by without my knowing that it was the Sabbath, and without thinking about the days. It was not more than a year before that a Sabbath eve meant a festive table, all the family together, white cloth, our best silver, mother whispering her blessing as she lit the candles, and father lifting the *kiddish* cup, as we all stood around and listened to his chant.

I blushed as the company asked me to chant the *kiddish*. It was an honor to be asked to say the prayers so I lifted the goblet and everyone rose. They listened and at the end all whispered "Amen."

It was getting dark and I had to catch a train back to Esweige.

Ed and I left the house and headed toward the railroad station. As we walked the street, we encountered patrols everywhere. There was a curfew in effect. Civilians were to get into their homes and off the streets. I, too, had to obey the curfew. Ed, who was in his G.I. uniform, thumbed a ride and was quickly picked up by a patrol jeep. They took both of us to his unit, which was near the railroad station.

Before Ed and I parted, he gave me his address in the States. "Look me up when you come to America," he said. Briskly Ed ran upstairs to his quarters and brought me loads of candy and cigarettes. We embraced, partly to hide a tear in my eye. I wondered if I would ever again make a friendship that did not come to a quick end? Would I ever live somewhere that I could call home?

I boarded the train with some apprehension. The trip to Esweige was longer than I had expected. On arriving in the D.P. Camp, I headed for the bulletin board to see if I had any messages and if my name was on a list.

There I saw it, in capital letters, a note for me to report to UNRRA office at once. "Were you looking for me?" I inquired of the lady behind the desk.

"What is your name?" she asked without looking up.

"Moric Mermelstein." She was startled, her voice rising. "Where have you been? We've been looking for you for weeks."

"What have I done?" I asked curiously. She paused, got out of her chair slowly, stood up straight and tall, and made her announcement with great ceremony. "You are going to America."

AMERICA! The word echoed thunderously in the inner chambers of my brain and my heart beat fiercely once again, but I stood before her without saying a word. Then I ran back to my barracks, gathered my meager belongings, made my rounds to bid goodbye to my friends and roommates, and returned to the UNRRA Office. There I was given a ration card, rations, and the necessary credentials and sent on my way. Upon arrival in Frankfurt, Germany, I was rushed to a reception center to be processed for immediate immigration.

On August 20, 1946, I sailed out of Bremerhaven on the SS *Marine Perch* for the United States. After a ten-day voyage across the rugged Atlantic, I disembarked in New York harbor on August 31, 1946, only to rediscover that I was the sole survivor of my entire family.

By Bread Alone

The Judgment

The four counts of the indictment were: 1—Conspiracy to commit crimes alleged in other counts; 2—Crimes against peace; 3—War crimes; 4—Crimes against humanity.

GUILTY on all 4 counts.
Death by hanging.

KEITEL

His guilt is unique in its enormity.

SAUCKEL

was in charge of
deportation for
slave labor of
5 million human beings.

Verdict: GUILTY on counts 3 and 4.
Sentence: Death by hanging.

JODL

Verdict: GUILTY on all 4 counts.
Sentence: Death by hanging.

FRANK

Governor-General of the occupied Polish territory.

Verdict: GUILTY on counts 3 and 4.
Sentence: Death by hanging.

Jew-Baiter Number 1.

Verdict: GUILTY on count 4.
Sentence: Death by hanging.

STREICHER

As early as 1938 he began to call for the annihilation of the Jews

GUILTY on all 4 counts.
Death by hanging.

GOERING

NOTE: CHEATED THE
GALLOWS BY SUCCEEDING
TO COMMIT SUICIDE IN HIS
PRISON CELL.

FRICK

GUILTY on counts 2, 3, and 4.
Death by hanging.

257

HESS: " . . . As deputy to the Führer, Hess was the top man in the Nazi Party

HESS

Verdict: GUILTY on counts 1 and 2.
Sentence: Life imprisonment.

GUILTY on all 4 counts.
Death by hanging.

ROSENBERG

Baldur von Schirach used the *Hitler Jugend* to educate German Youth 'in the spirit of National Socialism'

GUILTY on counts 3 and 4.
Death by hanging.

KALTENBRUNNER

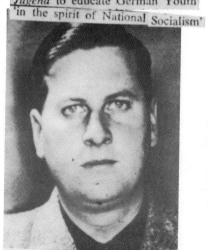

Verdict: GUILTY on count 4.
Sentence: 20 years imprisonment.

NUREMBERG DIARY

The Psychological Tests

The psychological testing program was virtually completed before the beginning of the trial while the prisoners were still in solitary confinement so that the validity of the results was safeguarded. Of the various tests given (Intelligence test, Rorschach and Thematic Apperception personality tests), the simplest to describe briefly, though not the most significant, was the Intelligence test.

I used my own German version of the American *Wechsler-Bellevue Adult Intelligence Test*, eliminating and compensating for those parts which are subject to cultural differences, like vocabulary and general information. The test battery consisted of

A. *Verbal tests of memory and use of concepts*
1. Memory span for number-series of increasing length.
2. Simple arithmetic of increasing difficulty.
3. Common sense questions.
4. Concept formation by verbal similarities.

B. *Performance tests of observation and sensory-motor co-ordination*
5. Substitution Code Test (substituting digits for symbols).
6. Object assembly (like jigsaw puzzles).
7. Converting designs on colored blocks.
8. Recognizing missing parts of pictures.

These tests have been well standardized for adults, giving a good sampling of the abilities ordinarily associated with academic intelligence. The IQ's were calculated according to the Wechsler-Bellevue method which (unlike the Stanford-

Binet) makes allowance for the deterioration of average intelligence with old age, rather than assuming a constant level throughout adulthood. This gave a fairer comparison of the IQ's of men of such widely divergent ages. It should be borne in mind, however, that the effective intelligence of older men like von Papen, Raeder, Schacht, and Streicher was 15–20 points lower than the IQ's indicated here but their relative standing in their respective age groups is accurately indicated.

NAME	IQ
HJALMAR SCHACHT	143
SEYSS-INQUART	141
HERMANN GOERING	138
KARL DÖNITZ	138
FRANZ VON PAPEN	134
ERICH RAEDER	134
DR. HANS FRANK	130
HANS FRITZSCHE	130
BALDUR VON SCHIRACH	130
JOACHIM VON RIBBENTROP	129
WILHELM KEITEL	129

NAME	IQ
ALBERT SPEER	128
ALFRED JODL	127
ALFRED ROSENBERG	127
CONSTANTIN VON NEURATH	125
WALTHER FUNK	124
WILHELM FRICK	124
RUDOLF HESS (estimated)*	120
FRITZ SAUCKEL	118
ERNST KALTENBRUNNER	113
JULIUS STREICHER	106

* On basis of retest after recovery.

Except for Streicher, the IQ's show that the Nazi leaders were above average intelligence (IQ 90–110), merely confirming the fact that the most successful men in any sphere of human activity—whether it is politics, industry, militarism, or crime—are apt to be above average intelligence. It must be borne in mind that the IQ indicates nothing but the *mechanical efficiency* of the mind, and has nothing to do with character or morals, nor the various other considerations that go into an evaluation of personality. Above all, the individual's sense of values and the expressions of his basic motivation are the things that truly reveal his character.

259

By Bread Alone

DOENITZ

Verdict: GUILTY on counts 2 and 3.
Sentence: 10 years imprisonment.

Verdict: GUILTY on counts 2, 3, and 4.
Sentence: Death by hanging.

SEYSS-INQUART

Nazism and Religious Bigotry

SCHACHT

Verdict: NOT GUILTY.

VON PAPEN

Verdict: NOT GUILTY.

Von Papen
had a more Christian con-
ception

*Von Papen continued his defense, ex-
plaining that the law putting Hitler into power was forced by
the seriousness of the political situation, but it was supposed
to be based on a Christian solution of social problems. He
concluded a Concordat with the Vatican, but Hitler proceeded to consider it merely a scrap of paper. His attitude
toward the Jewish problem is that which the Catholic Church
expects from every good Catholic.*

260

"Why, everybody knows what the Catholic Church's attitude is," he said to Schacht and me. "It is the principle that all men are equal before God and that racial differences are no indication of inequality."

Catholics in the dock as well as anti-Catholic Rosenberg began to discuss the attitude of the Catholic Church on anti-Semitism.

Rosenberg said that von Papen merely meant that in a Christian country there should not be too much Jewish influence. Seyss-Inquart remarked that 85 per cent of the lawyers in Vienna were Jews. He then went on to explain the tie-up between the priesthood and anti-Semitism.

He said that as a matter of fact, most of the priests were basically anti-Semitic, especially in Poland. That is where the pogroms have been going on for centuries even up to the present day, and it was the immigration of Polish Jews that carried a wave of anti-Semitism with it into Germany.

Frank agreed to this, giving a little more of the historical background. "Yes, the priesthood has been essentially anti-Semitic ever since the Inquisition. Hahaha! They tortured people all over Europe out of religious intolerance, and later they started burning witches."

Here Rosenberg added, glad of a chance to see Frank admitting that the Inquisition was a disgraceful chapter in Catholic Church history, "Yes, and that went on for four or five centuries—not just a momentary outburst of emotion!"

Frank sobered up and added, "The predecessors of Auschwitz were the torture chambers of the Inquisition.—It was a horrible period in our history really!" Frick and Rosenberg remarked that compared to the Inquisitors, Hitler was a white lamb. Frank disputed this, but with the same unfeeling perverted humor. "No, he wasn't a white lamb but it really was a hell of a period in history.—Hahaha! You see, my dear professor, mankind has always been in a terrible state. The beast in man keeps coming out again and again."

Rosenberg and Kaltenbrunner added further details of the tortures of the Inquisition, the adventures of Torquemada, etc. To keep the record straight, Frank pointed out that the Protestant rulers of northern Germany, not to be outdone in religious fanaticism took up the trying and torturing of "witches." These trials had apparently interested Frank as a lawyer. "I read some of the protocols of those trials out of the 15th and 16th centuries. They actually asked old women how many times they had sexual intercourse with the devil! It is recorded right in the protocols, and they tortured them until they got the answer.—Hahaha! Really it is grotesque!"

The Radio Division, FRITZSCHE

Verdict: NOT GUILTY.

Albert Speer, Hitler's Armaments Minister, personal architect and intimate of his circle

Verdict: GUILTY on counts 3 and 4.
Sentence: 20 years imprisonment.

VON RIBBENTROP *Verdict:* GUILTY on all 4 counts.
Sentence: Death by hanging.

Statesman

"I knew that Hitler was of the opinion that the Jews had started the war, but that was absolutely untrue, and I always told him that that was not right." His next thought was that if America had only listened to him, the whole catastrophe would have been avoided. He had sent somebody to America in 1940 to tell the Standard Oil people and the Jewish bankers not to let America get into the war. If they only had not been so hostile toward Germany . . .

262

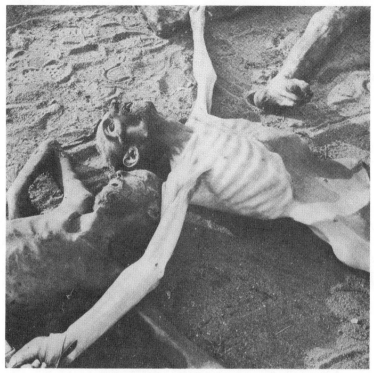

"For the Grace of God" "Ecce Homo" - 1945 After Christ

"Prayers Beside a Dead Man" (print), By M.K.

"Sick Prisoner" (print) by M.K. Mieczys-law Koscielak, a former inmate of Auschwitz-Birkenau and other death camps sketched these in secrecy while a prisoner and had them smuggled out of the camps to let the world know by way of his sketches what the Nazis were doing to us. But the world was silent and would not and could not believe us.

263

AUSCHWITZ-BIRKENAU
MEMORIAL

FORD AT AUSCHWITZ

BY RUDY ABRAMSON

Times Staff Writer

BREZINKA, Poland — The wind blows through the rustling barbed-wire fence, bends the expanse of blue and yellow wildflowers and rattles the doors of derelict wooden guard shacks.

Old women pick cabbage and shock wheat in nearby fields.

At eternal flame flickers atop the ruins of a crematorium the Nazis tried to destroy before they pulled out in 1945.

This is Auschwitz. Infamous Auschwitz.

Humanity was disgraced here by more than 4 million systematic murders, victims marched to the gas chambers for being born of parentage unacceptable to the Third Reich.

Now it is silent, but there is still a stench in the squat brick barracks where Jews from all over Europe were processed and tortured, awaiting death.

President Ford came here Tuesday and paid tribute to those who died.

His helicopter landed within the compound of Brezinka section of Auschwitz, and he walked slowly past the remains of a crematorium, past a railhead where prisoners were unloaded from boxcars, and laid a wreath at the foot of a marble monument, imprinted with the triangle the prisoners wore for identification.

"Horrible," the President was heard to say as he entered the camp. "Horrible. Unbelievable. Horrible."

A few steps behind him was Secretary of State Henry A. Kissinger, himself a German-born Jew, who told reporters, "I had some family members here."

Although the death camp has been an international monument for years, the Poles have left it much as it was, giving the feeling that it was vacated only yesterday.

At the peak of the Nazi effort to exterminate European Jews, Auschwitz Commander Rudolph Hoess sent 6,000 a day to their deaths, marching victims into underground chambers that held as many as 2,000 men, women and children at a time.

As Soviet troops moved on the area, the Nazis tried to hide what they had done, but they could not.

Hoess, a convicted murderer before he rose through the Nazi hierarchy to head Auschwitz, was convicted at Nuremberg. He was turned over to the Poles, and they hanged him not far from the spot where President Ford visited Tuesday.

It was the first time a U.S. President had visited any of the concentration camps where Hitler carried out his racist extermination program. Many of the compounds were liberated by American troops.

Later he called it "a ghastly and awesome reminder of man's inhumanity to man."

After he placed the red and white wreath at the base of the monument, Mr. Ford slowly moved down a row of stone tablets where messages in 18 languages denounced the atrocities.

He paused to read the English statement:

"Four million people suffered and died here at the hands of the Nazi murderers between 1940 and 1945."

Then, without ever acknowledging the silent crowd of several hundred Poles watching him, he walked away, beneath a banner reading, "Never more war, never more fascism."

Accompanied by Polish Communist Party Leader Edward Gierek, he signed a guest book, walked past gracefully towering birch trees to a barracks building where women inmates of Auschwitz had been incarcerated and talked with a man who survived five years in the camp.

Although he obviously was moved, the President purposely did not make the visit a major occasion. He was here only 20 minutes and did not visit the museum where the Nazi atrocities are illustrated in sickening detail.

When the President flew out, headed for the European Security Conference summit in Helsinki after a short stop in Krakow, the crowd drifted away, leaving Auschwitz quiet again.

There were only the sounds of footsteps on the cobblestone around the monument and the snapping of flags in the breeze.

GERALD R. FORD

PRESIDENT

OF THE UNITED STATES OF AMERICA

This monument and the memory of those it honors inspire us further to the dedicated pursuit of Peace, Cooperation and Security for all peoples.

Gerald R. Ford
President of The
United States of America.
July 29, 1975

H. A. K.

OŚWIĘCIM-BRZEZINKA , July 29, 1975

No President of the United States other than President Gerald R. Ford, visited Auschwitz-Birkenau while on his goodwill journeys to Europe.

NOTE:

While President Nixon and President Carter were in Poland on a state visit, they failed to take that extra step to visit the former facilities of Auschwitz-Birkenau, where four million men, women and little children were lured and driven into gas chambers disguised as shower rooms. Why?

Los Angeles Times

HOMAGE — President Ford places wreath at monument at Auschwitz, Poland, where 4 million Jews died. It was the first visit by an American President to any of the Nazi death camps.

'HORRIBLE, UNBELIEVABLE'

Ford Visits Auschwitz, Pays Tribute to Victims

Author

Wreath Laying Ceremony at Auschwitz-Birkenau 1980. Author and His Wife

The International Auschwitz Committee at work . . . October 1980 at Auschwitz-Birkenau. Author and His Wife as Delegates to the I.A.K. Conference.

269

By Bread Alone

THE JERUSALEM POST

INTERNATIONAL EDITION

THE LATEST
NEWS FROM
ISRAEL

Published in Jerusalem

יצא לאור בירושלים

No. 1,004. PUBLISHED WEEKLY. 24-30 AUGUST 1980 • 12-18 מ

REVISING THE HISTORY OF THE HOLOCAUST

To the Editor of The Jerusalem Post

Sir, — By now you may have heard of the so-called "prestigious" names: 1. Dr. Austin J. App (retired) La Salle College, Philadelphia

2. John Bennett, Victoria Council for Civil Liberties, Australia

3. Dr. Reinhard K. Buchner California State University, Long Beach

4. Dr. Arthur R. Butz, Northwestern University, Illinois

5. James E. Egolf, Duquesne University, Pennsylvania

6. Dr. Robert Faurisson, University of Lyon-2, France

7. Ditlieb Felderer, Bible Researcher, Sweden

8. Dr. James J. Martin, Institute of Historical Review

9. Udo Walendy, Verlag Fur Volkstum & Zeitgeschichtsforschung.

You may have also read about a recent publication of the so-called "Journal of Historical Review" which originated in Torrance, California. If by chance you have not heard of these gentlemen, nor read about the so-called "Journal of Historical Review," allow me to inform you that these university professors, some of them former Nazis of the old Hitlerite regime, have taken upon themselves to use and abuse our colleges and universities throughout the western world, in particular the United States, to spread lies, hatred and bigotry vis-a-vis the subject known as the "Holocaust." They even invented new titles to distort these awesome historical events. "The Hoax of the 20th Century," "The Myth of the Six Million," etc., etc.

What can one say, when once again we sit idly by as these highly acclaimed professors, in highly accredited universities are "at it again." They are teaching our new generation that the chumneys of Auschwitz were only those of the bakeries. That there were no gas chambers at Auschwitz-Berkenau. That Dachau was a peaceful town within Nazi Germany and that the "six million" European Jews fled Nazism and have been living peacefully in Israel ever since.

As one who survived the infernos of Auschwitz-Birkenau and Buchenwald, my eyes are still blurring from the vision of that nightmare and my ears are still ringing with the agonizing sounds of men, women and little children who were lured and driven into the gas chambers disguised as shower rooms, solely and exclusively because they were Jewish. These "prestigious" gentlemen mentioned above, as well as the bigoted organizations they represent, have the gall to offer any survivor of the Holocaust a $50,000, and possibly $100,000 award if he or she can prove that indeed gassings of men, women and little children had actually taken place during that awesome period known as the "Holocaust."

I shall be leaving for the 10th time to a survivors' conference in October to be held at Auschwitz. Perhaps some of those "prestigious" gentlemen would like to accompany me, at which time, I could physically point out the places from where I saw the actual gassings of men, women and little children in gas chambers disguised as shower rooms.

MELVIN MERMELSTEIN
Huntington Beach, California

REVISING HISTORY

To the Editor of The Jerusalem Post

Sir, — I have received some rather discourteous letters which include the most vile accusations. The problem seems to originate with a letter from Melvin Mermelstein which apparently was published in your paper on August 17 (which included the writer in a list of personalities active in denying the Holocaust — ED. J.P.). I am hoping to be able to reach Mr. Mermelstein to reassure him, and if possible, see him at Auschwitz in October where we can discuss the matter.

The letter has caused me a lot of suffering. I have nothing to do with Nazism. In fact, I have never been politically involved in my whole life and I was born in 1942 in the midst of the Nazi turmoil and our family suffered a lot during the war.

Furthermore, my relations with the synagogue here are of the best and I have participated in the services, although not being a regular member. There is a cordial relationship between us.

I hope this will reassure my many friends in Israel and elsewhere who otherwise get a distorted view of my good intentions.

DITLIEB FELDERER

Stockholm

To the Editor of The Jerusalem Post

Sir, — I recently arrived here from Sweden as a new immigrant. I was appalled to see in print the letter of Mr. Ditlieb Felderer from Stockholm in an issue of my daily paper, *The Jerusalem Post.*

This same Mr. Felderer is known as one of the biggest anti-Semites in Sweden. Some years ago he opened an office called Jewish Information at his private address outside Stockholm. Among his many activities at this office, he produced between 30 and 40 different leaflets denying that the Jews were exterminated during World War II. He has tried to propagate similar ideas among school youth. He has translated German books of an extremely anti-Semitic nature. He has also harassed several prominent Jews.

Mr. Felderer claims he is a good friend of Jews in Stockholm. To the best of my knowledge, he does not have a single Jewish friend in Stockholm and in fact the community has on several occasions tried to take him to court.

In order to avoid unpleasantness to my family in Sweden, I am omitting my family name.

FREDDY

(Name and address supplied)

Jerusalem

DENYING THE FACTS OF THE HOLOCAUST

To the Editor of The Jerusalem Post

Sir, — On October 14, you carried a letter from Ditlieb Felderer, Stockholm reporting a letter from Mr. Mermelstein of August 17 which had listed Felderer as one of the persons denying the Holocaust.

To put the record straight, we would like to point out that Felderer is indeed running a campaign in Sweden — through his obscure organization, Bible Researcher — denying the fact of the Holocaust. He is spreading leaflets in Swedish schools inciting pupils to ask their teachers about the "truth" of the Holocaust, offering huge sums to persons who can prove they saw gas chambers, denying Nazi atrocities and so on.

Felderer has certainly no "cordial" relationship with any synagogue in Stockholm. And furthermore, he has no good intentions in this matter. We urge your readers not to believe or trust the falsifications in Felderer's letter and not to help him in case he contacts them with obscure questionnaires.

JAN-ERIC LEVY
Executive director,
The Jewish Community
of Stockholm

By Bread Alone

INSTITUTE FOR
HISTORICAL
REVIEW

P.O. BOX 1306 ● TORRANCE, CA. 90505 ● USA

20 November 1980

Dear Mr. Memmelstein:

Your recent letter in the Jerusalem Post indicates that you can prove that
Jews were gassed in gas-chambers at Auschwitz.

At our 1979 Revisionist Convention we announced a $50,000 reward for proof of
this allegation. To date, no one has stepped forward, and at the 1980
Revisionist Convention we suspended the reward and replaced it with
a $25,000 reward for proof that The Diary of Anne Frank is authentic, and
another $25,000 reward for proof that Jews were turned into bars of soap by
the Nazis.

In the circumstances, we will re-open the $50,000 reward so that you can apply.
I enclose the necessary application forms. Please note that the evidence will
be judged along the same standards as evidence in a U.S. criminal court; not
the standards of the Nuremberg Trials.

If we do not hear from you, we will be obliged to draw our own conclusions, and
publicize this fact to the mass media, including the Jerusalem Post.

I look forward to hearing from you very soon.

Sincerely

Lewis Brandon
Director

Melvin Memmelstein
c/o Ideal Pallet Company
7422 Cedar Avenue
Huntington Beach
Ca. 92647   PERSONAL

(COPY OF ENVELOPE)

WILLIAM J. COX, LAWYER

December 18, 1980

708 GLADYS AVENUE
LONG BEACH, CALIFORNIA 90804
(213) 433-0961

Mr. Lewis Brandon
Director
Institute for Historical Review
P. O. Box 1306
Torrance, Calif. 90505

Dear Mr. Brandon:

I have been retained by Mr. Melvin Mermelstein to represent him in assisting his acceptance of the offer set forth in your letter to him dated November 20, 1980, a copy of which is attached as Exhibit "A".

Mr. Mermelstein fully accepts your offer and through the attached Exhibits "B" and "C" fully complies with your requirements of proof.

Inasmuch as your offer letter establishes that the standard of proof shall be that which prevails in United States Criminal Courts, Mr. Mermelstein assumes that the sufficiency of his evidence will be judged by an impartial fact finder, that all proceedings will be open to public and media observation, and that the matter will be resolved in a timely manner.

It is suggested that the proceeding be televised under a system which allows viewers to vote on the outcome and which ensures to all parties a just and fair basis for determining whether the contract now entered into has been satisfied. Such a program is available through Warner Communications, Station QUBE, in Columbus, Ohio.

The final paragraph of your letter emphasizes that you wish to resolve this matter "very soon." Since Mr. Mermelstein agrees with that premise, and shows a similar desire, it seems not unreasonable to demand that review and validation be completed in an equally timely manner as he has responded to your offer.

273

Therefore, if no response is had by January 20, 1981,
civil proceedings to enforce the contract will be instituted,
naming the Institute for Historical Review, and yourself
personally as defendants.

William Cox

I have read and approve the above acceptance.

Melvin Mermelstein

STATE OF CALIFORNIA)
) SS.
COUNTY OF LOS ANGELES)

On _December 18_, 1980, before me, the undersigned, a

Notary Public in and for said State, personally appeared

Melvin Mermelstein, known to me to be the person whose

name is subscribed to the within instrument and acknowledged

the he executed the same.

WITNESS my hand and official seal.

Signature: _Cheryl Bender_

CHERYL BENDER
NOTARY PUBLIC - CALIFORNIA
PRINCIPAL
LOS ANGELES COUNTY
My Commission Exp. 1983

INSTITUTE FOR HISTORICAL REVIEW

P.O. BOX 1306 • TORRANCE, CA. 90505 • USA

QUESTIONNAIRE AND CLAIM FOR $50,000 REWARD

A   Claimant Details

Name   *Melvin Mermelstein*

Address   *708 Gladys Ave.*

Long Beach   State *California*   Zip *90815*

Date of Birth   *September 25, 1926*   Place of Birth *Czechoslovakia*

Nationality at Birth *Czechoslovakian*   Current Nationality *American*

Ethnic Origin *Jewish/Hebrew*

Military Service? *U.S. Army*   Nation *American*   War *Korean*   Dates *1950-53*

Were you yourself interned in A German Concentration Camp? Which? Dates?

Yes. Auschwitz-Birkenau from May, 1944 to July, 1944. Gleiwitz I from July, 1944 to January 1945. Buchenwald from February 1945 to April 11, 1945.

B   Description of Evidence

On another sheet of paper, please describe your evidence in full. Your description must be typewritten in English. Answer as many of the following questions you can: Were you an eyewitness to gassing operations? If so, fully describe all of the mechanics invloved in as great detail as you remember. Give names, dates, exact locations of incidents. Do you have documentary evidence? Did you keep a diary or take photos? Specifically and carefully describe any documents you have which can be presented for examination. Do you have any forensic evidence to support your claim? If so, describe fully and send a photograph. Forensic evidence also must be exhibited for examination. As in American criminal court procedure, the standard of admissibility of evidence will be McCormick's Handbook on Evidence. Your claim will be considered and you will receive an acknowledgement and reply from the IHR. If the evidence as you describe it is deemed sufficient, you will be invited to personally present it for validation. Upon validation, vou will receive the reward.

CLAIM FOR REWARD (MUST BE NOTARIZED)

C   I hereby submit this claim for the $50,000 reward offered by the Institute for Historical Review. I certify that my answers to the Questionnaire and. my description of the evidence, both enclosed with this claim, are all true to the best of my knowledge and belief. I further certify that I am in possession of the evidence as described and that I am prepared to appear personally and possess said evidence for validation.

Claimant

Personally appeared before me this *18th* day of *December*, 19 *80*, and subscribed the within CLAIM FOR REWARD.

Personally appeared before me
(Mr) (Mrs) (Miss) (Ms) *Melvin Mermelstein*

275

EXHIBIT "B"

DECLARATION OF MELVIN MERMELSTEIN

I, MELVIN MERMELSTEIN, declare that:

1. I was born September 25, 1926 in the Carpathian region of Czechslovakia to Bernat and Fany Mermelstein, both of whom were of Jewish/Hebrew ethnic origin.

2. Prior to the outbreak of World War II, the Carpathian region was occupied by Hungarian military forces known as Magyars and ruled by Regent Horty Miklos.

3. In March of 1944, German armed forces including "SS" troops and Gestapo units were sent into the region.

4. On April 19, 1944 myself and my father, Bernat Mermelstein; my mother, Fany; my sisters, Etu and Magda; and my brother, Lajos, were rounded up by Hungarian militia and detained at a local brickfield called "Kalus Telep" for approximately one month.

5. At that time we were loaded into railroad boxcars and shipped out.

6. At Kassa, Slovakia, the guards on the train were changed from Hungarian militia to German "SS" troops.

7. After three days and two nights of travel, we arrived at Auschwitz-Birkenau on May 21, 1944.

8. We were told to disembark and to leave all our belongings on the boxcar.

EXHIBIT "B" (Cont'd)

9. That upon disembarking, the German troops separated everyone into two groups; one was for men, the other for women, children, ill and elderly. Myself, my father and my brother were placed in the first group. My mother and two sisters were placed in the second group.

10. I observed the crematoriums with their four tall chimneys spewing smoke and flame.

11. On May 22, 1944, I observed the buildings used as gas chambers and saw a column of women and children being driven into the tunnel that lead into the gas chambers, which I later determined to be gas chamber number 5.

12. The last time I saw my mother and two sisters was when they were driven into what I later discovered to be the gas chamber at Birkenau at dawn on May 22, 1944.

13. I observed an open pit in which there were burning bodies and that the guards ordered men to run around the pit and I heard groans and other sounds coming from the pit and I observed the guards shove and throw other men into the pit.

14. Myself, my father and my brother were processed into work details at Auschwitz.

15. I remained at Auschwitz for approximately six weeks, during which time I observed other transports arrive at the camp.

16. I was told that if I did not perform well at my appointed labor and stay healthy and strong that I would

1 EXHIBIT "B" (Cont'd)

2

3 be selected by the guards for death.

4   17. While at Auschwitz, the number A-4685 was

5 tatooed on my left forearm.

6   18. In July, 1944, I was transported to the

7 Gleiwitz camp where I remained imprisioned until January, 1945.

8   19. I was then made to force march to Bechenwald

9 camp where I remained until the camp was captured by Allied

10 forces on April 11, 1945.

11   20. After my liberation, I returned to my home-

12 town only to discover that I was the sole survivor of my

13 entire family. After a thorough search, as well as numerous

14 inquiries of friends and neighbors who were initially with

15 my mother and two sisters at Birkenau, I was given detailed

16 accounts of their fates at Birkenau by eyewitnesses at

17 the camp who observed the selecting and gassing at Birkenau.

18   21. I am the author of "By Bread Alone, The Story

19 of A-4685" which sets forth in more detail my experiences;

20 a copy of which is enclosed and incorporated by reference.

21

22

23 _____
                Melvin Mermelstein

24 STATE OF CALIFORNIA, COUNTY OF LOS ANGELES

25 On **December 18**   , 1980 before me, the undersigned, a Notary
26 Public in and for said State, personally appeared Melvin
      Mermelstein, to be the person whose name is subscribed to the
27 within instrument and acknowledged that he executed the same.

28 WITNESS my hand and official seal.

      Signature _Cheryl Bender_

CHERYL BENDER
NOTARY PUBLIC · CALIFORNIA
PRINCIPAL OFFICE IN
LOS ANGELES COUNTY
My Commission Expires Oct. 29. 1983

INSTITUTE FOR HISTORICAL REVIEW

P.O. BOX 1306 • TORRANCE, CA. 90505 • USA

William A Cox
708 Gladys Avenue
Long Beach
Ca. 90804

20 January 1981

Dear Mr. Cox:

re: Melvin Mermelstein

Thank you for your letter of 18 December 1980. I amended the Receipt Advice ("green card") to show your address, as your secretary had inadvertantly given our address as the sender.

I am still deliberating on your proposals with our Committee members and will get back to you just as soon as we have arrived at some concrete decisions.

Sincerely

Lewis Brandon
Director

By Bread Alone

WILLIAM J. COX, LAWYER

January 26, 1981

708 GLADYS AVENUE
LONG BEACH, CALIFORNIA 90804
(213) 413-0961

Mr. Lewis Brandon
Director
Institute for Historical Review
P. O. Box 1306
Torrance, Calif. 90505

Re: Melvin Mermelstein

Dear Mr. Brandon:

Your letter dated January 20, 1981 has been received and
discussed with Mr. Mermelstein.

We continue to consider a speedy resolution of this matter
quite important in that it is the honor of Mr. Mermelstein
that is daily put into question by your delay.

Therefore, unless you perform in accordance with the
contract in which you have now entered by February 6, 1981
we shall be forced to file an action in the Superior Court
to enforce his rights.

Sincerely,

William Cox

WC/j
cc: Mr. Melvin Mermelstein

280

INSTITUTE FOR HISTORICAL REVIEW

P.O. BOX 1306 • TORRANCE, CA. 90505 • USA

William A Cox
Lawyer
708 Gladys Avenue
Long Beach
Ca. 90804

27 January 1981

Dear Mr. Cox:

<u>re: Melvin Mermelstein</u>

I have now discussed your client's claim with my colleagues.

We also had another claim from Mr. Simon Wiesenthal. He wishes to claim the $50,000 for proof of gassings and the $25,000 for proof that Anne Frank's Diary is authentic. He declined to claim the $25,000 for proof that Jews were turned into soap.

In the circumstances, we have decided to deal with Mr. Wiesenthal's claim for the Anne Frank Diary authenticity, and then deal simulateneously with both his and your client's claim for the $50,000 later. I do hope that this will not inconvenience you or your client. Please assure him that we intend to deal fully and correctly with his claim.

Sincerely

Lewis Brandon

Lewis Brandon
Director

PM

INSTITUTE FOR HISTORICAL REVIEW • P.O. BOX 1306 • TORRANCE, CA. 90505 • USA

William J Cox
708 Gladys Avenue
Long Beach
Ca. 90804

(COPY OF ENVELOPE)

AIR EDITION 75¢

The New York Times

Copyright © 1981 The New York Times   —NEW YORK, WEDNESDAY, MARCH 11, 1981—

Auschwitz Survivor Suing

By ROBERT LINDSEY
Special to The New York Times

LOS ANGELES, March 5 — An unusual legal confrontation is under way in the Superior Court of Los Angeles County in which the principal issue is whether Nazi Germany used gas to murder Jews at Auschwitz.

Mel Mermelstein, a survivor of the World War II concentration camp in Poland, has filed a suit against the Institute for Historical Review.

Orange County Edition

Los Angeles Times

89 314 Sunday   **Thursday, March 12, 1981**   MF 190 pages Copyr

Extermination Camp Survivor Sues Institute

By MYRNA OLIVER and HENRY MENDOZA,
Times Staff Writers

Some nightmares never seem to end.

Nearly four decades ago, Long Beach businessman Mel Mermelstein was prisoner A-4685 at the Nazi extermination camp of Auschwitz, in Poland. His parents, two sisters and a brother died there. He survived.

Today, he is awaiting trial of a $6-million damage suit he filed in Los Angeles Superior Court against a Torrance organization that says it never happened.

"They will find out they were wrong," said the 54-year-old Mermelstein. "If anyone can prove it, I can."

Mermelstein said the attempt by the institute and by similar groups to rewrite history appears to be part of a resurgent anti-Semitism, visible also in recent attacks against Jewish institutions and against Israel.

"But this is one Jew who won't take it," he said. "This is one Jew who is through with nightmares and being insulted, libeled and pushed around.

"This time, I fight back!"

The Daily Breeze

Second Front Page

These eyes have seen the gas chambers. These ears have heard the cries of babies and mothers. These nostrils have smelled the stench of human flesh burning."

— **Mel Mermelstein,**
Long Beach businessman
and Auschwitz survivor.

Another view of history?

Torrance-based group's Holocaust-a-myth writings are labeled anti-Semitism

282

ORANGE COUNTY Jewish

heritage

VOL. 5741
No. 41

Award Winning Heritage

Pioneer Jewish Newspaper of Orange County
12181 Buaro St., Suite F, Garden Grove, Ca 92640

Friday, June 12, 1981

Single Copy 30c

EXCLUSIVE REPORT

Inside Liberty Lobby — a network of hate

By Herb Brin

"Willis Carto?"

"Yes."

That simple conversation took place in Washington D.C. last week in front of the Liberty Lobby offices on Independence Avenue and the remarkable lawsuit of Mel Mermelstein took a new and dramatic turn.

Willis Carto, chief honcho of the anti-Semitic Liberty Lobby, was formally served with notice to appear for deposition.

While legal problems for Carto started when Mel Mermelstein filed a $17 million lawsuit as the Institute for Historical Review, a Liberty Lobby offshoot, refused to honor an offer for proof that the German murders of our Six Million had taken place — Carto this week emerged as the suit's chief target.

Carto promptly countered with issuance of a "White Paper on the ADL" which was distributed to members of Congress and which denounced the Anti-Defamation League of B'nai B'rith as an "unregistered foreign lobby".

ADL has had a running battle with Carto's Liberty Lobby for years. Carto dropped a lawsuit against ADL when he refused to open his files to ADL investigators.

This week, through our own independent sources, Heritage can lay bare some intriguing aspects of the Carto-Liberty Lobby operation.

These questions arise:

What is the connection between Willis Carto and the once respected American Mercury Magazine, until recently owned by the Texas based Legion for the Survival of Freedom?

The American Mercury, edited by LaVonn Furr, has emerged as a vicious anti-Semitic publication — a far cry from its days of glory under H.L. Mencken.

According to recent reports, the Legion for the Survival of Freedom has sold the magazine to a Ned Touchstone, of Shreveport, La. Some of the proceeds from the sale have been turned over to the Noontide Press and the Institute for Historical Review. Continued on City Desk

LIBERTY LOBBY IN COURT — Mel Mermelstein, seated right, has his first day in court against the Liberty Lobby and their gaggle of pseudo-scholars who dared to suggest that the German mass murder of Jews was a hoax. Mermelstein is suing Liberty Lobby for $17 million in damages. His attorney, William Cox, standing, won court order naming three other Liberty Lobby defendants in the case. Approving the order is Superior Court Judge Edward M. Ross. Representing the anti-Semitic Liberty Lobby, seated, is Atty. Richard Fusilier. Artist David Rose sketch for Cable News Network.

By Bread Alone

Across the CITY DESK
Herb Brin

Continued from Page 1

The IHR shares a Post Office Box in Torrance with the Liberty Lobby.

It is the IHR which collected a gaggle of pseudo-scholars to attempt to rewrite history so that the German guilt for the mass murder of Six Million Jews would be whitewashed.

Touchstone publishes the Counselor out of Post Office Box 73523, Houston, Texas, 77090. The Counselor is a tabloid of the Louisiana White Citizens Council. LaVonn Furr is its editor.

Does Willis Carto control in a substantive way all activities of the Legion for the Survival of Freedom? That is a question which will be answered in the Mermelstein lawsuit.

His wife, Elisabeth Carto, served as a director of the Legion for the Survival of Freedom, which on June 30, 1966, merged with a Washington D.C. corporation known as the Committee for Religious Development.

Debts assumed by the Legion for the Survival of Freedom, in the merger, included six notes to W.A. Carto in the amount of $22,871.15.

The merger documents were signed by Willis A. Carto as vice president and LaVonn D. Furr, secretary.

Last March, Mrs. Carto resigned from the corporation.

According to a Writers Guide market report, the Legion for the Survival of Freedom had acquired American Mercury and installed LaVonn Furr as the editor.

The Legion for the Survival of Freedom, in addition to operating the Noontide Press, also owns an entity known as Independence House. A third head of the Legion hydra is the Institute for Historical Review.

Thus the network of Willis Carto consists of the Legion for the Survival of Freedom (publishing); Liberty Lifeline Foundation and the Liberty Lobby.

In a deposition 10 years ago, Carto bragged: "I am the Liberty Lobby."

He also happens to be a public admirer of Adolf Hitler.

Last week, at a Superior Court hearing in Los Angeles, Mel Mermelstein, through his attorney, William Cox, won approval from Judge Edward M. Ross, to add the following defendants to the "Holocaust" case:

Council on Dangerous Drugs and its successor, the Liberty Lifeline Foundation, and the related publisher, Indepedence House.

At last report, Willis Carto has returned to his home in Palos Verdes Estates after leaving for Washington D.C. when he learned that process servers were seeking to serve him in the Mermelstein case.

Atty. Richard Fusilier has accepted service in the case on behalf of the Legion for the Survival of Freedom, Noontide Press and I.H.R. He told the court that he was unable to contact Lewis Brandon — also known as David McCalden — the former director of the Institute for Historical Review who had issued the offer of $50,000 for proof that a single Jew had ever been gassed to death by the Germans.

Fusilier told the court: "His telephones have been ---connected and I have no address on him but I am told ... s not left the jurisdiction."

Continued on Opinion C

More: City Desk from Page B

Brandon had entered an answer to the Mermelstein case. On June 25, a hearing has been set in Superior Court by Atty. Cox demanding that Brandon be brought in for depositions. "If he doesn't show up, we will ask that his answer be stricken and a default judgment entered against Brandon-McCalden," said Cox.

Fusilier said: "I don't think he's one they're really after. Maybe he's flown the coop."

Brandon-McCalden is a former resident of Ireland and England where he was neo-nazi.

Meanwhile, Mermelstein submitted to an intensive five hour interrogation.

"I'll be there until hell freezer over," he later told Heritage.

S. I. HAYAKAWA
CALIFORNIA

GENE PRAT, PH. D.
ADMINISTRATIVE ASSISTANT

𝔘nited 𝔖tates 𝔖enate
WASHINGTON, D.C. 20510

COMMITTEES:

AGRICULTURE, NUTRITION
AND FORESTRY

FOREIGN RELATIONS

SMALL BUSINESS

October 20, 1980

Mr. Mel Mermelstein
c/o Ideal Pallett System
7422 Cedar Street
Huntington Beach, California 92647

Dear Mr. Mermelstein:

Thank you for the letter you had written regarding the
Holocaust.

I am, of course, sensitively aware of the horrors of the
"Holocaust." In all the world's history, this attempt at
genocide of a people will be a blot on what is labeled the
"civilized world."

The truth of the "Holocaust" is documented in many places
particularly in "Holocaust Libraries" in cities in this
country and in Europe.

I assure you I would not permit the "Holocaust" truth to
be tampered with or erased.

I have taken the liberty of forwarding your letter to the
President's Holocaust Memorial Council for their review.

Again, thank you for writing.

Sincerely,

S. I. Hayakawa

S. I. Hayakawa

SIH:fem

285

S. I. HAYAKAWA
CALIFORNIA

GENE PRAT, PH. D.
ADMINISTRATIVE ASSISTANT

𝔘𝔫𝔦𝔱𝔢𝔡 𝔖𝔱𝔞𝔱𝔢𝔰 𝔖𝔢𝔫𝔞𝔱𝔢
WASHINGTON, D.C. 20510

COMMITTEES:
AGRICULTURE, NUTRITION,
AND FORESTRY
FOREIGN RELATIONS
SMALL BUSINESS

May 18, 1981

Mr. Melvin Mermelstein
President
Ideal Pallet System, Incorporated
7422 Cedar Street
Huntington Beach, California 92647

Dear Mr. Mermelstein:

Thank you for your letter and enclosures of March 16.
Please forgive the tardiness of this response.

Like most Americans, the only knowledge I have had of
your case was through reports in the newspapers and on
television. After reading the material that you sent me I
must tell you that I was saddened to be reminded that such
burning, single-minded hatred exists in our time.

I have noted your request for a law that "Jews can be
criminally libelled if a defendant claims that the murder of
Jews has been a Zionist swindle." While I can appreciate your
call for such a law, it might have First Amendment problems.
I believe that you have proceeded properly in taking the
offensive against those individuals and groups who have harassed
you. By winning your case you will be setting a precedent that
similarly minded persons will take note of.

I wish you the best of luck and will follow your case with
interest.

Sincerely,

Sam Hayakawa

S. I. Hayakawa

SIH:BMd

286

ALAN CRANSTON
CALIFORNIA

United States Senate
WASHINGTON, D.C. 20510

October 13, 1980

Honorable Jimmy Carter
The White House
Washington, D.C. 20500

Dear Mr. President,

It's a great pleasure to recommend a Californian and friend, Melvin Mermelstein of Long Beach, California, for appointment to the newly created Commission on Wartime Relocation and Internment of Civilians.

A survivor of the Nazi concentration camps and a deeply public-spirited man, Mel Mermelstein has devoted a good deal of time and money to civic and humanitarian activities. He very much wants to serve on a commission which could use his experience and unique perspective on the problem of internment for racial or religious reasons. In this connection, I think he would make an excellent choice to serve on this Commission to study the internment of Japanese and Aleut Americans in our country.

I urge you give Mel Mermelstein your most thoughtful consideration. He has been highly recommended to me by friends in California who know him well and feel he could make a valuable contribution on a commission of this nature. I hope you will give him the opportunity to do so.

Best wishes,

Sincerely,

Alan Cranston

Author
and his wife
and
their four children

Symbol of Holocaust Survivors Gathering.
Jerusalem, Israel 1981.
Plaque on display at the Auschwitz
Study Foundation Holocaust Exhibit.

NOTE: Barbwire is original from Auschwitz-Birkenau's death camp.

289

By Bread Alone

And so I go back to the South not in despair . . . I go back to the South not with the feeling that we are caught in a dark dungeon that will never lead to a way out. I go back believing that the new day is coming . . . I have a dream! It is a dream deeply rooted in the American dream. I have a dream . . . that one day right down in Georgia, Mississippi and Alabama the sons of former slaves and the sons of former slave owners will be Able to live together as brothers. I have a dream . . . that one day little white children and little Negro children will be able to join hands as brothers and sisters . . . I have a dream that one day every Valley shall be exalted . . . every hill and mountain shall be made low, the rough places will be made plain and the crooked places will be made straight and the glory of the Lord shall be revealed that all flesh shall see it together. I have a dream . . . that the brotherhood of man will become a reality in this day . . . and with this faith I will go out, and carve a tunnel of hope through a mountain of despair. With this faith I will go out with you and transform dark yesterdays into bright tomorrows . . . with this faith, we will be able to achieve this new day, when all of God's children, black men and white men, Jews and gentiles, Protestants and Catholics, will be able to join hands and sing with the Negroes in the spiritual of old . . . Free at last . . . free at last . . . thank God Almighty . . . we are free at last!

DR. MARTIN LUTHER KING
DETROIT — JUNE 23, 1963

I believe, in spite of all, that there is still much good left in us to attain the goals of what Dr. Martin Luther King, and others like him, set out to attain; BROTHERHOOD, UNDERSTANDING AND PEACE AMONG ALL.

Mel Mermelstein

Los Angeles Times

Saturday, October 10, 1981

Holocaust Given Legal Recognition
Judge Makes Ruling in Court Action by Auschwitz Survivor

By MYRNA OLIVER, *Times Staff Writer*

A Los Angeles County Superior Court judge officially recognized Friday that "Jews were gassed to death at Auschwitz concentration camp in Poland during the summer of 1944."

Los ANGELES
HERALD EXAMINER

Judge says Holocaust 'just simply a fact'

Saturday
October 10 1981

Rules against institute that claims mass murder of Jews is myth

By Nicole Yorkin
Herald Examiner staff writer

A Los Angeles Superior Court judge yesterday declared it an irrefutable fact that "Jews were gassed to death at the Auschwitz concentration camp in Poland in the summer of 1944," as claimed by the plaintiff in the landmark $17 million "Holocaust case."

PRESS-TELEGRAM (AM/PM)/MONDAY, OCT. 12, 1981

PRESS-TELEGRAM

Judge affirms reality of the Holocaust

A judge says he knows what everybody knows — that the Nazis killed 6 million Jews in the Holocaust — and a Nazi whitewash scheme suffers a notable defeat in court.

The Daily Breeze

Holocaust ruled not to be hoax

Saturday, Oct. 10, 1981

By Dan Weikel
Staff writer

A Superior Court judge, declaring Friday that Jews were gassed to death at Auschwitz concentration camp in 1944, ruled against a Torrance-based group being sued over its theory the Holocaust is a hoax.

Daily Pilot

BER 10, 1981

ORANGE COUNTY, CALIFORNIA

Auschwitz Holocaust ruled historical fact

The Register

Saturday
October 10, 1981
8 sections/122 pages
15 cents

Judge upholds Holocaust as 'established fact'

PRESS-TELEGRAM

LONG BEACH, CALIFORNIA/SATURDAY, OCTOBER 10, 1981 **25c**

Holocaust no myth, judge rules in emotional case